SOLDIERS
AND
CIVILIANS

Detail from "Civilians and Soldiers." Top: recruits on the day they enlisted. Bottom: the same men after 12 days under the drill sergeants. (Source: War Department pamphlet, "Experiences of a Recruit in the United States Army," 1916.)

SOLDIERS AND CIVILIANS

*The U.S. Army
and the American People*

Edited by
Garry D. Ryan
and
Timothy K. Nenninger

Distributed by Scholarly Resources, Inc.

National Archives and Records Administration
Washington, DC

Library of Congress Cataloging-in-Publication Data

Soldiers and civilians.

    Includes index.
    1. Sociology, Military—United States.   2. United
States.   Army.   3. Civil-military relations—United
States.   I. Ryan, Garry D.   II. Nenninger, Timothy K.
UA25.S66   1987   306′.27′0973   86-21664
ISBN 0-911333-52-5

PUBLISHED FOR THE
NATIONAL ARCHIVES AND RECORDS ADMINISTRATION
BY THE
NATIONAL ARCHIVES TRUST FUND BOARD
1987

ISBN 0-911333-52-5

Contents

v

Preface

In recent years a new military history has emerged in American scholarship. This new history, in contrast with the traditional "drum and
trumpet" version of America's martial past, concentrating on operations
and commanders, emphasizes the development of the military as an institution and its interrelationship with the rest of American society. Some
practitioners of the new military history have been influenced by social
science concepts and methodology, especially sociological. Others
have relied on more traditional means of historical research, analysis,
and writing. Regardless of the approach taken, an appreciation of the
impact of the military on American life throughout our history is implicit
in all of this recent scholarship.

At the same time, at least since 1975, when the nation was finally freed
from its obsession with Vietnam and the attendant problems, debate on
national defense matters has focused on the viability of the all-volunteer
army and the related need to return to some form of conscription; on
American commitments to the North Atlantic Treaty Organization
(NATO), South Korea, and the Middle East, and the force levels and
strategy to support these commitments; on the state of readiness, organization, and capability of the army; on the quality of army leadership;
and on the role of women and minorities in the service. The ongoing debate reminds us that scholarship, historical and otherwise, does not take
place in a vacuum. It also reminds us that the U.S. Army today is truly a
product of its history (a point emphasized in Professor Weigley's paper),

is deeply affected by the concerns and mores of the wider American society, and in turn influences that society.

When the National Archives began planning the 19th in its series of scholarly conferences, the selection of a military theme for the conference that combined the fruits of recent historical scholarship along these new lines of interest with an examination of the current status of the U.S. Army and American society seemed appropriate. As a result, the conference brought together historians, sociologists, and other academic professionals as well as army officers, archivists, and other government officials to discuss the interrelationships between the U.S. Army and the American people during the past 150 years. Because the values, mores, internal dynamics, and organization of the army affected the time, place, and nature of its interaction with the broader civilian community, the conference first examined the social world of the U.S. Army before turning to its interaction with the American public. Within this framework, topics included military policy as a reflection of American society, the social makeup of the army community (officers, enlisted men, and their families), the lasting results of the army presence on certain American localities, and the army as an agent of social change and as a means of social control. Although the principal context of the conference lay in the past, the final session consisted of a wide-ranging discussion of the current status of the U.S. Army vis-a-vis American society and the prospects for that relationship during the 1980s.

The essays included in this volume are a product of that conference. The diverse backgrounds of the authors meant that a variety of methodologies, approaches, and perspectives were used in examining the several aspects of the theme "the U.S. Army and the American people"; naturally, the conclusions reached were equally diverse. We hope that the essays will contribute to a broadening of the horizons and of the definition of military history and will help to link the study of American military policy, institutions, and influence to a more general examination of American history and society.

The essays in this volume are essentially as they were first presented at the conference, but each author has recently reviewed his contribution to ensure that it responds to recent scholarship. Because of the interesting questions raised in Professor Linderman's commentary on the papers by Professors Lane and Weigley, we continued the dialogue by allowing them to respond in writing to his comments. Similarly, in order to recapture some of the essence of the excellent discussion following the papers presented at the conference on "The People of the Army," we asked Professor Coffman, who was moderator of that session, to provide a commentary on the essays encompassing some of that discussion. Finally, with apologies to Shirley J. Bach, Robert G. Gard, Jr., William L. Hauser, Charles C. Moskos, Jr., and George C. Wilson, we have not included an account of their largely spontaneous oral remarks during the final conference session, which was a lively panel discussion on "the Army in the 1980s."

The editors are in debt to a number of people who contributed significantly to the conference and to this publication. In addition to their moral and financial support, James E. O'Neill and Mable E. Deutrich offered sound advice in the many months during which the program was planned. The session chairmen, James L. Collins, Jr., Edward M. Coffman, Dale E. Floyd, Forrest C. Pogue, and Harry J. Middleton, kept the participants within their allotted times and skillfully conducted the lengthy and spirited discussions that were an integral part of each of the sessions. Elsie Freeman, J. Samuel Walker, and Deloris Lott handled registration and myriad other administrative details as well as organized the reception held during the conference. Matherine Cain, Mary Washington, Catherine Bush, and Kitty Carter cheerfully and efficiently handled the typing and other clerical chores generated by the conference and the preparation of this volume. Finally, we would like to thank Timothy Walch, who took an interest in the conference papers and saw them through to publication.

Garry D. Ryan
Timothy K. Nenninger

SOLDIERS
AND
CIVILIANS

INTRODUCTION

Goodpaster, Andrew Jackson (Cadet), USMA Class of 1939.
(*Source: USMA Archives*)

West Point, the Army, and Society:
American Institutions in Constellation

Andrew J. Goodpaster

When I returned to West Point in 1977 after a lengthy absence, it was difficult for me to avoid comparing the academy then with the academy as I recalled it from cadet days 40 years earlier. Many things were of course very much the same, but there had nevertheless been some big changes—new buildings, new people. Some of the most interesting changes, however, were smaller in scope. One was the increased use of electronic gadgets. From hand-held calculators to the giant computers, new and powerful machines assist the learning process by simulating an almost unending number of real world situations. In earlier days, to the extent that they could do so, models and mechanical devices filled that role. There were models of just about everything—bridges, machines, weapons, even models of the solar system. One of the last named was particularly interesting. It was an ingenious mechanical device that depicted a portion of the solar constellation (the sun, the earth, and the moon), and if someone turned the right cranks, these bodies were set into wonderful and seemingly random motion. Now we learned, of course, that those movements, far from being random, responded to a rigorous and explicit set of physical laws; there was a unity to the apparent randomness that might easily escape the casual observer.

It occurs to me that our American society and its component institutions, military and civil, are much like the device that attracted us in our youth. Though their activities sometimes seem independent, even

3

random and contradictory, in reality they respond to a set of principles or ideals. Whereas the principles governing the earlier device were quite rigorous, explicit, and even simple, however, our society's institutions are viewed much more tentatively in their highly complex interaction.

The ideas underlying the creation of the United States were relatively simple ideas. They were manifested in goals that the founders laid out in the Constitution. These men desired "a more perfect Union" and "Justice." They sought a means to "provide for the common defense" and to "promote the general welfare." Moreover, they desired "Liberty" and the "Blessings" it could bring, not only for themselves, but also for their children and their children's children. Through the years, the shared dedication to those goals has united Americans both in and out of uniform. It continues to do so. That shared dedication, which we now take so much for granted, was itself a novelty in the nation's infancy.

In earlier days the military had always been an appendage of the crown. The mechanisms for allegiance to a constitution were uncertain at best. The business of providing the United States with a common defense seemed to require some kind of standing army, but the founding fathers had been schooled in the Whig philosophy that stressed the danger that such an institution could pose to the government. They had learned through an English heritage and from firsthand experience how such a force could be used to subvert their liberties. There was no reason, at the time, to believe that an American army would react differently. After all, their own officers had almost rebelled at Newburgh. The nation was seemingly faced with the necessity of maintaining an institution that inherently endangered its very existence.

The nature of the American concern, and to a large degree the solution, became clear in an early confrontation. As the officers of the revolutionary army disbanded, they created an organization that would perpetuate the relationships of the days just passed. To some other Americans, however, the Society of Cincinnati symbolized one of the greatest concerns about a military establishment. It seemed to create and to perpetuate an officer caste that would somehow stand apart from the people, an elite and privileged class outside the mainstream of American life and aspiration. In many ways this early episode set the tone, and to a large degree the substance, of America's civil-military relations. Americans would not tolerate a military force that did not emanate from and reflect the breadth of American society and the ideals that animated it. Concerns about the military establishment repeatedly surfaced as a fear of growing elitism, of a tendency for the army, or at least the officer corps, to become divorced from the larger society that it was supposed to serve. The fundamental civil-military relationship in any society is of course one of service; the military serves the parent civil society. In American society, however, the military establishment is expected to mirror the attitudes of the society it serves. I myself have long held that the American military establishment is and must be designed, operated, and supported to serve the goals and interests, particularly the security goals and interests, of the society at large. Equally important, it should be consciously designed, insofar as possible, to reflect the goals and interests of that same society. All that the military is and therefore all that it does reflects the parent society it serves, for in America the military force should in truth be a representative segment of that society.

Nevertheless, the military task and function impose special requirements of order, discipline, dedication, and sacrifice, not to mention training and operational readiness, that go beyond the norms of society and must go beyond them if the society and its norms are to be safeguarded. Here is a true paradox. It is interesting to see how our nation resolves it today and has resolved it in the past.

The support the armed forces receive, the degree to which they are accepted and respected, depends on the extent to which the nation sees the military as an inherent, if specialized, societal component, and the nation's view is shaped in important part by the extent to which it perceives that the military institution mirrors the large society. Insofar as the nation believes that the military institution is taking on a set of goals of its own, and to the extent that the ideals of the large society itself are in flux, the relationship is likely to be troubled. When it is, a kind of adversary relationship may begin to emerge. The military establishment may be viewed as a competing, burdensome entity that seems to endanger society's offspring while it draws the country into distant and perilous adventures, even though the commitment to such intervention has been a matter of high political decision. Whatever its origins, however, whenever situations of this kind exist, the military can expect attacks aimed at realigning its relationship with the parent society.

In colonial days the military establishment was deeply rooted in the democratic process. Through the militia system the citizens contributed directly to the common defense. In a large sense the military and civil institutions were one and the same, and as long as the threat of Indian raids or the dangers of attack by the colonies of other countries were immediate, they continued as one. As the threats receded into the distance, however, the mechanism of an armed citizenry fell into disarray. Laws requiring each man to arm himself were so widely disobeyed that legislatures soon found it necessary to purchase weapons for any force they hoped to raise. Where the militia persisted, it sometimes became an anachronism, practicing only a meager charade of war. Yet the republican nature of the militia was appealing. When the national forces raised during the revolutionary struggle took on the trappings of a European-like regular establishment, they were viewed in many quarters as suspect. At the first opportunity the regulars were demobilized in favor of the militia, with which the country was more comfortable. America had not yet conceived a force compatible with its own republican society.

Not surprisingly, following the Revolution the new nation soon faced problems of national defense that rendered the traditional militia system obsolete. Indian problems in the West were too remote, and the old hostility toward England as well as the new friction with France touched too few lives to arouse the citizenry to action. The old militia-oriented defense proved inadequate, and the nation turned, with some reluctance, to a standing army. The move was not uniformly popular. More than a few observers were concerned that the army would be used to enforce the repressive measures to which the Federalists had turned at the end of the 18th century. Such concern was magnified when Republicans found themselves excluded from the officer ranks of an army in which Hamiltonian political persuasions seemed the most important qualification. Such a situation was bound to stir dissatisfaction, and it did. If dedication to the crown was sufficient for most armies, it was downright dangerous in the American lexicon. In America, allegiance to a regime (to the government in power) was not enough. The army would have to demonstrate broader identification and dedication—dedication to the values of the society as a whole and identification with a broad segment of the society, not simply with the upper class or with an elite political faction.

Jefferson possibly deserves the credit for creating an army that the new nation would find acceptable, though it is not so certain that he was farsightedly following such a master plan. More likely lesser motives were at work. Jefferson, like leaders before him, may have been seeking merely to ensure that the officer corps of the army under his presidency would be politically loyal. Toward that end he actively recruited Republicans from all parts of the country. This effort produced a possibly unexpected but certainly fortuitous effect. The appeal of the Republican faction was so much broader than that of the Federalists that the men recruited represented a much broader segment of American society. Their loyalties lay with the people from which they had come—in effect with American society at large—not with a small military or political caste. Madison's argument in the *Federalist*, No. 10, that the republic would draw strength and security from the diversity of its members, proved equally true of the officer corps. "Extend the sphere," he wrote, "and you take in a greater variety of parties and interests; you make it less probable that a majority of the whole will have common motive to invade the rights of other citizens; or if such a common motive exists, it will be more difficult for all who feel it to discover their own strength, and to act in unison with each other."[1] The republic was finally made secure when the agency responsible for its security passed irrevocably into the hands of the people. It was truly a republican solution, with leadership drawn from every segment and corner of the nation. Jefferson, who had conceived of a people's army in a militia format, ultimately created one from the regular establishment. By the end of the Jeffersonian era, the change that had been wrought was obvious. In 1826 one writer observed:

> Our national defences are no longer regarded with the prejudiced feeling of past days; they are not now looked upon as the creations of particular administrations or parties. . . . The time has past in the United States, when any just fears are entertained of such a standing army, as may be required by the present system of general defence. It is a gratuitous assumption, that the officers of the army are less identified with the country, have less interest in its institutions, and are less desirous of maintaining them, than any other class of citizens. The military establishments of most countries form an appendage of the crown. . . . But in our country, on the contrary, the army is dependent upon the people, and is mingled with them; it participates in the same habits, imbibes the same sentiments, and regards itself in every respect as part of the great community.[2]

The American army had learned to move in concert with the rest of American society, and it had finally become a corporate part of that society.

Jefferson also created the instrument ensuring that the army could continue to draw the bulk of its regular officers from the broadest possible cross section of the country—the U.S. Military Academy. The founding of the academy has traditionally been explained in terms of the importance of engineering to the new nation, but recently a further explanation has emerged (from our own turf, I might add), namely that the school was created originally to ensure that Republican sons from the hinterland could receive the training necessary to make officers of them. The military academy, according to this explanation, would provide Republican officers for the new army.[3] Wherever the truth lies, the new academy, in the hands of the Republicans, socially broadened the officer corps in a way that made it at once more responsive and more acceptable to the whole of American society, in effect creating a new officer corps. Since that time America has never had a military caste, either social or political. The officer corps has been drawn from all corners and all levels of society. If the academy admitted enough sons of high officials, civil and military, to raise the hackles of a few, it always also included a significant number of lads whose fathers were cobblers, mechanics, and farmers. Many students also returned to the civil society from which they had sprung. Far from being disturbed, forward-looking faculty members such as Dennis Hart Mahan saw in this pattern a positive virtue. The academy's graduates would spread learning among the lesser-trained militia.

Since that time many of the challenges to the nation's military institutions have come when people believed that the force was straying away from this republican path. Elitism and special privilege had no place in an army pledged to defend a republican society. These attacks have sometimes mistakenly been viewed as manifestations of some incipient Whig antimilitarism. In fact, they represent a republican insistence that the army mirror in its fundamental commitments the society that it is sworn to protect. Ultimately such insistence becomes society's best insurance that this force will not undertake some demagogic transformation. As often as not, attacks on the military focused on the military academy, the source of most of the officers for the nation's regular force. As early as 1822 one critic complained that appointments were being given to "the sons of the most wealthy or most influential persons."[4] John C. Calhoun, the Secretary of War, responded that such charges had no basis in fact and noted that one set of important criteria was the applicant's poverty and the service the boy's family had rendered the nation. A lad whose father had fought in the Revolution and was now indigent would supposedly be greatly preferred.

James Barbour, the next secretary, sought recommendations from Congress and appointed one cadet from each congressional district, a custom that assured the broadest possible geographical distribution of office and broad political and social distribution. This practice proved so desirable that it was formalized by Congress in 1843. Congress also insisted on one further point: the academy would keep what one report called "eminently popular, republican, and equal conditions of admission"—in other words, entrance requirements would be maintained in such a way that no arbitrary requirements would restrict entry into the military academy.[5] Admission would remain open to the broadest possible sector of society. In the meantime the academy was repeatedly reminded that it would not be allowed to become a haven for any particular class. The academy responded to Jacksonian attack by keeping records regarding the circumstances of the parents of the cadets admitted. Beginning in the early 1840s the father's occupation and economic standing and the size of the community from which the cadet entered the academy became a matter of official record, a practice that was not discontinued until 1910. This record attests to the diversity of the cadets' backgrounds.[6]

Well into the second half of the 19th century, old Jacksonians spoke bitterly of aristocracy and monopoly at West Point, but the diversity of the selection process, which was undertaken by all the members of Congress, ensured the nation of an officer corps drawn from a broad social and geographic base. In the military academy that Jefferson created, the fashion in which appointments were made promised to perpetuate an army as republican as the nation it was called on to support. Attempts to tinker with either admission procedures or standards met immediate opposition. In the early decades, no matter how many times the superintendents complained that candidates were not sufficiently prepared (sometimes "unable to spell the simplest word," to quote one document), Congress made no change that would restrict democratic access to the nation's military establishment.[7] Weaker students often found the academic demands more than they could handle and resigned or were discharged. Some struggled mightily until they overcame the deficiencies in their preparation. Not until free public schools had long since provided the necessary preparatory education were changes made. Democracy had become a secure tradition at the institution; in 1898 Elihu Root assured the nation that the "country's liberty" could never be endangered by an army "inspired by the spirit of the Military Academy."[8]

Though citizen soldiers frequently resented the discipline that West Pointers had grown to expect and demand, the necessarily undemocratic nature of a military establishment should not obscure the fundamental loyalty that academy graduates have demonstrated to the society at large. The academy has traditionally reflected in its constituent makeup the society it has served. The diversity of its roots, the democratic access to its officer ranks, has provided an army that is in touch with and in harmony with the nation at large.

As an integral part of the social fabric of the nation, the military establishment has been a corridor of upward mobility for many minority groups. In the mid-19th century it provided opportunities for the newly arrived Irish. More recently, it has served a similar function for blacks and Hispanics. Again, the army has kept in step with American society at large. West Point has been an active agent in this process. It has provided access to the officer ranks for each new group integrated into the larger society.

Today the military academy stands as a continuing link between society and the army, though it no longer stands alone, as it formerly did. Many institutions now connect society and the military services. Industrial, social, and educational ties are more complex than before and more extensive. As in the past, however, no other single institution reflects and accepts the challenge of bonding and preserving the ideals of the nation and the army to the extent that the U.S. Military Academy does. Our recent national and institutional history shows that challenge to have proven a difficult but worthy one to the leaders of both the nation and the army.

The increasing societal awareness in the early 1960s that greater efforts were essential if blacks were to be more fully integrated into the mainstream of American life was reflected by the military academy. West Point has played an important role in the effort to increase the number of black officers in the service and has substantially increased black enrollment. It was not necessary, as has sometimes been charged, to lower admission standards, because there has been no lack of black youth who can meet and exceed the required standards. The problem has been one of competition with other leading institutions for the highly talented and best prepared youth. Historically, admission standards have never barred, and should not bar, democratic access to the military academy and to the officer ranks. We do not operate on a quota basis, but we do have a continuing dedication to producing qualified officers whose racial numbers reflect the racial composition of the general population. This commitment has led us to increase our efforts to recruit from all minority groups that have been traditionally underrepresented in the officer ranks. Again, we are making significant progress, but the competition has been stiff for the best young people of all groups, and the 5-year postgraduate commitment that our young people must undertake sometimes discourages applicants.

Another area of recent effort has related to the admission of women to the Corps of Cadets beginning in 1976. This move, once again, plainly reflects a corresponding shift in American society at large. I would be less than honest, however, if I did not acknowledge my pride, and that of West Point, in the way that both the young women and the young men have risen to the challenge. Whether or not there is less than a total agreement in society—or in the army, for that matter—about the issue, the consensus is clear, and the military establishment has moved to comply with scrupulous, and I believe characteristic, dedication.

The importance that I attach to the interaction of the various American institutions seems to me well reflected in a new course that we are currently pursuing and evaluating. The course is designed to expose students to some of the salient institutions in our society in order to promote understanding of their functions, their history, and the values they represent. In an increasingly complex world it seems to me that such an understanding is indispensable for the future leaders we educate, since consensus about issues of importance to the nation requires the synthesis of multiple and often disparate interests, processes, and points of view.

Far from being isolated in its mountain setting in the Hudson highlands, the military academy is, and has been, very sensitive to the movement of the mainstream of American society. The picturesque setting, the seeming seclusion, and the ties of tradition may project a deceptive image. In fact the aims of the larger society and of the institution continue to be fused in many ways. The military academy has close and historical ties to both the executive and the legislative branches of

Recognition Day, 1978, at the U.S. Military Academy at West
Point, NY. (*Source: U.S. Army*)

our government. Our elected representatives play a key role in the governance of the institution. The Board of Visitors, a collection of men and women distinguished in many fields, makes annual visits and has broadly influenced the development of the academy over the years. Undoubtedly the most important element, however, is the continuing geographic, social, ethnic, and political diversity of the cadets who enter the institution each year. Observers who think they see emerging from the academy plastic people with interchangeable parts have never probed beyond the surface. Each graduating class manifests all the diversity of the society from which the students came just 4 years before. We take it as a high compliment that even our critics recognize the degree to which the cadets talk with each other and work with each other with a considered unity of purpose. Nevertheless, such abilities should by no means be allowed to obscure the existence within the corps of the same diversity that has been the key to the strength of the republic and to the republican nature of the army. Essential to an understanding of the historic relationship between the U.S. Army and the American people is an appreciation of the extent to which these institutions have moved in concert.

As with the astronomical device that so captured our interest many years ago, we are now intrigued and preoccupied with the necessity of ensuring that the American army will continue to reflect the same ideals that motivate our society at large.

Notes

1. Alexander Hamilton, John Jay, and James Madison, *The Federalist*, ed. Henry Cabot Lodge (New York: G. P. Putnam's Sons, 1888), pp. 58–59.

2. *North American Review* 23 (Oct. 1826):273–74.

3. Theodore J. Crackel, "Securing the Republic: Jefferson, Politics, and the Army, 1801–1809" (paper delivered at the Missouri Valley History Conference, Omaha, NE, 1977).

4. *Niles' Weekly Register*, n.s., 10, (Mar. 16, 1822):33.

5. Stephen E. Ambrose, *Duty, Honor, Country: A History of West Point* (Baltimore: Johns Hopkins University Press, 1966), pp. 83, 128.

6. "Lists Relating to Economic and Social Status of Cadets' Parents," 1842–1910, 2 vols., Records of the U.S. Military Academy, Record Group 404, USMA Archives, West Point, New York.

7. Ambrose, *Duty, Honor, Country*, p. 179 (statement of Alexander H. Bowman in 1864).

8. *The Centennial of the United States Military Academy at West Point, New York, 1802–1902*, 2 vols. (Washington, DC: U.S. GPO, 1904), 1:53.

1

ROOTS OF AMERICAN MILITARY POLICY AND INSTITUTIONS

Alexander Hamilton. Photograph of an etching by Albert
Rosenthal, Philadelphia, 1888. *(Source: National Archives)*

Ideology and the American Military Experience: A Reexamination of Early American Attitudes Toward the Military

Jack C. Lane

A recent study on the relationship between the American public's view of the Vietnam war and its attitude toward the military produced some surprising results. The authors found that the "growing disaffection for Vietnam did not for most people mean increasing moral rejection of the war, but probably reflected growing pragmatic opposition to a costly disappointment."[1] Hence, they argued, it is a mistake to generalize that antiwar sentiment produced an antimilitary attitude. This conclusion should not have been very surprising. Earlier studies during the Vietnam period revealed a consistently positive public attitude toward the military, and a study on public views during the Korean war reached similar conclusions.[2]

Yet viewed historically, the recent discovery of a promilitary attitude does seem somewhat anomalous, because generations of Americans have been taught and have uncritically accepted the idea that the American public has historically displayed a fundamental and unwavering hostility toward the military. This hostility, they have learned, was the principal reason for America's anemic military policy in the 19th and early 20th centuries. In study after study, military historians have carefully constructed a believable antimilitary scenario: the colonists inherited the English Radical Whig bias against the military, and this inheritance was reinforced by the colonial and prerevolutionary experience. After the Revolution, the dominant American liberal

15

ideology embraced the antimilitary tradition and made it a permanent fixture in American life.[3] One prominent military historian has well summarized the early manifestations of this perceived tradition: antimilitarism, he declares, has expressed itself

> in resentment of red-coat garrisons in the colonies before the American Revolution, their presence becoming the primary cause of the Revolution; in the effort of the writers of the Constitution to divide military powers among the federal legislature, the federal executive, the states and the people, thus minimizing the dangers of military influence; in continual warnings of statesmen against standing armies; in Jacksonian efforts to destroy the Military Academy at West Point and with it the professional officers corp; and in habitual peacetime neglect of military preparation.[4]

We must do more, however, than simply discover expressions or manifestations of antimilitarism. We must probe deeper into the meaning of such expressions because they do not occur in a vacuum; they are inextricably bound up in the nation's system of widely shared ideas, values, conventions, and attitudes. Thus it can be argued that powerful historical forces, not some inherited beliefs, have shaped the American public's attitude toward the military. Gordon Wood's statement concerning ideological precepts provides a pertinent insight here: a society's beliefs, he has noted, are determined "as much by the character of the world being confronted as by internal developments of inherited or borrowed conceptions."[5] From this perspective, then, what appears on the surface as an antimilitary tradition with a life and substance of its own actually proves to be an aspect of a complex ideological system. Thus we must look beyond antimilitary expressions to the more complicated motivations that gave rise to them.

A number of strategies may be used to achieve this deeper meaning. Period studies on military affairs, properly conceived, can provide an integrated picture of the multiple forces that bear on military affairs. Richard Kohn's study of Federalist military policy is a model in this genre.[6] Marcus Cunliffe has uncovered an intense martial spirit in ante bellum America.[7] William Skelton is successfully probing the relationship of military policy and societal developments in the age of Jackson,[8] and parts of Russell Weigley's history of the U.S. Army contain insightful discussions on the interrelationships in other periods.[9] In addition, Gerald Linderman has shown the influence of prevailing attitudes and values on American reaction to the Spanish-American War, and Thomas Leonard has examined how the society's shared idealistic images of the Civil War led it to see war not in its bloody, cruel aspects but as an intellectual game of strategy or as a way of socializing young people.[10] Here I would like to suggest and then to explore another strategy—a conceptual framework—around which such a reexamination could be built.

If, as I have stated earlier, the American public's attitude toward the military must be treated as an aspect of the society's ideological beliefs, we must understand the dynamics of ideological systems. Social scientists have produced a rich and varied literature in this field, but there seems to be a common agreement that Clifford Geertz has written the most incisive synthesis of the recent studies on ideology. In an article entitled "Ideology as a Cultural System," Geertz presents a complicated argument. For our purposes two major insights stand out: first, Geertz agrees with the traditional view that society uses ideology as a way of responding to a stressful situation, but he expands upon this traditional view by arguing that those responses need not take such pathological forms as Nazism or McCarthyism. According to Geertz, a society constructs an ideological cultural system in order to make sense of unsettled times. Like road maps, that system helps society chart its course in shifting developments. Not surprisingly, revolutionary conditions always bring forth sudden bursts of ideological expressions, because, he notes, such formulations "come most crucially into play in situations where the particular kind of information they contain is lacking, where institutionalized guides for behavior, thought, or feelings are weak or absent."[11]

Ideology, then, helps transform physical experience into sentiments and attitudes, thus creating a "subtle interplay" between ideas and social realities. This interplay, he argues, produces an "intricate structure of inter-related meanings" that helps society respond to crises. This structure in turn provides scholars with a vehicle for better understanding the responses, because, in Geertz's phase, they are "extrinsic sources of information," blueprints of the sociopolitical structures of society. Ideology thus provides both a matrix for a political order and a "map of problematic social reality."[12]

Geertz's second insight further refines his conception of an ideological cultural system: ideologies, he claims, are most clearly seen as cultural symbol systems, of which verbal expressions are the most common. On the surface we see symbols of ideology, but they are mere "feeble representations" of the intricate structure of interrelated meanings that lie beneath the surface. Drawing upon the studies of Kenneth Burke and others, Geertz depicts ideological word symbols as systems of symbolic action, as bridges between the mind and the real world. For Geertz, then, words are symbols of an ideological cultural system, and the power of words as ideological symbols is that they express a "more complex meaning than [their] literal reading suggests." Thus not only is an ideological symbol more complex than it appears on the surface, but an analysis of that symbolic structure allows us to trace the interworking of the sociopolitical process itself.

From the ideological perspective, then, it is possible to view the antimilitary tradition in a more substantive fashion than has heretofore been possible. If antimilitarism is simply an aspect of a larger ideological system—if it is an ideological symbol itself—then, according to Geertz's thesis, we must avoid interpreting it merely as a literal expression of traditional opposition to the military. On the contrary, we must look beyond that symbol to some deeper, more complex meaning, because the symbol is standing for something within the sociopolitical life of a society. Its significance most likely transcends military affairs.

I would like to explore Geertz's theory as particularly applicable to one of America's most venerable antimilitarisms: opposition to a standing army. This tradition is an excellent example of the power, complexity, and persistence of an ideological symbol. Formulated as a response to the prerevolutionary crisis with Great Britain, it helped substantiate the colonial view of British tyranny; employed as a catchphrase to rationalize the revolt against Britain, in time it took its place as a leading symbol of the revolutionary movement. Finally, as we shall see, long after the British threat had disappeared, it persisted as an ideological symbolic response to the stressful uncertainties of building a new nation.

Opposition to a standing army was actually a late addition to the American colonial ideological system. As John Shy has indicated, the colonists were quite favorably inclined toward the British army before 1763.[13] Major developments after the French and Indian War, however, led to a change in American attitudes. By 1775 the British regular army had begun to arrive in large numbers in the colonies, and American contact with British soldiers left a bitter taste. As Richard Kohn has written, "Civil-military conflict flared at all levels. Army recruiters plied country boys with rum, enlisted indentured servants and apprentices, and arrested colonial deserters."[14] English Radical Whig ideology, which the colonists had read and absorbed, had warned that a standing army was a threat to constitutional and individual rights, and now the colonists had evidence to support such claims.[15] Incidents such as the Boston Massacre and the use of British troops to quell discontent immediately prior to the outbreak of the Revolution crystallized growing sentiment against the standing army. By 1776, the revolutionaries had made it a fixture in their ideological system, and as with their political beliefs, they tended to generalize their prejudice against the army.

Thus although the revolutionary generation's fear and distrust of a standing military force was grounded in large part on its practical experience with the British army, the revolutionaries pushed that experience a step further. During the political debate with Great Britain they made distrust of a standing army an essential part of their ideological struggle against the mother country. Again in Richard Kohn's words: "The British army represented that monstrous 'Conspiracy against Liberty' which Americans saw emanating from the ministry in London; it was the agent of European corruption come to sap American virtue, the iron fist of customs regulation, the tyranny of trial without jury."[16] In short, opposition to a standing army symbolized many of the colonial grievances against the British, a logical outcome, for as Gordon Wood has noted, the revolutionaries' "rhetoric was never detached from the social and political reality; indeed it becomes the best entry into an understanding of that reality."[17]

Most historians, including Kohn, argue that the belief was so strong after the Revolution that even in the absence of a British military threat the bias against the standing army carried forward as a powerful tradition. A subtle yet significant shift nevertheless occurred after the Revolution. A standing army came to be depicted not only as a threat to individual liberties and as a subverter of republican governments, but also as an instrument for opponents and supporters of the creation of a strong central government. Suddenly Americans transformed the issue of a standing army into a powerful political symbol. The revolutionary nationalists made a national standing army a symbol for the increased authority of central government, while opposition to a standing army became a weapon in the arsenal of people who opposed political centralization. The issue of a standing army as a military establishment became obscured in the process.

As we know, conditions after the war produced a centralist sentiment that resulted in the calling of the Constitutional Convention and the framing of a nationalist Constitution. The nationalists succeeded in creating a stronger central government at the expense of state sovereignty, but they were also forced to bow to the localist exigencies of American political, social, and economic life. Consequently, although they created a supreme central government, it was constructed within a federalist political system that divided authority between the state and central governments.

Nothing better illustrates the nationalist-state-centered compromises than the constitutional solution to the problem of a military establishment. The nationalists were determined to give the new nation a meaningful military force, by which they meant a national standing army. From this determination came the constitutional authority for the central government "to raise and support armies," "to provide and maintain a navy," and "to make rules for the governing and regulation of the land and naval forces." At the nationalist-dominated convention, no serious differences arose on these military matters.

Instead the cause of a bitter debate was the proper nature of the military establishment that would support the regular army in emergencies. The nationalists were willing to accept the state militia as a reserve force but only if Congress was given the authority to organize, arm, and discipline it. Alexander Hamilton forcefully stated the nationalist position: the militia of all the states, he said, should be placed "under the sole and exclusive direction of the United States, the officers of which to be appointed and commissioned by them."[18]

The advocates of states' centrality in the convention, however, seized upon the issue as critical to their cause. Led by Elbridge Gerry and Luther Martin, they were determined to leave some military power in the hands of the states. Gerry sounded the call that would ultimately force the nationalists to compromise. Typically he played upon the traditional fear of standing armies, repeating again and again the well-worn phrase that standing armies were dangerous in time of peace. Gerry's main goal, however, was to tie the militia question to the larger issue of strengthening the central government at the expense of state sovereignty. The militia, Gerry contended, was critical to state power, a matter, he said, "on which the existence of the State may depend." Give the national government control of the militia, he warned, and "such power may enslave the States."[19] Although states were willing to support a strong central government, that government's power must be limited, and placement of the entire military under the central government would exceed the limits. Luther Martin vigorously concurred with Gerry. Giving the general government control of the militia, he thought, "was the last coup de grace to the State governments," because the first attempt "by a state to put the militia in a situation to counteract the arbitrary measures of the general government would be construed as an act of rebellion or treason."[20]

The convention solved the military impasse in the same fashion that it had settled its political problems: it federalized the militia by placing it within what became known as the federal system. The Constitution gave Congress the authority to call the militia to "execute the laws of the union, suppress insurrections and repel invasions." It was responsible for organizing, arming, and disciplining the militia, but the authority for appointing officers and training the men was reserved to the states. Thus power over America's reserve force was divided between the national and state governments.

Not surprisingly, in the ratification debate, the Anti-Federalists seized upon the military clauses as evidence of potential tyranny of the central government. They were convinced that republican government was possible only in small political units such as the states. They believed that, in a nation as large as the United States, the central government would be so distant that it could enforce its authority only by means of soldiers.[21] Therefore, they argued, any military power in the hands of the central government was dangerous. Patrick Henry forcefully articulated the position set forth earlier by Gerry. The military clause, Henry argued, was simply one of the transparent efforts to create an overpowerful central government. The states, he said, were the only barriers to tyranny by centralization, and the militia seemed to him the final state instrument for resisting such potential tyranny. "Where are means for resisting," he asked, "when our only defense, the militia, is put in the hands of Congress?" Already the Constitution had given Congress the dangerous power of taxation. Now, he declared, with their powerful authority of "raising an army, and by their control over the militia, they have the sword in one hand and the purse in the other. Shall we be safe without either?"[22] States'-rightists reasserted the theme in the ratification debates in other states. Many states joined Virginia in suggesting that a strong amendment regarding the militia should be added to the Constitution. The result was the second amendment: "As well-regulated militia being necessary to the security of a free state, the right of the people to keep and bear arms shall not be infringed." The wording of the amendment suggests the degree to which the military establishment had become a political matter and the degree to which the Anti-Federalists saw the militia in terms of security, not against an external force, but against the threat of the central government.[23]

Thus in the controversy over the new nation's military establishment one issue at stake was much larger and much more significant than a standing army. In fact, even at this early date, opposition to a standing army had become a conventional ideological symbol. To the Anti-Federalists, the major struggle pitted state authority against national authority. Many observers sincerely believed that central government of the kind created by the Constitution threatened state authority, and because they saw the states as the best guarantee of republican government, they believed that a powerful central government placed individual liberties in jeopardy. They argued not against a standing army as such but against a *nationalist* standing army created and controlled by the central government. They had no quarrel with a state army—the militia. In fact, as we have seen, they saw the militia as a counter to the central government's authority, a basic reason why they fought so stubbornly against the Federalist effort to nationalize the militia, which they considered another effort to reduce state sovereignty in favor of centralization.[24]

In much the same way that the framers had accepted a federal solution to political problems, the Anti-Federalists accepted, in the militia clause and in the second amendment, a federal compromise on the military issue. Thus William Riker is quite correct in observing that the clause precisely expressed "a coherent theory of federalism."[25] In the Constitution the military function, like the other functions of government, was divided between the central government and the states.

The federal solution provided the framework, and the ratification process set the tone and created the rhetoric, for subsequent debates on the military issue. In the next three decades, efforts to nationalize the militia and even attempts to strengthen the national regular army were consistently seen as threatening the federal system. At such times state-centered advocates and opponents of strengthening the central government predictably played on prejudices against a standing army to support their position.

In the decades that followed, the symbol of opposition to a standing army, like all established ideological precepts, appealed to all factions across the political spectrum. The Jeffersonian Republicans employed the symbol against the Federalist attempts to enlarge the regular army, and the Federalists later accused the Republicans of military tyranny during the War of 1812. When Secretary of War John C. Calhoun tried to reorganize the regular army during the Monroe administration, he aroused old Jeffersonian Republicans from their slumber.[26]

The Jacksonian response to the military issue is a perfect example of the way in which sentiment against the standing army had become pure ideological symbol. By the 1830s very few people, and least of all Andrew Jackson, took seriously the belief that a standing army threatened republican principles. Jackson not only wanted to draft eligible young men into the militia but also consistently asked for appropriations to support a stronger regular establishment.[27] Yet historians have continued to interpret Jacksonian military policy as an example of the persistence of an antimilitary bias.[28]

If we view it from the standpoint of ideological symbolism, however, the Jacksonian approach to the military takes on a somewhat different meaning. The Jacksonians were quite consistent in following the prescribed ideological pattern established earlier by the Jeffersonians. They were as fully state-centered as their Jeffersonian predecessors if not more so. Like the early Anti-Federalists, they believed strongly that the state rather than the central government offered the best political structure for realizing the principles of republican society. The combination of President Jackson's militia experience and this state-centeredness made the Jacksonians fervent champions of the state militia system as the bulwark of democratic republican society.

Scholars have also detected a strain of equalitarian populism in the Jacksonian approach to the military.[29] That tendency, however, did not come, as they have supposed, from some widespread grass-roots opposition to the military. The Jacksonians' attack on the military academy, for example, was consonant with their ideological opposition to privilege. Jacksonians—whether facing the recharter of the U.S. Bank, entrenched public office holders, or special benefactors of internal improvements—consistently expressed a hatred of special privilege. To them, no institution seemed more obviously a bastion of elitist, perhaps even aristocratic, privilege than the military academy at West Point. It would have been surprising indeed if the Jacksonians had paid no attention to it.

The President's response to the academy prompted a classic Jacksonian confrontation; its resemblance to the Bank issue is uncanny. Like the Bank, the academy was seen as a privileged institution. Also like the Bank, it was ruled by a self-centered authoritarian, Sylvanus Thayer. Finally, yet again like the Bank, in the end the conflict over the academy proved to be less a struggle over policy than a clash of two obstinate personalities. Except for a radical fringe, the Jacksonians made no attempt to destroy the academy. They wanted from West Point no more than they demanded from the political, social, and economic system: equal opportunity for all individuals to compete on the basis of talent, not privilege—patently a reasonable demand. Thayer nevertheless saw it as an attack on the military profession. He resigned, but the academy did not collapse. It later changed in the way that the Jacksonians had said it should, and it was stronger for having done so.[30]

Antimilitarism, then, was not the source of the Jacksonians' military policy. Their attitude toward the military academy arose from a system of ideological beliefs that centered on the abhorrence of special privilege in a democratic society. In the era of Jackson, the military academy had simply replaced the standing army as the object of antimilitary prejudice.

In the foregoing analysis, in a suggestive rather than a comprehensive way, I have attempted to probe beyond the conventional view of the American public's historical attitude toward the military. My employment of a conceptual model—ideology as a cultural system—may appear at first glance too restrictive as a frame of reference, but in fact the model rests firmly on the concept that historical developments are dynamic factors in shaping American military attitudes.[31] This model suggests that beliefs and ideas are powerful forces but that they are historically developed and are much too complex to be given a universal interpretation. Thus my purpose has been, in the first place, to caution military historians against a too casual acceptance of a pervasively historical antimilitary tradition and, in the second, to encourage them to investigate more seriously the complex and pluralistic nature of American attitudes toward the military. I have offered a strategy that may help in this investigation. It might also surprise us by uncovering the kind of promilitary sentiment that social scientists have discovered recently among the American public.

Notes

1. John Blair and Jerald Bachman, "The Public View of the Military," *The Social Psychology of Military Service*, eds. Nancy Goldman and David Segal (Beverly Hills, CA: Sage Publications, 1976), pp. 216–227. This conclusion is supported further in the following: David Segal and John Blair, "Public Confidence in the U.S. Military," *Armed Forces and Society* 3 (Fall 1976):3–11; C. Richard Hofstetter and David Moore, "Watching TV News and Supporting the Military," *Armed Forces and Society* 5 (Winter 1979):261–269; and Jerald Bachman, John Blair, and David Segal, *The All-Volunteer Force* (Ann Arbor: University of Michigan Press, 1978).

2. David Segal, "Civil-Military Relations in the Mass Public," *Armed Forces and Society* 1 (Summer 1975):513–526; and A. Modegliani, "Hawks, Doves, Isolationism, and Public Distrust: An Analysis of Public Opinion on Military Policy," *American Political Science Review* 66 (Sept. 1972):960–978.

3. The view that the colonists inherited the English Radical Whig antimilitary tradition is expressed in Lois G. Schwoerer, *"No Standing Armies": The Anti-Army Ideology in Seventeenth Century England* (Baltimore: Johns Hopkins University Press, 1974); Bernard Baylin, *The Ideological Origins of the American Revolution* (Cambridge, MA: Harvard University Press, Belknap Press, 1967); Lawrence D. Cress, "Radical Whiggery on the Role of the Military: Ideological Roots of the American Revolutionary Militia," *Journal of the History of Ideas* 40 (Jan. 1979):43–60; Cress's larger study, *Citizens in Arms: The Army and the Militia in American Society to the War of 1812* (Chapel Hill: University of North Carolina Press, 1982); Robert E. Shalhope, "The Ideological Origins of the Second Amendment," *Journal of American History* 69 (Dec. 1982):599–614. The view that colonial and prerevolutionary experience reinforced the Whig inheritance may be found in Arthur Ekirch, *The Civilian and the Military* (New York: Oxford University Press, 1956), pp. 3–17; C. Joseph Bernardo and Eugene Bacon, *American Military Policy: Its Development Since 1775* (Harrisburg, PA: Stackpole Press, 1955); Marvin Kriedberg and Merton Henry, *History of Military Mobilization in the United States Army, 1775–1945* (Washington, DC: Department of the Army, 1955); Walter Millis, *Arms and Men* (New York: Putnam's, 1956), pp. 11–12; and William A. Ganoe, *A History of the United States Army* (New York: Appleton-Century, 1924). Samuel P. Huntington in his classic work *The Soldier and the State: The Theory and Politics of Civil-Military Relations* (Cambridge, MA: Harvard University Press, 1957) posits the theory that liberalism was basically antimilitary.

4. Russell F. Weigley, ed., *The American Military: Readings in the History of the Military in American Society* (Reading, MA: Addison-Wesley Publishing Co., 1969), pp. xi–xii.

5. Gordon Wood, "Rhetoric and Reality in the American Revolution," *New Perspectives on the American Past*, eds. Stanley Katz and Stanley Kutler (Boston: Little, Brown and Co., 1969), pp. 101–123.

6. Richard Kohn, *Eagle and Sword: The Federalists and the Creation of the Military Establishment in America, 1783–1802* (New York: Free Press, 1975).

7. Marcus Cunliffe, *Soldiers and Civilians: The Martial Spirit in America, 1775–1865* (Boston: Little, Brown and Co., 1968).

8. William Skelton, "Professionalization of the U.S. Army Officer Corps During the Age of Jackson," *Armed Forces and Society* 1 (Summer 1975):443–471.

9. Russell F. Weigley, *History of the United States Army* (New York: Macmillan, 1967).

10. Gerald Linderman, *The Mirror of War: American Society and the Spanish-American War* (Ann Arbor: University of Michigan Press, 1975); Thomas Leonard, *Above the Battle: War Making in America from Appomattox to Versailles* (New York: Oxford University Press, 1978).

11. Clifford Geertz, "Ideology as a Cultural System," *Ideology and Discontent*, ed. David E. Apter (New York: Free Press of Glencoe, 1964), pp. 47–76.

12. Ibid., p. 62.

13. John Shy, *Towards Lexington: The Role of the British Army in the Coming of the Revolution* (Princeton: Princeton University Press, 1965), pp. 393–398.

14. Kohn, *Eagle and Sword*, p. 5.

15. Significantly, even Radical Whig ideology was concerned with the standing army less as a military force than as a political issue. The Whigs believed that the standing army was dangerous as an instrument of monarchial tyranny, but more to the point, they distrusted it because it encouraged citizens to avoid service and was therefore a corrupter of public virtue. As one historian has noted, the Radical Whigs' support of militia "reflected as much their concern about the imbalance of the English Constitution as their determination to develop a military alternative to a standing army" (Lawrence Cress, "Radical Whiggery on the Role of the Military," p. 50).

16. Kohn, *Eagle and Sword*, p. 6.

17. Wood, "Rhetoric and Reality," p. 117.

18. Quoted in James Scott, "The Militia," *S. Doc. 695*, 64th Cong., 2d sess. (Washington, DC: U.S. GPO, 1917), p. 31. For Madison's views, see James Madison, *The Papers of James Madison*, eds. Robert A. Ruthland and Charles Hobson (Charlottesville: University Press of Virginia, 1977), 11:142–144.

19. The arguments concerning the militia are scattered throughout the debates. For Gerry's and Martin's view, see Max Farrand, ed., *The Records of the Federal Convention of 1787*, 4 vols. (New Haven: Yale University Press, 1911), 2:329–332 and 385–388.

20. Quoted in John Mahon, *The American Militia: A Decade of Decision, 1789–1800* (Gainesville: University of Florida Press, 1960), p. 8.

21. Kohn, *Eagle and Sword*, p. 82.

22. Ibid., p. 83.

23. For a debate over other meanings of the second amendment see Shalhope, "Ideological Origins of the Second Amendment"; Lawrence Cress, "An Armed Community: The Origins and Meaning of the Right to Bear Arms," *Journal of American History* 71 (June 1984): 22–41; Shalhope and Cress, "The Second Amendment and the Right to Bear Arms," *Ibid.*, 71 (Dec. 1984): 587–593.

24. Jackson T. Main, *The Anti-Federalists: Critics of the Constitution, 1781–1788* (1961; reprint ed., New York: W. W. Norton and Co., 1974), pp. 147–148.

25. William Riker, *Soldiers of the States: The Role of the National Guard in American Democracy* (Washington, DC: Public Affairs Press, 1957), pp. 15–18.

26. On the employment of the symbol by Jeffersonians, see Kohn, *Eagle and Sword*, pp. 129–131, 223–224, 260, and 269. On its use by Federalists and old Jeffersonians, see Ekirch, *Civilians and the Military*, pp. 52–59.

27. Richard L. Watson, "Congressional Attitudes Toward Military Preparedness, 1829–1835," *Mississippi Valley Historical Review* 34 (Mar. 1948): 611–613.

28. Examples include Weigley, *History of the U.S. Army*, pp. 154–156; Leonard White, *The Jacksonians: A Study in Administrative History* (New York: Macmillan, 1954), pp. 208–212; Bernardo and Bacon, *American Military Policy*, pp. 147–160; Stephen Ambrose, *Duty, Honor, Country: A History of West Point* (Baltimore: Johns Hopkins University Press, 1966), pp. 106–124. Ekirch, *Civilians and the Military*, and Cunliffe, *Soldiers and Civilians*, see the Jacksonians—correctly, I think—as basically promilitary.

29. Most of the sources listed in n. 3 reflect this attitude, but Samuel Huntington, *Soldier and the State*, has concluded most forcefully that the Jacksonians provided America with

one of the major strains of antimilitarism, which he terms military popularism, or the intrusion of popular politics into military affairs (pp. 203–211).

30. Ambrose, *Duty, Honor, Country*, pp. 120–123. The relationship between the Jacksonian concept of privilege and its approach to the military is described also in D. W. Brogan, "The United States: Civilian and Military Power," in *Soldiers and Governments*, ed. Michael Howard (London: Eyre and Spottiswood, 1957), pp. 169–185. Marcus Cunliffe, *Soldiers and Civilians*, makes a good case for the theory that the organized opposition to the military academy in the 1830s and 1840s was inspired by one man, Alden Partridge, a disgruntled former superintendent who had been summarily dismissed. Cunliffe concludes that opposition is thus not "proof of national indignation" (p. 155).

31. Gordon Wood puts it this way: "Although words and concepts may remain outwardly the same for centuries, their particular functions and meanings do not and could not remain static—not as long as individuals attempt to use them to explain new social circumstances and make meaningful new social behavior;" in "Intellectual History and the Social Sciences," *New Directions In American Intellectual History*, eds. John Higham and Paul Conkin (Baltimore: Johns Hopkins University Press, 1979): 27–41. In this collection of essays, Clifford Geertz is cited more than any other single authority. For a discussion and evaluation (not always favorable) of the ways historians have employed Geertz, see Ronald G. Walters, "Signs of the Times: Clifford Geertz and Historians," *Social Research* 47 (Autumn 1980): 537–556.

The Long Death of the Indian-Fighting Army

Russell F. Weigley

For 106 years, from the inception of the first American regiment in 1784 to the suppression of the final pathetic spasm of Indian military resistance at Wounded Knee Creek in 1890, the U.S. Army in its uniforms of dusty blue was preeminently the Indian-fighting army. It was rarely an army used or even intended as a weapon to serve the international policies of the United States. Thus it was scarcely an army at all in the terms of the contemporary armies of the European great powers. It was not a force in international relations; it was a domestic constabulary, intended to maintain law and order within the United States.

When the history of the Indian frontier at last ended, the U.S. Army could not readily find a new raison d'être to replace the police mission that had sustained it for so long. In its psychology, attitudes, and organization, it long continued to be the Indian-fighting army. Through the 1930s and until the eve of World War II, the only divisions in the army that were not skeletonized but reasonably ready for some sort of military action were the 2d Infantry Division and the 1st Cavalry Division (the latter traditional horse cavalry), both in the VIII Corps Area, whose headquarters were at Fort Sam Houston, TX. Both were ready for action because their mission was to protect the Mexican border against incursion by Mexican irregulars in the manner of Pancho Villa in 1916: the army of the 1930s was still designed first for an extension of its old

27

Indian-fighting, constabulary role, for the kind of service that it historically knew best.[1]

Within a few short months of the passage of the Selective Service
Act of 1940, the army had to wrench itself abruptly away from traditional
habits of mind to take on global responsibilities as a military instrument
of American world power, in direct competition with the armies of the European great powers. For no American institution did the swift movement of the United States to the center of the world political stage in
1940–45 demand a readjustment of greater magnitude than for the
army. The history of the Indian-fighting army had little to do with the ex-
ercise of world power, yet within 5 years the U.S. Army found its
concerns dramatically expanded from the spillover of Mexican revolution along the Rio Grande to the maintenance of world order from the
Elbe to Korea. In the meantime, the American army had to fight against
the most formidable of the veteran great-power armies. If we are to understand either the strengths or the deficiencies of the U.S. Army in its
new role as arbiter of global power since 1940, we must remind our-
selves of how short the army's global history has been and of how long
the army was the Indian-fighting constabulary in its attitudes and values even well beyond the last Indian wars.

The long history of the army as a police force for the Indian frontier
above all else shaped the army's institutional personality and its relations with the society it served. The U.S. Army in the first century of its
existence was a small army whose small strength was scattered across
vast territories, less because of any democratic ideological suspicion of
strong armies than because the army's reason for being demanded no
force of substantially larger size or more concentrated deployment.
Americans have not been so ideological a people that the antiarmy
thought inherited from 17th- and 18th-century English liberalism would
have been likely to deter them from creating a strong army if they had
felt a need for such a force. In the 1790s, when inherited suspicions of
standing armies retained much of the added impetus lent them in America by the presence of the British army in the 1760s and 1770s, the U.S.
Congress nevertheless voted a series of remarkable increases in military strength against the threat of the Quasi-War with France.[2] But most
American experience in the 19th century posed no such threat, nor did
the circumstances of the United States for many decades after the close
of the Indian wars present a substitute for the Indian-fighting mission
that would cause much of a change in the profile of the American army
formed during the Indian wars.

The army "has but little opportunity for active service," wrote Secretary of War William Crowninshield Endicott, describing the Indian-
fighting army and its needs during the final years of the Indian
campaigns, "and what it has is not of the most agreeable or inspiring

kind. The control and pursuit of Indians, difficult and hazardous as it often is, and developing as it does the individual character and gallantry of officers and men, is yet war on a very limited scale, and bears but slight resemblance to the great contests which follow the collision between nations."[3] The limited scale of warfare to which Endicott referred, and the logistical difficulties that large forces would have met in campaigning across the Great Plains and the deserts of the Southwest, confined the regular army to 25,000–30,000 officers and men during the generation after the Civil War. Army officers impatient over slow promotion, and militaristic zealots such as Bvt. Maj. Gen. Emory Upton, might complain that the country needed a larger force, but they were hard put to offer convincing demonstrations of need.

The commanding general of the army, reporting in 1890 to Endicott's immediate successor as Secretary of War, could no longer cite even war against the Indians on a limited scale as a reason for the existing U.S. Army or as a rationale for its form of organization:

> The past year, like the two or three preceding, has been marked by an almost total absence of hostilities with any of the Indians, or any indication on their part of a determination to again go on the warpath. . . .
>
> This improved condition in the vast interior of the country has enabled the military authorities during the past few years to give greater attention to the need of the country, respecting its relations to foreign powers.[4]

But what indeed were the military needs of the country in relation to foreign powers? The American military journals of the late 19th century, for the army most notably *The Journal of the United States Military Service Institution* and *The United Service*, attest that the soldiers of the day shared a sufficient awareness that with the end of the Indian wars a military epoch was passing: "During the past decade few disturbances have ruffled the great calm of national life; the Indian troubles are, in the opinion of those best qualified to judge, almost at the end," said a representative article in the *United Service* in 1889.[5] The professional journals, however, could speculate more freely than could official reports about the implications of the army's loss of its historic raison d'être. The tone was apt to be gloomy: "The army to-day is seldom brought to the attention of the people, and a soldier of the United States has become almost as rare a sight in the great centres of population as a wild Indian. The national uniform is unknown."[6] Without the duties of an Indian constabulary, whither the U.S. Army? What organizing purpose remained?.

The soldiers who had tested their vision and judgment against the distances and dangers of the Great Plains while the Indian wars lasted

"The Indian Fighting Army." Signal Corps photograph of a
Frederic Remington painting. *(Source: National Archives)*

were mostly too farsighted and realistic to believe that "relations to foreign powers" of the sort that sustained European armies could provide a
substitute reason for being for the American army in any predictable future. Occasional publicists might conjure up prophecies of enemy fleets
and invading armies assailing the American coast, but thoughtful American soldiers knew better. They knew, without coining the phrase "free
security,"[7] that the oceans secured their country against any foreign military threat to its vital interests. "A glance at the condition of affairs at the
present time will show that causes which might lead to war between the
United States and a great European power are difficult to find," said the
same *United Service* writer who had noted the absence of the national
uniform in the cities' streets. Only with a few Latin American states
might causes of war be reasonably conceived, and no major sustained
new employment for the army was part of the conception.[8] Furthermore,
even if possible causes of war against a major power had been more
likely to arise, it remained altogether unlikely that a foreign power could
project across the oceans enough military strength to imperil the United

States. As Philip Sheridan, commanding general of the army, reported to the Secretary of War in 1884:

> I do not think we should be much alarmed about the probability of wars with foreign powers, since it would require more than a million and a half of men to make a campaign on land against us. To trans-port from beyond the ocean that number of soldiers, with all their munitions of war, their cavalry, artillery, and infantry, even if not molested by us in transit, would demand a large part of the shipping of Europe.[9]

Capt. John Bigelow, writing in his *Principles of Strategy* in 1894, noted that two steamers were usually considered necessary to transport a reg-iment of infantry on a long ocean voyage. Logisticians calculated that at least 30 steamers would be required for a division of 10,000 men and 135 steamers for a corps of 33,000 men. Only Great Britain and possibly France possessed enough ships to carry 50,000 troops across the Atlantic. Using all its shipping, Great Britain might conceivably transport half a million troops—but Britain could hardly turn all its shipping to an attack upon the United States. No European power could invade the United States.[10]

General Sheridan had conceded that coastal cities might be vulnerable at least to bombardment and raids. While a plausible scenario for such bombardment or hostile raiding from overseas was itself difficult to construct, the defense of the seaboard cities against a raid was in any event primarily the responsibility of the navy and then not of the army at large but of the numerous coastal fortifications. The army could find little new sense of purpose here.

Nor, as the military writers at the end of the 1880s implicitly feared, was the army destined to find much new sense of purpose for many years to come. Trouble with Spain briefly provided a possible international war for which to prepare later in the 1890s, and then came the "splendid little war" itself. From the war with Spain there developed a renewal of the sort of mission to which the army was accustomed, albeit on a new stage. The pacification of the Philippine archipelago brought campaigning essentially not unlike the army's historic campaigning against the North American Indians. The war with Spain having ended, the army reverted from instrument of international policy to police force within the American dominions.

Intractable as many of the inhabitants of the Philippines proved to be, so that the army's suppression of the initial Filipino Insurrection centered on Luzon was followed by years of sporadic conflict in Mindanao and the Sulus, the army's renewed police duties could hardly be expected to afford as long-lasting a mission as had the Indian campaigns across nearly the whole breadth of North America. It was not for an indefinitely renewed career as a constabulary that the army reformers from Secretary of War Elihu Root to Maj. Gen. Leonard Wood sought to reorganize the army during the first decade and a half of the 20th century. The reformers looked, rather, toward a destiny of world power. Yet the shape and scope of that military destiny eluded them. The American army in its day-to-day activities grasped all the more tightly the reality of police duties—including those on the Mexican border, when that old trouble zone flared up again after 1910—because the shape of a larger future remained so uncertain. General Wood and the preparedness advocates of the second decade of the new century spoke often in terms of continental defense as the new mission of the army in an era of world power, but the likelihood of a foreign invasion of the continental United States from across the Atlantic, to say nothing of the Pacific, remained as remote in terms of the practical logistical impediments to such an enterprise as it had been when clear-sighted Phil Sheridan denigrated the danger a generation before.[11]

In 1912 the *Infantry Journal* editorially addressed the question of the army's uncertain purposes. Referring to recent evidence that the army and the nation were awakening to new prospects in a new century and that there was an intellectual awakening in the officer corps, the *Infantry Journal* nevertheless found a central problem in "the tendency of armies to lose sight in peace of the real reason for their being." Among foreign armies there had developed recently the concept of a coherent national "doctrine" of war, which would unify all of an army's military activities. The *Infantry Journal* hoped it might encourage the formulation of an American doctrine of war. The editor, however, also recognized an almost insurmountable obstacle to the American army in its search for a unified, coherent doctrine of war:

> Without a doctrine well established through the military services there can be no national conception of war and no correct interpretation of what war has meant in the life of the nation. And it is this last that is vitally important. Yet reasoning here moves in a circle since it is in what war has meant in the life of a nation that the national conception of war should lie. In other words, a national conception of war is not to be implanted in a people through the blind adoption of another people's doctrine, with another habit of thought. The two doctrines of war best known to-day which have led to the French and German conceptions of war have something more than the mere difference of military training dividing them. They have different national characteristics, different historical development. The rest of the military world has tried for some time rather blindly to copy either the French or German doctrine, but without much success. Very naturally so. . . .
>
> No other nation can hope to take either doctrine and apply it in the same way and with equal success to its own problems. . . . Therefore, though we take not merely the text of our regulations from abroad, but the fundamental facts of a doctrine also, we must still attempt to formulate the latter to fit the facts of our national development just as we try with our regulations to adapt them to national characteristics. Until we do this anything like an American conception of war is impossible.[12]

Yet where did such reasoning lead save in a circle? What conception of war and definition of military doctrine could animate the American army when its sustained historic mission had never been the waging of large-scale war and no clear conception of a future mission in war could be suggested by the *Infantry Journal* editorship? The French and German armies could have a coherent military doctrine because their mutual rivalry shaped both armies. The American army had no comparable source of direction and doctrine.

World War I did not resolve the army's search for a new reason for being, nor did it fundamentally alter the character of the army, which remained essentially the Indian-fighting army because its major formative experiences lay on the Indian frontier. The American experience of European war in 1917–18 was not only too brief to alter old habits of thought in more than a limited way; its impact was further limited by the evident determination of civilian policy almost immediately after the guns ceased firing to disavow any prospect that a mass American army would ever again intervene in Europe's quarrels. The army moved into the 1920s and continued into the 1930s as little able as it had been in 1912 to formulate a doctrine and conception of war in the German or French manner with reference to a likely rival army. (With the U.S. Navy, the case was different, for naval strategists rightly discerned the shadow of the coming naval war against Japan. "An Orange war is considered the most probable," said a naval officer, referring to the color code for the war plans to deal with Japan.[13] The army could draw up strategic plans for no similarly probable war to be fought mainly on land.)

Lacking a plausible rival against whom to draw strategic plans, the army could capitalize on its World War I experience almost solely in the logistical and administrative areas. Here at least the memory of World War I economic mobilization inspired army planners of the 1920s and 1930s to draw up blueprints for a similar economic mobilization in a future war. As long as policy precluded the possibility that mass military power might again be used overseas, it remained very unclear against which great power a new economic mobilization might be directed.[14]

Economic mobilization planning aside, in matters concerned directly with its combat role the U.S. Army of the 1920s and 1930s went about its business of policing the Philippines and the Mexican border in the old ways inherited from its Indian-fighting history, the brief encounter with European war in 1917–18 standing as an almost irrelevant interlude. That it remained for the old Indian-fighting army to lurch abruptly toward a new conception of itself when the threat of war with Germany at last brought a strategic mission in sight is suggested symbolically by the lingering reluctance of George S. Patton, Jr., to forsake the horse cavalry for tanks. As late as 1940, Patton still hesitated to abandon the old army's means of mobility, and he grasped at various straws: "It occurs to me that, since mechanized cavalry depends for its success on a very large use of the radio, much advantage could be gained over them [by horse cavalry] should you be able to set up radio interference."[15] More substantially, the twilight influence of the Old Indian-fighting army upon preparations for a new war may well have contributed to a major operational problem of World War II: a disjunction between American strategy for the war and the kind of army that the veteran regular army officers fashioned to fight it.

American strategy in World War II aimed to effect as prompt as possible a direct confrontation with the main enemy forces opposed to the Western Allies—with the German forces in northwest Europe—to overpower the enemy's main strength and thus to bring the whole structure of the Axis empire tumbling down. British influence in the strategic councils of the Allies much compromised this American strategy, but if the Americans had had their way, the Western Allies would have employed a straightforward power-drive strategy to overwhelm the Axis with superior force. Once British commitment to OVERLORD had been secured, Anglo-American strategy did take the form desired by the Americans.[16]

Not only British strategy, however, but also the design of the U.S. Army compromised a power-drive strategy of direct confrontation with the enemy's main forces. As it emerged from its long Indian-fighting era, and especially from the final Indian wars waged across the distances of the Great Plains, the American army was designed more for mobility than to generate power. It needed to move rapidly and over long distances more than to mass overwhelming force for direct assault. As the British were often dourly to observe, though the Americans advocated a power-drive strategy, the concentration or massing of strength that would seem a logical concomitant of such strategy was not the American army's forte.

In the interwar years, when British theorists and German practitioners developed the fusing together of power and mobility in the armored division that became the foundation of the blitzkrieg, American soldiers tended to remain doubtful that mobility could be linked with power without serious loss of mobility. Gen. Charles P. Summerall, who as chief of staff of the army from 1926 to 1930 sponsored the first American prototype of an armored division, recognized the need to seek to combine "superiority of fire and superiority of movement," but he perceived "the tendency of the present age . . . toward an ever-increasing substitution of machines for man power" as calling into question the mass army with all its power. He also saw the relatively small motorized striking force as a likely arbiter of strategy in the future. He thought the brightest hope for a modern tank that could form the backbone of the new armored division lay in Walter Christie's models: light, highly mobile tanks, embodiments much more of mobility than of power.[17]

Summerall, for all that, wanted to combine the maximum feasible power with mobility in the prototype armored division. His successor as chief of staff, Gen. Douglas MacArthur, retreated from Summerall's quest for a balanced armored force. MacArthur broke up Summerall's Experimental Mechanized Force, returned to the infantry the responsibility to "give attention to machines intended to increase the striking power of the Infantry against strongly held position," and made cavalry the home of "combat vehicles . . . in roles of reconnaissance, counter-reconnaissance, flank action, pursuit and similar operations."[18]

That is, MacArthur separated mobility from power. Thereafter the infantry maintained a subsidiary interest in employing tanks, and the 2d Armored Division was eventually to emerge from the infantry's tank regiments. In the meantime the principal doctrinal development toward American armored divisions, and particularly the work of Adna R. Chaffee, Jr., as executive officer and then commander of the 7th Cavalry Brigade (Mechanized), took place in the cavalry traditions and shaped a World War II armored force whose salient characteristic was mobility rather than power. The affirmation of the commanding general of the armored force on December 7, 1942, that no requirement existed for an American 60-ton heavy tank summed up the commitment of the American armored arm in World War II to mobility above all other aspects of military force. As a result, until almost the end of the war the U.S. Army had no tank that could match the power of the Tiger or the Panther. The preference for mobility over power that had been built into the Sherman tank also assured that the U.S. Army would have no tank appropriate to the strategy of direct confrontation with the main German armies in the West.[19]

While General MacArthur in dismantling the Experimental Mechanized Force had seemingly relegated power, as distinguished from mobility, to the infantry, the American infantry also remained faithful nevertheless to an inheritance drawn not from large-scale wars but from patrolling the distances of the Great Plains. The essence of the American infantry division of World War II, the feature that set it apart from the infantry divisions of other armies, was its mobility. Everything in the American infantry division was motorized except the rifle companies, and with the addition of a few quartermaster truck companies the riflemen could be mounted as well. No other army's infantry had such potential for swift movement. In the pursuit of the Germans across France in August 1944 and across western Germany in April 1945, the American army's mobility served strategy supremely well. The American triangular infantry division of World War II, however, proved to be a very shallow reservoir of sustained fighting power. The basic combat strength of the 5,184 men in its 27 rifle companies was exhausted with dismaying rapidity when a division fighting in the Bocage of Normandy or in the Huertgen Forest might readily suffer 4,000 casualties in a month and these almost entirely among its riflemen.[20]

In the kind of direct, head-on confrontation with the enemy that the American power-drive strategy demanded in the Normandy battles and again along the German West Wall, the American army's lack of sustained combat power did not serve as well. The American infantry divisions lacked the reserves of combat strength and endurance that were needed to

overwhelm German infantry divisions even with the reduced German tables of organization of 1944. American armored divisions, designed for
exploitation rather than for the fusion of mobility with power that had made
the enemy's panzer divisions so fearsome, could not compensate for the
infantry's deficiencies, as the panzer divisions had offset shortcomings in
German infantry formations. The prolonged and costly deadlocks in Europe from June 6 to July 25, 1944, and from early September 1944 to late
March 1945 were in large part the products of the American army's inability to mass power against strong defenses. An army still designed in 1944
and 1945 for the mobility that had been the American army's historic tactical hallmark could not readily serve its own country's World War II strategy
of direct confrontation.

Any discussion of such brevity inevitably oversimplifies. Surely
other factors besides the legacy of the Indian wars helped frame the
American army's penchant for mobility in World War II. The most mechanized society on earth could hardly have failed to create a highly
mobile army, though a deficiency in combat power was not equally implicit in the army's societal origins. Yet institutions are products of their
histories, and it is worthwhile for military historians to remind themselves habitually that the history of the U.S. Army has been, during most
of its existence, the history of the Indian-fighting army.[21]

Notes

1. Jim Dan Hill, *The Minute Man in Peace and War: A History of the National Guard*
(Harrisburg, PA: Stackpole, 1964), pp. 358–359.

2. For the army of the 1790s and its political background, see Richard Kohn, *Eagle and
Sword: The Federalists and the Creation of the Military Establishment in America, 1783–
1802* (New York: Free Press, 1975).

3. *Annual Report of the Secretary of War for 1886*, 4 vols. (Washington, DC: U.S. GPO,
1886), 1:16–17.

4. *Annual Report of the Secretary of War for 1890*, 4 vols. (Washington, DC: U.S. GPO,
1890), 1:44.

5. First Lt. George P. Scriven, "The Army and Its Relation to the Organized and Unorganized Militia," *United Service*, n.s. 1 (May 1889):520. Similar approaches to a changing
military epoch include those taken in W. H. Carter, "One View of the Army Question," *United Service*, n.s. 2 (June 1889):573–578; Thomas F. Edmands, "Is Our Nation Defenceless?"
North American Review 152 (Mar. 1891):381–384; 1st Lt. A. D. Schenck, "The Efficiency of
the Army," *United Service*, n.s. 6 (July 1891):1–15; An Officer of the Army, "Army Reorgani-
zation," *United Service*, n.s. 6 (July 1891):52–59; Maj. G. W. Baird, "Recent Army
Legislation," *United Service*, n.s. 10 (Dec. 1893):501–507; and Capt. John A. Dapray, "Are
We a Military People?" *Journal of the United States Military Service Institution* 23 (Nov.
1898):371–391.

6. Scriven, "The Army and Its Relation to the Organized and Unorganized Militia," p. 520.

7. A resonant phrase in the writing of American history since its use by C. Vann Woodward in his presidential address to the American Historical Association, "The Age of Reinterpretation," *American Historical Review* 66 (Oct. 1960):3.

8. Scriven, "The Army and Its Relation to the Organized and Unorganized Militia," pp. 521–524, quotation from p. 522.

9. *Annual Report of the Secretary of War for 1884*, 4 vols. (Washington, DC: U.S. GPO, 1884), 1:49.

10. John Bigelow, *The Principles of Strategy Illustrated Mainly from American Campaigns* (1894; reprint ed., New York: Greenwood, 1968), pp. 54–55.

11. On the preparedness advocates' inability to conjure up more than a "specter" of an enemy, see John Patrick Finnegan, *Against the Specter of a Dragon: The Campaign for American Military Preparedness, 1914–1917* (Westport, CT: Greenwood, 1975).

12. "Doctrine, Conception, and History of War," *Infantry Journal* 9 (Sept.-Oct. 1912):256–258.

13. Cdr. R. B. Coffey, "The Navy War Plans Division: Naval Plans and Planning," Army War College, War Plans Division Course No. 10, March 11, 1924, p. 6, copy in box 280, Tasker H. Bliss Papers, Library of Congress, Washington, DC.

14. On economic mobilization planning, see Paul A. C. Koistinen, "The 'Industrial-Military Complex' in Historical Perspective: The Interwar Years," *Journal of American History* 65 (Mar. 1970):819–839; Marvin A. Kreidberg and Merton G. Henry, *History of Military Mobilization in the United States Army, 1775–1945* (Washington, DC: U.S. GPO, 1955), pp. 385–394, 406–423, 441–459, 493–540.

15. Martin Blumenson, *The Patton Papers, 1885–1945*, 2 vols. (Boston: Houghton Mifflin, 1972–74), 1:947.

16. I have developed this interpretation of Anglo-American strategic debate at length in my work, *The American Way of War: A History of United States Military Strategy and Policy* (New York: Macmillan, 1973), pp. 312–333, 343–354. For a similar view, see, in the series *United States Army in World War II: The War Department*, Maurice Matloff and Edwin M. Snell, *Strategic Planning for Coalition Warfare, 1941–1942* (Washington, DC: Office of the Chief of Military History, 1953), and Maurice Matloff, *Strategic Planning for Coalition Warfare, 1943–1944* (Washington, DC: Office of the Chief of Military History, 1959). Regarding efforts to deemphasize Anglo-American differences, see Kent Roberts Greenfield, *American Strategy in World War II: A Reconsideration* (Baltimore: Johns Hopkins University Press, 1963), and Richard M. Leighton, "OVERLORD Revisited: An Interpretation of American Strategy in the European War, 1942–1944," *American Historical Review* 68 (July 1963):919–937.

17. Gen. Charles P. Summerall in *Report of the Secretary of War to the President, 1928* (Washington, DC: U.S. GPO, 1928), p. 81 (first quotation), and *Report of the Secretary of War to the President, 1930* (Washington, DC: U.S. GPO, 1930), pp. 122 (second quotation) and 124–126.

18. Summerall in *Report of the Secretary of War to the President, 1931* (Washington, DC: U.S. GPO, 1931), p. 43.

19. For the statement of the commanding general of the armored force that no requirement for a heavy tank existed, see Constance McLaughlin Green, Harry C. Thomson, and Peter C. Roots, *The Ordnance Department: Planning Munitions for War*, in *United States Army in World War II: The Technical Services* (Washington, DC: Office of the Chief of Military History, 1955), p. 278. The issues of controversy in American tank development are further explored in the same work, pp. 199–200, 236–239, 278–287. For larger discussions of armored force development and doctrine, see Kent Roberts Greenfield, Robert R. Palmer, and Bell I. Wiley, *The Organization of Ground Combat Troops*, in *United States Army in*

World War II: The Army Ground Forces (Washington, DC: Historical Division, US Army, 1947), pp. 56–72, 319–335; Donald E. Houston, *Hell on Wheels: The 2d Armored Division* (San Rafael, CA: Presidio Press, 1977), pp. 1–118; and Richard M. Ogorkiewicz, *Armoured Forces: A History of Armoured Forces and Their Vehicles* (New York: Arno, 1970), pp. 86–96, 188–205. The most comprehensive work on the subject, and the best on Chaffee, is relatively uncritical: Mildred Harmon Gillie, *Forging the Thunderbolt: A History of the Development of the Armored Force* (Harrisburg, PA: Military Service Publishing Co., 1947).

20. On the shaping of the World War II infantry division, see Greenfield, Palmer, and Wiley, *Organization of Ground Combat Troops*, pp. 265–318. Some of the problems involving the staying power of the triangular division were discovered early in maneuvers before commitment to combat and are discussed in Jean R. Moenk, *A History of Large-Scale Army Maneuvers in the United States, 1935–1964* (Fort Monroe: Headquarters, US Continental Army Command, 1969), pp. 21–107. The issue of rifle company casualties and the staying power of American divisions arises repeatedly in the *European Theater of Operations* volumes of *United States Army in World War II*. Regarding the Normandy campaign, see Martin Blumenson, *Breakout and Pursuit* (Washington, DC: Office of the Chief of Military History, 1961), especially pp. 71, 76, 175–176; for the Huertgen Forest, Charles B. MacDonald, *The Siegfried Line Campaign* (Washington, DC: Office of the Chief of Military History, 1963), pp. 373–374, 428–429, 438–439, 492–493.

21. A recent book that begins to assess the long-term impact of the army's experience on the Indian frontier, especially as expressed in Robert M. Utley's keynote address, is James P. Tate, ed., *The American Military on the Frontier: Proceedings of the Seventh Military History Symposium, US Air Force Academy, 1976* (Washington, DC: US GPO, 1978).

Commentary on "Roots of American Military Policy"

Gerald F. Linderman

Any conference would be fortunate to have essays as perceptive and provocative as those of Professors Lane and Weigley, and I am pleased to have been asked to comment briefly upon them.

Professor Lane suggests that historians have given excessive weight to American antimilitary sentiment per se, that, for example, one of that sentiment's components, popular animosity against a standing army, although it may be taken at face value within the revolutionary environment that engenders it, is subsequently enmeshed in the evolution of a complex ideology. He also suggests, as I understand his argument, that by this process a bias reasonable at a particular time eventually becomes a powerful tradition periodically invoked and thus intensified by interests that view the opportunity to employ antimilitary sentiment as a vehicle capable of serving varieties of their own interests. Behind the debates regarding the locus of control over American military forces, for example, there lies the larger conflict between centralists and localists; antimilitary sentiment becomes the weapon of the latter. Behind the debates regarding the U.S. Military Academy's future, there lies the larger battle against privilege; antimilitary sentiment becomes a Jacksonian weapon. At issue is not the existence of either standing army or military instruction, as it would have been had antimilitary sentiment

I thank John Shy and Maris Vinovskis of the University of Michigan for their reactions and suggestions.

had an independent existence, but rather their nature and thus their control. Professor Lane cites in support of his argument public opinion polls of the Vietnam years revealing that antiwar sentiment is not antimilitary sentiment; studies that reexamine antimilitary sentiment within the context of such ideological cultural systems, he believes, will uncover "the kind of promilitary sentiment that social scientists have discovered recently among the American public."

Professor Lane's paper valuably cautions that our view of antimilitary sentiment has been a simplistic one, that we have too often regarded it as a given when we should have been investigating where and in what fashion partisans of other issues exploit it. The road that he here sets out is a promising one. I very much doubt, however, that it will carry us to the destination he proposes. It is possible that antimilitary feeling has less often a vitality of its own, but I doubt that its entanglement in other issues has hidden an underlying promilitary sentiment.

There is, for example, an alternative hypothesis by which we might account for the Vietnam polls: not that 19th-century antimilitary sentiment was illusory but that any contemporary promilitary sentiment might mark a relatively recent and very significant change. Could we not argue that World War II basically altered the relationship of American military and civilian sectors; that the civilian population was led by the experience of that war and the ensuing Cold War to grant, as it had not before, the necessity, the essential function, of the army; that military expansion and peacetime draft diminish the previously powerful distinction between a professional army and a citizen army; and that these factors increase the number of social surfaces on which civilians and soldiers interact and thus reduce the impotence and isolation that invite public animosity in the 19th century? I have seen in my own research the common grievance in 1898 that professional soldiers unjustifiably challenge the citizen soldier's competence to wage war. The complaint carries force in a war whose main components remain, at least in the public mind, the man and his rifle, but surely by 1945 Americans had conceded that war's requirements, patterns, and weaponry extend beyond ordinary civilian endowment, that special professional competence is required. Such an argument, then, would seek to locate points of significant change rather than to uncover a hitherto unrecognized promilitary sentiment.

Here I find instructive the case of professional diplomacy, whose past, too, is burdened by European taint and whose 19th-century existence is, like that of the standing army, caught up in patterns of larger conflict—Jacksonian interregional rivalries, for example. The distinction, however, is that events have offered professional diplomats no opportunity to demonstrate enduring essentiality or to link themselves extensively to the patterns of American daily life, as has the professional soldier. Even when he or she is not a factor in larger ideological debate, the professional diplomat remains a figure of popular suspicion and distrust, and so it was, I think, with the professional soldier and the professional army throughout the 19th century.

Professor Weigley contends with skill that the end of Indian fighting was by no means the end of the Indian-fighting army, that in the absence of any persuasive subsequent mission, the principles of the constabulary continued for half a century to inform army organization. The Indian-fighting army's emphasis on mobility over power, the unwillingness to fuse the two—these persist into the years of World War II. Although American strategy in that war gave primacy to the power drive straight at the German enemy in western Europe, American land forces lacked the organizational fundament for the power required. The results, a legacy of the constabulary, are those "prolonged and costly deadlocks" of June–July 1944 and September 1944–March 1945.

My reservation rests on a suspicion that Professor Weigley's central idea is asked to explain more than it can. Is there not a more economical explanation for the deadlock on the western front? Given the necessity of landing on narrow beaches such numbers of men and such volumes of material, of establishing and maintaining supply lines over such distances and against such opposition, could any army have performed measurably better? And if the answer is yes, how are we to know that the difference resides in that single organizational factor, the stress on mobility over force? Why not just as reasonably attribute the first deadlock to the Germans' greater measure of combat experience or the second to the severity of logistical strains?

It remains for us to demonstrate the American army's predisposition to mobility at other junctures and in a comparative context. Although Professor Weigley finds that World War I was for the army "an almost irrelevant interlude," might we not expect to find in it instances of the constabulary influence? Do American and British approaches to problems of war, then or later, diverge not at all because of an American predisposition to mobility?

Although substantiation thus remains a problem, the contention itself is original and inventive. Professor Weigley proposes connections that others of us miss and offers them in a paper revealing both a profound familiarity with history's pieces and the imagination to refit them, here to our clear advantage.

Russell F. Weigley

I am grateful that Professor Linderman found my paper stimulating. I can scarcely quarrel with his suggestion that there were other explanations for the deadlock on the western front of World War II besides the

ones I have mentioned in my paper, for I myself have written a book—
The American Way of War—largely addressing the tendency of modern
war toward deadlock for the causes that he mentions, and thus I saw no
reason to belabor the issues of massive armies and massive weights of
material all over again.

Nor do I want to belabor such issues now. Rather I take this opportunity to say how much I admire Professor Lane's paper and how much I
believe it merits careful consideration by everyone interested in the history of American civil-military relations. I agree wholeheartedly with
Professor Lane's conclusion that historians have given excessive weight
to antimilitary sentiment in America. I may have helped contribute in the
past to the impression that a deep gulf of mutual suspicion separated
American soldiers and civilians, but I do not now believe that such a gulf
existed. Rather, I believe that the leaders of the American Revolution
seized upon the antimilitary rhetoric of the British tradition of political
radicalism as a convenient means of expressing and adding grandeur
to their practical grievances against the presence of British regular soldiers in America, for those expenses they were expected to help defray.
Having seized upon an antimilitary rhetoric to justify the Revolution,
Americans were stuck with it; to repudiate the rhetoric would seem to be
to repudiate the Revolution itself. Yet to suggest that Americans were
committed to an antimilitary ideology is to make Americans appear a
more ideological people than they have ever been. Their political leaders continued to give voice, on patriotic occasions, to the old antimilitary
rhetoric of the Revolution. Rhetoric was not ideology, however, and it
never prevented the Americans from establishing in practice a military
force of whatever size and strength that practical expediency appeared
to decree. When the military forces were small, the reason was not
antimilitary ideology but that military needs were small.

Even if the notion of an antimilitary ideology and a deep gulf between American soldiers and civilians in the past is mainly a myth, as I
think it is, it can cause suspicion and confusion in civil-military dialogues
today. Professor Lane has done a considerable service in helping eliminate the myth, and I hope that this symposium can further dissolve
barriers that have hampered the soldier and the civilian in their efforts to
understand one another.

Jack C. Lane

First, let me thank Professor Linderman for his careful reading of my
paper. He has grasped my meaning and has articulated it quite well. I
do feel, though, that he was misled by the phrase in the last sentence of
my paper in which I state that the employment of a strategy based on the
concept of a cultural ideological system might uncover "a promilitary

sentiment" in the past. I must admit that my choice of words was unfortunate, because I had consciously approached the subject not to find a promilitary attitude in the past (which I certainly did not do) but to urge us to think more deeply about an American myth—namely, the belief in an all-pervading antimilitary tradition. I said about the American historical attitude toward the military that it has been inextricably entwined in the historical process and deeply enmeshed in American ideology. I tried to show that when this concept is applied to incidences of perceived antimilitarisms in a specific period—in this case the early national period—a picture emerges in which, to paraphrase Professor Linderman, antimilitary sentiment becomes a vehicle for a variety of interests. I certainly had no intention of substituting a promilitary myth for an antimilitary myth.

Actually, we have much to learn about the precise nature of past American attitudes toward the military. I suspect, however, that when sophisticated studies have been made on this important subject, we will find, if not a stronger promilitary sentiment than we heretofore suspected, at least a significant affinity with things military. Marcus Cunliffe, as I indicated in my paper, has suggested this affinity in the ante bellum period, and there are suggestions that it was even stronger after the Civil War. When we find such educators as William Torrey Harris extolling the virtues of the military ethic as it applies to public schooling, and when we hear post–Civil War businessmen called "captains of industry" commanding an "industrial army," we should begin to realize that American attitudes toward the military are much more complex than antimilitary shibboleths suggest.

Having established, I hope, that I have not attempted to uncover a "heretofore unrecognized promilitary sentiment," I do not find myself at odds with Professor Linderman's analysis of post–World War II American attitudes toward the military. Indeed, I argued precisely his point: that historical forces, not "some fear of or revulsion against the military," shaped those attitudes. I would phrase his argument somewhat differently, however: the nationalization, even internationalization, of American life in the 20th century has made Americans much more amenable to all national institutions, including the military. That, however, is precisely my point. As I have argued elsewhere, 19th-century Americans viewed military institutions from a localist, not a nationalist, perspective and thus found them not detestable but irrelevant. Nineteenth-century localism and 20th-century nationalism are key elements in America's changing cultural ideological systems and necessarily produced differing sentiments toward military institutions. We ought to be exploring these shifting sentiments under changing ideological beliefs, not some mythical antimilitarism.

2

THE PEOPLE
OF THE ARMY:
The Military
Social World

Officers and their guests under a cactus, Fort Thomas, AZ, 1886.
(Source: National Archives)

Perceptions of the Army Wife:
Her Role in a Changing Society

Elizabeth M. Finlayson

> When a man enters the service, the government has gained not one, but two—the man and his wife. If the wife is well informed as to what is expected of her, the probability is greater that her husband will have an easier and more successful career. As he progresses through the ranks, she too should have accustomed herself to the increasing responsibilities that become hers, and accept them with confidence and assurance, permitting her to progress as her husband does.
>
> —Mary Preston Gross, *Mrs. NCO* (1969)

In most of her book *Mrs. NCO*, Mary Preston Gross focuses on the proper role of "Mrs. NCO" as a contributing member of the military family and a helpmate to her husband in meeting his career obligations. Similar books have been written for "Mrs. Lieutenant" and "Mrs. Field Grade."

Some wives read such books as these and, faithfully following the advice of the author, become integrated into the military and its way of life—a life resplendent with social and professional customs and traditions. Other wives find even the implications of such titles as "Mrs. NCO" unacceptable. After all, have they not been schooled to believe that wives have no rank?

The portrayal of the army wife as a helpmate is common throughout the literature of post–World War II years. To illustrate, we may assemble an interesting composite of the army wife from the catchy phrases of several authors. The army wife "is the epitome of womanhood; her ability to cope with the new and unexpected is unsurpassed; and always she complements the high calling of her husband."[1] She is the "diplomat without portfolio" who "never complains when she has to move," whose "only tragedy that upsets her is separation from her husband."[2] She is "an independent dependent"[3] who "finds satisfaction and

47

fulfillment in her home,"[4] who "rears her family, generally, under conditions which would seem impossible to her civilian sisters," accomplishing all this as "a good soldier, whose sense of Duty, Honor, and Country
are those of the Army itself."[5] "In these things [she] will find enough of
glamour, interest, satisfaction, life."[6] Nancy Shea, the original "Emily
Post" for military wives, writes in an early edition of *The Army Wife*: "As
a wife you have a most important role in your husband's Army career. It
does not matter whether he is an enlisted man, noncommissioned officer, warrant officer, or commissioned officer. Although no serviceman's
career was ever made by his wife, many have been hindered or helped
by the social skills of their wives, their flexibility, and their loyalty toward
the Army and its customs."[7] Certainly wives who read the literature are
alerted to the concept of the army unit as a husband-wife team and the
promise that there are career benefits for the serviceman whose team
plays the game well.

    While several recent studies have focused more on the effect of
these expectations on the serviceman's wife in terms of role stress and
conflict, time itself appears to have done little to change the attitudes of
the military. In fact, the *Officer's Guide,* not in the truest sense an official
publication, reads very much in its 1977 edition as it did in 1942:

> The wife of an officer exerts a powerful influence upon the success of
> his career. In many assignments her personality, character, and ca-
> pacities are a strong and necessary complement to her husband.
> She can be an asset or burden; an inspiration and help, or a stone
> about his neck . . . . She must learn about the Army, its standards
> and requirements, its codes and opportunities, its established ways,
> so that she may understand the problems faced by her husband.
> This knowledge will help her to assist her husband to achieve most
> from his service.[8]

Or, in the words of Nancy Shea, "Never ask your husband to help with
the dishes at night; he has been working for the government all day."[9]

    These reports of the typical army wife obviously do not describe the
many servicemen and their wives who have not been career minded,
who have seen their army life as temporary, unsettling, and disruptive.
While we may say that the literature was not written for these wives, the
fact remains that World War II and Vietnam saw an influx into the military of short timers and draftees who far outnumbered the careerists.
The noncareerist wife would probably not respond very favorably to social demands placed upon her by virtue of her husband's temporary
stint in the army as she tried to cope with the frustration of frequent
moves and frequent separations from her husband. Ellwyn R. Stoddard
and Claude E. Cabanillas report in *The Army Officer's Wife: Social
Stresses in a Complementary Role:*

Huge numbers of ROTC and OCS officers brought into the military service during World War II and the Korean War and again during the Vietnam conflict had often been married prior to their officer training. And the wives of these non-Academy officers are more likely to have developed loyalties and interests divergent from those rigidly specified for the traditional officer's wife. In this sense, there has been an increasing rate of nonparticipation in strictly military affairs by the modern Army officer's wife, who is a converted civilian with civilian tastes and loyalties at odds with the stringent boundaries formerly placed around an aspiring officer's wife.[10]

Certain situations in the military are, of course, more conducive to participation in military affairs than others. Studies show that wives who live on post, and those who share with their serviceman husbands an overseas assignment, identify with the military to a substantially greater degree, and feel greater satisfaction, than do wives whose only contact with the military is an occasional social event or a visit to a nearby commissary. Most wives say they prefer to live on the post; it is convenient and relatively inexpensive, and a wealth of social and military activities are available to them, in which they participate in varying degrees.[11] For wives who live on post, as Morris Janowitz remarks in *The Professional Soldier*, "the military profession is more than an occupation; it is a complete style of life."[12] Unfortunately, for many families, on-post and overseas assignments are few and far between. The fact is that most tours are spent in civilian housing.

Army wives who live in civilian communities report that they do not feel the close ties to the military, that they lose touch with the style of life that on-post living makes possible. For the most part, their husbands go to work in the morning and come home at night, not unlike the husbands of their neighbors. When husbands are away from home on temporary duty (TDY) assignments, wives report that they miss the support of other military wives that on-post living provides. Some wives feel that the geographical isolation from the military and the constant moves from one civilian community to another create feelings of detachment and alienation from the military. Such feelings are particularly common among young wives, whose husband may have neither the rank nor the position that would tend to bring their wives the social companionship of other army wives.

For wives who have developed no outside interests of their own, the army can be a lonely and frustrating experience. On the other hand, women who have learned to rely on their own resources often welcome the chance to be free of military obligations while living as "civilians." These are women who adjust well to change and who, more than likely, report enthusiastically that the opportunities for travel and for meeting new people more than compensate for the inconveniences of military mobility.

While the attitudes of the military establishment may be slow to change, one primary force of change in society at large is affecting the army wife's perception of her role. The women's liberation and civil rights movements have both done much to alter the lives of women in our society. New army wives will probably not be willing to forfeit the freedom and independence made possible for them through these movements.

Several publications of recent years address the issue. In *The Professional Army Officer in a Changing Society*, Sam C. Sarkesian writes:

> Changing outlooks on the role of women and the impact of the women's liberation movement have had some influence on perceptions of the role of officer's wives. Some are speaking out against meaningless social functions and demanding that a wife should have an identity of her own, separate from her husband's career in the military. . . . Obviously, the professional world cannot remain immune to social changes and the women's liberation movement. But given the nature of the military profession and its demands on a wife, it is unlikely that many women who are oriented towards women's lib would be attracted to the profession, and if they are initially, but changed their mind, it is unlikely that they would allow their husbands to remain long in the profession. There will be some changes in attitude on the part of the military, but these will hardly be enough to cause any dramatic revision of the need for husband-wife career drive within the military.[13]

In a report prepared at the U.S. Army War College, William Bennett takes an overall look at changing social attitudes for women and the military:

> The Army wife plays an important role in her husband's career. She is expected to stand behind him and make his life easier, be the mainstay in raising children and provide support socially. In this changing society, many women are no longer satisfied to be relegated to this passive support role. Some Army wives have their own careers. Some want to pick their own friends and chose their own type of leisure.[14]

As one wife succinctly remarked, "I don't want to spend my life in a role which is like being a den mother to a grown man. I want my own identity and so do my friends. We want to be able to choose what we do, instead of having our lives programmed for us by the wives of our husbands' fellow Army officers."[15] Ellwyn Stoddard and Claude Cabanillas believe that "the growing influence of the Women's Liberation Movement in trying to destroy the demeaning female stereotypes of the past and give a new positive image of independence and self-respect is not lost on many officers' wives, who review their own circumstances in the light of this new perspective."[16]

The demands that the army makes of the wives of servicemen conflict with the wife's concept of what she must experience if she is to find army life personally rewarding. As one woman recently observed, "If I were to devote my entire life to my husband's career, then what resources would I have to fall back on when he is gone—which is frequently—and I must spend my days without his support. I must have a life of my own, and my husband shares with me in this belief."[17]

Unsurprisingly, when I met with several groups of army wives recently, I found that most of them felt under no pressure to participate in army functions. Rather than perceiving the role expectation as stressful or conflicting, many contemporary wives seemed somewhat startled by the notion that the army might care how they spend their time. They found the idea new and novel. Army wives today tend to participate in the social life of the military to the extent that they feel inclined to do so, with no feeling of needing to do more because it is expected. They reported that, on assignments when their husband's position required additional responsibilities of them, they were able to respond to the extra demands—as would any other wife—without feeling pressured to do so. Wives also questioned the idea that they bore some responsibility for their husband's advancement. They do not see themselves as being instrumental in their husband's career promotions. In fact, as a group they reported having been told by their husbands, "You don't have to help me with my career. I can make it on my own."

The army seems to be experiencing some fallout from the overall societal changes that are freeing women from some of the bondages of the past. The reason may be in part that the people of the pre–World War II "old army," who felt very strongly about military traditions and customs, have reached the age of retirement and are no longer on active duty, where their influence can be felt. Perhaps too it is time we stopped thinking in terms of the typical army wife, since in reality there is no such person. Military men, just like men in any other profession, marry women of many backgrounds. As wives they are not enlisted or commissioned; in that sense, they are not military. In many respects, they evaluate the pros and cons of their husband's career just as would their civilian counterparts. If the army wishes to retain in the volunteer army the men who have successfully enlisted or have been commissioned, it would do well to court their wives. Many career decisions are made when families are young, when the serviceman has not attained a rank or position that gives him financial or professional security. Neither the enlisted man nor the officer is at all likely to make the army his career unless his wife can live with his decision. The army's position, therefore, should offer encouragement and opportunity to the modern wife so that she too can find personal fulfillment and growth within the military environment. In the long run, her partnership with her service husband and with the military could well be strengthened if she is also able to stand alone in her own right.

Notes

1. *The Officer's Guide*, 8th ed. (Harrisburg, PA: Military Service Publishing Co., 1942), p. 318.

2. Nancy Shea, *The Army Wife*, 3d ed. rev. (New York: Harper and Brothers, 1954), passim.

3. Nancy Shea, *The Army Wife*, 4th ed. (New York: Harper and Row, Inc., 1966), p. 114.

4. Betty Kinzer and Marion Leach, *What Every Army Wife Should Know* (Harrisburg, PA: Stackpole Co., 1965), p. 28.

5. *The Officer's Guide*, 8th ed., p. 318.

6. Russel B. Reynolds, *The Officer's Guide*, 31st ed. (Harrisburg, PA: Stackpole Co., 1966), p. 95.

7. Shea, *The Army Wife*, 4th ed., p. 1.

8. *The Officer's Guide*, 39th ed. (Harrisburg, PA: Stackpole, Co., 1977), p. 105.

9. Shea, *The Army Wife*, 3d ed. rev. (1954), p. 149.

10. Ellwyn R. Stoddard and Claude E. Cabanillas, "The Army Officer's Wife: Social Stresses in a Complementary Role," *The Social Psychology of Military Service*, eds. Nancy L. Goldman and David Segal (Beverly Hills, CA: Sage Publications, 1976), p. 158.

11. Elizabeth M. Finlayson, "A Study of the Wife of the Army Officer," *Families in the Military System*, eds. Hamilton I. McCubbin, Barbara B. Dahla, and Edna J. Hunter (Beverly Hills, CA: Sage Publications, 1976), pp. 19–41.

12. Morris Janowitz, *The Professional Soldier: A Social and Political Portrait* (New York: Free Press, 1960), p. 175.

13. Sam Charles Sarkesian, *The Professional Army Officer in a Changing Society* (Chicago: Nelson-Hall Co., 1975), pp. 40–41.

14. William M. Bennett, Jr., et al., "Army Families" (Group Research Project, Army War College, Carlisle Barracks, PA, 1974), pp. 3–4.

15. Mildred Kavanaugh, "Coffees, Teas, but Without Me!" *Family* 9 (Aug. 1973):5.

16. Stoddard and Cabanillas, "The Army Officer's Wife," p. 152.

17. Interview with the wife of a colonel in the regular army at James Madison University, Harrisonburg, VA, April 1, 1979.

The American Soldier:
Myths in Need of History

Richard H. Kohn

Anyone who remembers the controversy about the behavior of American prisoners of war in Korea, and anyone who has listened to the exaggerated predictions of violence by Vietnam veterans, knows about the myths and misrepresentations that have attached to the American soldier.[1] These myths do *not* bear repeating here. They survive with remarkable staying power because they are so useful: in inspiring patriotism, in criticizing American participation in a war or the government's military policies, in celebrating our national virtue. American and foreign observers, assuming that we are somehow unique, have created stereotypical images in attempting to discover the military essence in our character as a people. These myths are perpetuated also by scholars, who in the pursuit of "social science" or in the service of a government practicing "human engineering"—psychologist Robert Yerkes's charming phrase in 1941—ask the same questions, using the same categories, in the same search for all-encompassing generalizations about Americans in service.[2] Far and away the most pernicious myth of all is that there was, or is, any such thing as the American soldier—a prototypical American in uniform—or that our military forces, either as institutions or as collections of individuals, reflect our true character as a people and as a nation.

It is time for some common sense on this subject. It is time to cease trying, in the face of logic and sound scholarship, to generalize about

something as varied as military service that has been experienced by so
many diverse people under such disparate circumstances for as long as
three centuries. Consider, for example:

- There has never been one American army, but a bewildering potpourri
  of different kinds of forces and units at different times. Peacetime regulars in the 19th century consisted mostly of drifters and immigrants.[3] Not
  even mass wartime armies have been homogeneous: in 1775 and 1861,
  the armies swelled with enthusiastic volunteers who probably differed
  considerably in background and certainly in motivation from the coerced masses of draftees, drafted substitutes, and bounty and
  draft-induced volunteers of 1777 and 1863.[4] In 1898, a flood of men ena-
  bled the regular army to reject three out of four volunteers.[5] During the
  1940–41 buildup, the army was a tangled mixture of different groups:
  regular and Reserve Officers Training Corps (ROTC) officers, old regular noncoms, drafted enlisted men—and National Guardsmen.[6]
- The army has always included categories of units that were special by
  composition or function. I suspect that, for their eras, the coast artillery
  and the airborne were not representative of the army as a whole. We
  should also remember the segregated black regiments, the experimental Indian companies, the Philippine scouts, and the Japanese-
  American units. Even our mass armies have been skewed: the World
  War II infantry enlisted ranks could not have been a cross section of the
  population if a large proportion of the college men became officers and
  the skilled or technically apt were skimmed off for the technical branches and the air corps.[7]
- We should not expect the army as an institution to reflect society unless a
  centralized, stratified, cohesive, authoritarian, and autocratic institution
  can reflect a decentralized, heterogeneous, individualistic, democratic
  society. The army reflects society only by comparison with other armies.
- While there are some universal truths about military organization and
  experience, the changes in the course of history will explain more than
  the similarities. Battle, for example, has evolved since medieval times.
  What motivates men and enables them to endure the stress has depended on the men, the nature of battle itself, and the conditions of service. With respect to the period since 1940, social scientists have
  emphasized different factors motivating men in battle, and John
  Keegan, having reviewed this literature for his own study, suspects that
  the will to survive, and coercion, have been far more important than primary group cohesion or shared values.[8]

I have no wish to appear before you as some "nattering nabob of
negativism." My purpose is not to provoke you but to plead with you: give
the American soldier a history. In point of fact, despite a vast literature,
rich source material, and some excellent recent scholarship, we know
precious little about American soldiers: who they were, why they enlisted or allowed themselves to be coerced into service, what their leaving and returning meant to their communities, what they thought, why
they fought, how they behaved, and what impact service had on them

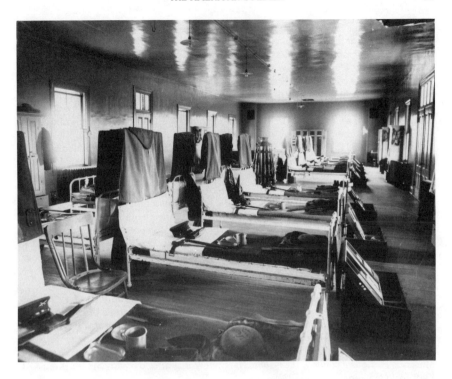

Squadroom prepared for inspection, Fort Totten, NY, 1908.
(Source: National Archives)

and on society.[9] Unless we abandon not only our stereotypes but also our propensity *to think in terms of stereotypes,* American soldiers will remain as anonymous as that mausoleum across the river in Arlington makes them. Until we deal with enlisted men and their experiences within the perspective of change and time, the American soldier will have no history—and therefore no identity.

Notes

The author published a fuller version of this paper as "The Social History of the American Soldier: A Review and Prospectus for Research," *American Historical Review* 86 (June 1981): 553–567.

1. On the Korean controversy, see Albert D. Biderman's classic *March to Calumny: The Story of American POW's in the Korean War* (New York: Macmillan, 1963); Peter Karsten, "The American Citizen Soldier: Triumph or Disaster," *Military Affairs* 30 (Spring 1966):34–40; H. H. Wubben, "American Prisoners of War in Korea: A Second Look at the 'Something New in History' Theme," *American Quarterly* 22 (Spring 1970):3–19. An excellent review of the predictions and realities of Vietnam veterans is Jack Ladinsky, "Vietnam, the Veterans, and the Veterans Administration," *Armed Forces and Society* 2 (Spring 1976):435–467.

2. Soldiers and military service have been used for the purposes of social science at least since the Civil War and the publication of Benjamin Apthorp Gould's *Investigations in the Military and Anthropological Statistics of American Soldiers*, Vol. 2 of U.S. Sanitary Commission, *Sanitary Memoirs of the War of the Rebellion* (New York: Hurd and Houghton, 1869), and this use continued in Samuel A. Stouffer et al., *The American Soldier*, Studies in Social Psychology in World War II (Princeton: Princeton University Press, 1949), 2 vols. See also the introduction, Stouffer's "Some Afterthougts of a Contributor to *The American Soldier*, and Daniel Lerner's, "*The American Soldier* and the Public" *Studies in the Scope and Method of "The American Soldier,"* eds. Robert K. Merton and Paul F. Lazarsfeld, (Glencoe, IL: Free Press, 1950), pp. 9, 10, 198, 200–201, 216–219, 222–232. For Yerkes's statement, submitted as a memorandum to the Secretary of War in January 1941, see Robert M. Yerkes, "Man-Power and Military Effectiveness: The Case for Human Engineering," *Journal of Consulting Psychology* 5 (Sept.–Oct. 1941):205–209.

3. Marcus Cunliffe, *Soldiers and Civilians: The Martial Spirit in America, 1775–1865* (Boston: Little, Brown, and Co., 1968), pp. 116–120, 125; Francis Paul Prucha, *Broadax and Bayonet: The Role of the United States Army in the Development of the Northwest, 1815–1860* (Madison: State Historical Society of Wisconsin, 1953), pp. 37–45; Victor Hicken, *The American Fighting Man* (New York: Macmillan, 1969), pp. 341–343, 350–351; Jack D. Foner, *The United States Soldier Between Two Wars: Army Life and Reforms, 1865–1898* (New York: Humanities Press, 1970), pp. 6–10.

4. The best single study of manpower in the Revolution is Mark Edward Lender, "The Enlisted Line: The Continental Soldiers of New Jersey" (Ph.D. diss., Rutgers University, 1975). For a broader discussion, see Charles Royster, *A Revolutionary People at War: The Continental Army and American Character, 1775–1783* (Chapel Hill: University of North Carolina Press, 1980). The Civil War draft system is discussed in Eugene Converse Murdock, *Patriotism Limited, 1862–1865: The Civil War Draft and Bounty System* (Kent, OH: Kent State University Press, 1967).

5. Marvin A. Kreidberg and Merton G. Henry, *History of Military Mobilization in the United States, 1775–1945* (Washington, D.C: Department of the Army, 1955), p. 163.

6. For a discussion of some of the problems, see Stouffer, *American Soldier*, 1:61–81.

7. Ibid., 245–247; Robert R. Palmer, Bell I. Wiley, and William R. Keast, *The Procurement and Training of Ground Combat Troops*, in *United States Army in World War II: The Army Ground Forces* (Washington, DC: Department of the Army, 1948), pp. 3–4, 6, 10, 11, 16–18.

8. John Keegan, *The Face of Battle* (New York: Viking Press, 1976), especially chapter 5. See also Keegan's statement in "The Historian and Battle," *International Security* 3 (Winter 1978–1979):147. The subject continues to attract considerable interest. See, for example, Frederick J. Kviz, "Survival in Combat as a Collective Exchange Process," *Journal of Political and Military Sociology* 6 (Fall 1978):219–232. Kviz (p. 219) calls for just the kind of generalizations that I believe should be avoided. An example of such generalizing is Peter Maslowski, "A Study of Morale in Civil War Soldiers," *Military Affairs* 34 (Dec. 1970): 122–127.

9. The best review of the literature is Peter Karsten, *Soldiers and Society: The Effects of Military Service and War on American Life* (Westport, CT: Greenwood Press, 1978), pp. 31–48. Karsten notes (pp. 3–4) that we really know very little, but he structures his sources topically for generalizations across time. He states (p. 12): "I was struck by the degree to which the experiences and attitudes of eighteenth-, nineteenth-, and twentieth-century American soldiers were more alike than they were different. . . .there were differences. . . . But, on balance, the differences appear (to me, at least) to be less significant than the similarities."

Comments on the Noncommissioned Officer

Ernest F. Fisher, Jr.

When we examine the noncommissioned officer throughout the U.S. Army's long history, we are led to ask three questions concerning him. Who was he? What was his role? What was his status? Seeking answers to these questions, we find that the answers generally vary, depending upon the period of the army's history that we are studying. The answers vary not only in the context of time but also within the context of the current military organization and weapons development.

Turning to the first question—who was the noncommissioned officer and what were his origins?—we find that during the War for Independence he might, in a state militia unit, have been the younger brother of a popularly elected captain of a company. Often the noncommissioned officer might also be a substantial farmer with some influence among his neighbors. As for the Continental Line, noncommissioned officers were more often men who by nature were drawn to the military life but lacked either the social standing or the education to become commissioned officers. Later in our nation's history, as the tide of European immigration swelled, the noncommissioned officer was sometimes a peasant boy from Central Europe, a former professional soldier from Prussia, a cashiered lieutenant from the French army, a gymnasium graduate from one of the smaller German states, or a destitute Irishman or Englishman seeking his fortune in the American West, where he sometimes took his discharge after completing his enlistment. Examples of these categories and more are to be found in extant company descriptive books maintained within regiments throughout much of the 19th century. Most of these men, despite the diversity of their ethnic backgrounds and education, shared a desire to better themselves and looked upon the U.S. Army as offering the means of doing so. In most cases, they were not disappointed.

During periods of hard times and high unemployment, especially in the latter half of the 19th century but also in the 20th, the noncommissioned officer was sometimes a former business clerk, a mechanic, or a salesman. When the nation resorted to the draft in the Civil War and in the major wars of the 20th century, some noncommissioned officers were college graduates and unemployed carpenters. In any case, the noncom was a man who had impressed his company commander as able and firm, capable of being a foreman, or a leader of men. The noncommissioned officer's role as administrator/supervisor or as combat leader has been equally varied. He has, from the army's beginning, played an important administrative or supervisory role—keeping duty rosters, issuing rations, overseeing quarters, enforcing discipline, and assisting in

Noncommissioned officers and men relaxing at Fort Keogh, MT, circa 1890. *(Source: National Archives)*

training recruits in the school of the soldier. The greatest variations in his function, however, are evident in the changes in his tactical role since the 18th century. From the War for Independence through the Civil War, the linear battle formations prescribed by regulation and by training manuals assigned to the noncommissioned officer mainly the roles of file closer and guide. He was to help the troops keep their alignment during the many elaborate drill evolutions that units practiced on the parade ground and took with them onto the battlefield. Under fire the noncommissioned officer continued to perform his traditional role of forcing the men to hold their ranks when every instinct suggested flight.

There were, however, exceptions to these roles. The first appeared during the Indian wars, both before and after the Civil War, when the challenge of fighting small bands of highly mobile Indians made it necessary to adopt tactics involving small units. These tactics often elevated the noncommissioned officer to combat commander of a small unit. War Department records include reports from the field that frequently mention noncommissioned officers who had distinguished themselves in such a role. The second exception was an outgrowth of the evolution of weapons and equipment since World War I. Crew-served weapons, capable of a high rate of fire and mounted on vehicles able to traverse many kinds of terrain, have gradually placed in the hands of combat-arm noncommissioned officers firepower far greater than that controlled by a regimental commander in the Civil War or, in some cases, than that of a company commander in World War II.

More than a century before Rudyard Kipling penned the phrase that has since become a cliché—"The backbone of the Army is the noncommissioned man"—officers of the U.S. Army had described the noncommissioned officer in similar terms. Yet in spite of frequent affirmations of his worth, not until the post-Vietnam decade did the noncommissioned officer gain the status of careerist in his own right, possessing his own system of selection, education, and evaluation paralleling that long enjoyed by the commissioned officer.

Early in the 19th century in the more technical branches of the service, such as artillery, signal, ordnance, quartermaster, and medical, noncommissioned officers had often received, in varying degrees, formal and systematic training in special branch schools. This practice contrasted markedly with the custom of many European armies that had long maintained special academies for the formal training of noncommissioned officers. As with the noncommissioned officer's tactical role, however, the growing lethality of weapons and their increasing complexity made necessary more systematic training or schooling for the noncommissioned officer, especially in combat arms. In 1971 the army responded to this demand with the creation of a noncommissioned officers' educational system consisting of a graduated training and testing program that replaced the traditional ad hoc and on-the-job training methods for these ranks. At the apex of this educational system is the Sergeants Major Academy established at Fort Bliss in 1972. Improvements in the noncommissioned officer's selection, training, and promotion procedures have greatly improved his position in the army. The noncommissioned officers' corps, whose senior representative is the sergeant major of the army, has through these developments won from the army establishment growing recognition of its status as a professional corps coequal in importance to the officer corps, so that the two operate in tandem, leading and administering the U.S. Army on a day-to-day basis.

The Army Officer as Organization Man

William B. Skelton

Historians and social scientists have studied 19th-century army officers in a wide variety of roles: as policemen of the frontier, as agents of manifest destiny, as formulators of the "American Way of War," as explorers and railroad builders, and as nascent military professionals. One additional role has received relatively little scholarly treatment, yet it is central to an understanding of the regular army as a social institution. I am speaking of the army officer as bureaucrat—as one of the first representatives of that now ubiquitous species the organization man.

The nature of modern military organization makes it obvious that officers would fill this role. Even at the army's lowest ebb, when it was scattered in tiny garrisons along the western and seacoast frontiers, it was a large institution that involved the full-time services of several thousand officers, enlisted men, and civilian employees. It was hierarchical in organization and was relatively highly specialized internally; it operated by fixed rules and regulations, possessed mechanisms to enforce compliance among group members, and aspired to the ideal of "efficiency" in the performance of its functions.

Moreover, the army was one of the very few large bureaucracies in the United States through much of the 19th century. Despite the economic revolution of the ante bellum era, most economic activity remained fragmented and decentralized until the Civil War. It was carried on in business offices and in shops employing at most a small staff of clerks or a few dozen manual workers. Political parties, though appealing to a mass voting public and increasingly directed by full-time managers, had little permanent or formal organization. They relied on patronage and on the force of mutual interest to unite diffuse regional and ethnic co-alitions. As social historians have emphasized recently, ante bellum Americans did experiment with a variety of institutional forms that were specialized in function and were organized along bureaucratic lines: they included the penitentiary, the factory, and the urban public school system. These, however, were usually small and local in scope. Only the other branches of the federal government—such institutions as the Post Office Department, the customs service, the Public Land Office, and the navy—approached the army in size, complexity, or cohesion, and none surpassed it in these qualities.

Army officers were thus among the first Americans to function within a restrictive bureaucratic environment. This condition shaped the internal life of the officer corps in various ways. We may first consider the elusive problem of career motivation. Important to the self-image of the military profession is the view that the military service is a "calling" rather than merely an occupation. Young men are supposedly drawn to a military career by strong positive forces—family traditions of military leadership, dreams of martial glory, patriotic devotion—rather than by such mundane considerations as money and security. Certainly some individuals in the old army made career choices in accordance with this stereotype, following in the footsteps of heroic forebears or feeling inspired by the "martial spirit" allegedly so pervasive in American society.

Most officers, however, seem to have selected their careers for more prosaic reasons. Officers' biographies and memoirs, and especially the thousands of letters of application for military appointments that are scattered through the collections of the National Archives, contain relatively few references to the romantic appeal of military life. Far more common are tales of tragedy and economic deprivation—of well-to-do families reduced to poverty; of widows struggling to support numerous children; of educational careers thwarted by the lack of funds or by a parent's death.[1] Even the applications of sons of army and navy officers mention economic circumstances more frequently than positive motivations.[2] There are constant reminders that the vaunted social mobility of the 19th century was not entirely upward. Middle- and upper-class families often declined in fortune, and not everyone fit Richard Hofstadter's depiction of the "typical American" of the ante bellum period as "an expectant capitalist, a hardworking, ambitious person for whom enterprise was a kind of religion, and [who] everywhere . . . . found conditions that encouraged him to extend himself."[3] Although there were many exceptions, the army as a large, permanent organization probably appealed most strongly to aspiring officers—attracting them with its offer of a free education and of a "respectable," if not very lucrative, career, protected from the rough and tumble of contemporary civilian society.

Officer's commission for William Bradford, signed by President
Andrew Jackson. *(Source: National Archives)*

Thus a certain type of person was most likely drawn to a military
career, a person who, because of temperament or family circumstances,
placed a high value on the security that a bureaucratic institution could
provide. Still, what effects did the career itself have? Did it eventually
lead to the development of a service ethic or cause men to regard the
army as offering a psychically rewarding way of life? For some officers,

military service seems indeed to have had this effect. A specialized education at West Point, prolonged service at isolated posts, the exhilerating, if infrequent, experience of combat, perhaps marriage to the sister or daughter of a fellow soldier—all worked to separate regulars from the mainstream of civilian society and to bind them to a unique military milieu. "I never could be happy out of the army," wrote Lt. Earl Van Dorn after 6 years of active duty. "I have no other home—could make none that would be genial to my feelings. The minds of civilians and ours run in different directions."[4]

On the whole, however, regulars appear to have found army life remarkably unrewarding. They filled their letters and journals with complaints about low pay, slow promotion rates, frequent family separations, the monotony of garrison duty, and the lack of esteem for the military profession in the larger society. Nearly every officer for whom adequate information is available considered resignation at one or more times during his career. The greatest attraction of military service—and the force that kept the attrition rate low in the 19th-century officer corps—remained the security of belonging to a large organization, an attraction that expanded in mid-career, as officers saw their alternative prospects fade. While Maj. William H. T. Walker was "tired of the glory of serving such an ungrateful old scoundrel as Uncle Sam," he considered himself "too poor and proud to resign. . . . To pull off my coat & commence at the bottom of the ladder without money or credit is rather too bitter a pill for a man of forty to swallow." After 19 years in the army, Cap. John R. Vinton admitted that he had little of the "adventurer's spirit" and dreaded trusting his fortunes to chance. "The mere *certainty* of our small pittance of pay, is therefore a consideration more satisfactory to me than twice its amount would be if depending on the contingencies of luck or trade." "When are you going to resign?" Lt. Cyrus B. Comstock asked an army friend. "We can all agree that the Army is not the place for a man of energy & ability—but how fearful we all are of the plunge."[5] Many officers who left the service, either by resignation or because of disbandment, tried to return or sought berths in other branches of the governmental bureaucracy that offered a similar refuge from the vicissitudes of a freewheeling, competitive society.

To say that officers placed a high value on security is not to say that they lacked ambition. The quest for personal advancement and recognition permeated American culture in the 19th century, and the army could hardly have escaped its influence. In contrast to their European counterparts, most American officers did not come from aristocratic social backgrounds that could offer them status and financial security independent of their military commissions. The drive to advance, to achieve and maintain status, was thus an all-absorbing drive in the army, as it was in the larger society. Officers stood apart from their civilian contemporaries by virtue of the type of advancement they sought. While most 19th-century citizens would have defined success as some form of independent entrepreneurship—the ownership of a farm, plantation, or small business—regulars viewed it in organizational terms, as upward mobility within the army's rigidly defined hierarchy of ranks. In doing so, they anticipated the dominant values of 20th-century organizational society.

If there were a way of gauging mental energy, it would almost certainly determine that old army officers expended more of that resource in the pursuit of bureaucratic goals—promotion, higher pay, favorable assignments—than in any other phase of their professional lives. In part this preoccupation reflected the closed, even stifling nature of military bureaucracy. Strict seniority governed ordinary promotion through the grade of full colonel. The army lacked a retirement system until 1861; aged commanders either resigned voluntarily or, more likely, died in service. Although Congress occasionally added to the permanent military establishment, most of the original commissions in the new regiments went to citizen appointees rather than to promotion-hungry junior officers. Hundreds of West Point graduates started their careers as brevet second lieutenants, an anomalous grade intended merely to keep them in service until permanent vacancies opened. In 1836, the Adjutant General estimated that a cadet receiving his first commission at the age of 21 could expect to command a regiment when he reached 79.[6]

Under such circumstances, the officer corps seethed with frustrated ambition. Officers turned on each other in angry quarrels over relative rank, published their grievances in the press, and plotted circuitous routes around promotion bottlenecks. They did not hesitate to solicit political support outside the army. When Congress considered adding new regiments in 1854, for example, the Georgia legislature passed a resolution backing Lt. James P. Flewellen for promotion; another young officer bolstered his application with the recommendations of 79 Pennsylvania legislators, 15 congressmen, and the state governor; and a third had the support of the entire congressional delegations of all six New England states.[7] Thwarted by the seniority rule in their quest for advancement, many regulars placed their hopes in brevet rank, a type of honorary rank higher than an officer's regular grade that was granted for gallant or meritorious conduct or for 10 years' service in one grade. Bitter controversies over brevet rank, especially the pay and command prerogatives attached to it, erupted repeatedly during the 19th century and at times threatened the stability of the army. Officers showed an unseemly interest in the health of their superiors. Lt. Jacob E. Blake wrote a friend in 1834: "Promotions will be exceedingly good no doubt, Capt. Ford has resigned already, Lieut. Bradford has shot himself accidentally in loading a pistol, Noland has just resigned, and Capt. Hunter proposes following. By the bye I nearly rose one a few days since; Capt. Wickliffe now at Leavenworth, hurt himself very seriously in loading a double-barrel gun, but he is likely to recover."[8]

Officers' ambitions for personal advancement interacted closely with another aspect of their bureaucratic lives—intraservice alignments and tensions. By the ante bellum period, the army had achieved a relatively high degree of internal specialization, greater than that of any other large organization of the time. Most basic was the distinction between the line regiments and the general staff, the latter term designating the supply and support departments. Within the line, three distinct combat arms developed: infantry, artillery, and mounted troops. The various staff departments—engineering, medical, ordnance, quartermaster, and others—had relatively permanent cadres of officers and were virtually autonomous in most of their operations, being responsible directly to the Secretary of War. As with 20th-century organization men, army officers tended to identify more strongly with their particular departments or branches than with the larger institution. The concept of politically neutral national service, the officially sanctioned ethic of the military professions, was an abstract and lofty ideal that was primarily useful to justify the army's existence before an indifferent and often hostile public. In the absence of significant intraservice rivalry, the organizational interests of the army as a whole seldom compelled united action. On the other hand, branch and departmental interests formed immediate, tangible goals, directly affecting officers' command prerogatives, compensation, and opportunities for promotion.

Bureaucratic warfare along branch and departmental lines thus permeated 19th-century military administration. While the regiments and the staff branches often squabbled among themselves, the deepest divisions ran between staff and line and involved remarkably intense emotions. Line officers saw their staff colleagues as "silk-stocking and boudoir gentlemen" who enjoyed special privileges in stations and pay for performing essentially civilian duties.[9] They suspected, with considerable justification, that the permanent location of staff headquarters in Washington gave those branches an inordinate amount of influence in formulating military policy and legislation. For their part, staff officers struggled to defend and expand their departmental prerogatives, insisting that the army's widely scattered garrisons and its diversified functions made a large staff apparatus necessary. All branches developed arsenals of bureaucratic weapons to push their causes: appeals to the War Department and commanding general; mobilization of influential friends and relatives; publication in the civilian press; lobbying in Congress. At times intraservice controversies assumed a legalistic opaqueness reminiscent of medieval scholasticism or of 20th-century bureaucratic jargon. A report of the Chief of Ordnance in relation to a clash with the artillery over officers' quarters at Fort Monroe captures the flavor:

> The ground of the [artillery] application can only be laid on an erroneous idea of the meaning of the 966th paragraph of the General Regulations for the Army, edition of 1841. That paragraph gives the right of choice of quarters from the highest to the lowest grade; but only to quarters which have been designated by the officer of the Quartermaster's Department. Now, it is well known that the quarters at Fort Monroe Arsenal are not, and never have been, under the control, in any degree or manner, of the Quartermaster's Department, and that they never have been, nor can be, *while arsenal quarters*, under such control, either for designation or any other purpose, of the officers of that department.[10]

Although 19th-century officers resembled today's organization men in important ways, the parallel was not exact. The old army lacked one basic feature of most modern bureaucracies, whether civilian or military—advancement on the basis of personal evaluations by a man's superiors. Whatever may be said for such evaluations as a method for recognizing "merit" and enhancing efficiency, they have the important unofficial function of maintaining discipline and control within the organization. In other words, they reinforce the official hierarchy of authority. Robert Presthus, a perceptive student of bureaucracy, considers this system central to organizational psychology. "Such conditions mean that the typical organization man will be disciplined, anxious, and sensitive in his relations with others. He will understand that mobility requires the support of prestigeful seniors, the gatekeepers who control the entrance to the avenues of authority, status, and income."[11]

Frustrating as it often was to ambitious young officers, the seniority system of the old army eliminated the need to conform rigidly to organizational standards or to curry the favor of immediate superiors. Longevity, or in some matters political influence, rather than merit evaluations determined career mobility. The absence of informal bureaucratic sanctions encouraged indiscipline. Bitter quarrels over minor prerogatives or obscure points of honor permeated the old army; some of them ran for years and resulted in courts-martial and even duels. Subalterns did not hesitate to take on senior commanders when they considered their rights violated, and personal animosity aggravated the more permanent institutional divisions within the army. On the other hand, the seniority rule functioned in the manner of academic tenure to afford military men at least potentially the freedom to attack abuses in the "system." Maj. William H. Chase of the Corps of Engineers, for example, carried on a long-term feud with the leaders of his branch, opposing such departmental sacred cows as units of engineer troops, an extensive program of coastal fortifications, and pay differentials favoring staff over line officers.[12] Lieutenants Braxton Bragg and Daniel H. Hill both published articles in civilian journals that blasted their superiors, civilian and military, and called for reforms in military administration.[13] On numerous occasions officers brought charges of misconduct against their seniors. Whatever basis there may be for the stereotype of today's career officer as a closed-lipped ticket puncher, who is unwilling to rock the organizational boat lest he damage his career chances, the 19th-century regular acted otherwise.

I do not wish to imply that officers' absorption in bureaucratic, "careerist" matters undermined their official conduct. Through the 19th century, the army performed rather effectively a variety of duties that had been assigned it by the government, including some that were exceedingly complex and unpleasant. I do believe, however, that historians should devote more attention to the structure of the army as a large organization, considering its impact on the sociology and social psychology of the military profession. For one thing, such problems as career motivation, the politics of promotion, and intraservice tensions and alignments are intrinsically important to an understanding of the values and lifestyle of the officer corps, whether in the 1840s or the 1970s.

Second, internal organizational pressures often had wider implications, influencing the development of military policy and the army's relationship to the larger society. I have discussed elsewhere how such forces in the ante bellum officer corps created a distinct pattern of political activity, emphasizing the pursuit of professional objectives to the exclusion of issues unrelated to military affairs.[14] One of the main pillars of 19th-century American defense policy, the system of seacoast fortifications, depended for its survival on the intensive lobbying of the Corps of Engineers, which considered the program essential to its autonomy and elite status within the army. Similarly, the army's support of West Point and of a "professional" view of military leadership arose largely from careerist motivations—officers' desire to distinguish the regular army from the militia and volunteers and thus to assure its survival in the face of widespread public criticism. Any attempt to write the social or institutional history of the U.S. Army must therefore consider the officer in one of his most important though least studied roles—that of America's first organization man.

Notes

1. This generalization largely reflects my research in applications for military appointments, a rich source of biographical information virtually untouched by military historians. The following two collections are the most important for the pre–Civil War period: U.S. Mili-

tary Academy Cadet Application Papers, 1805-1866, and Letters Received by the Adjutant General, 1805-1889, the latter of which includes applications for direct citizens' appointments to 1821. Both series are among Records of the Office of the Adjutant General, 1780's-1917, Record Group 94, National Archives, Washington, DC (Hereafter, I shall indicate records in the National Archives using the symbol NA, preceded by the record group, or RG, number.) Records of the Office of the Secretary of War, RG 107, NA, also includes several series of applications that are especially useful for applications received from citizens during the 1850s. The files vary in length, of course, and most do not indicate the applicant's career motivation. Aside from biographies and memoirs, however, which usually treat the careers of exceptional men, these records are virtually the only source of information on an important problem.

2. See, for example, the cadet application papers of the following officers: Frank S. Armistead, File 1851/10; Electus Backus, File 1819/49; Edmund C. Bainbridge, File 1851/13; John W. Davidson, File 1840/20; Lunsford L. Lomax, File 1850/182; John O. Long, File 1849/205; William E. Merrill, File 1853/194; Larkin Smith, File 1828/1. All are among the U.S. Military Academy Cadet Application Papers, 1805-66, RG 94, NA, National Archives Microfilm Publication M688, 242 rolls.

3. Richard Hofstadter, *The American Political Tradition and the Men Who Made It* (New York: Vintage Books, 1954), p. 57.

4. Van Dorn to Sister, January 13, 1848, *A Soldier's Honor: With Reminiscences of Major-General Earl Van Dorn*, ed. E. V. D. Miller (New York: Abbey Press, 1902), p. 26.

5. Walker to Molly Walker, [1858], William H. T. Walker Papers, Duke University Library, Durham, NC; Vinton to Maj. Edmund Kirby, December 2, 1836, Jacob Brown Papers, William L. Clements Library, Ann Arbor, MI; Comstock to Lt. James B. McPherson, August 13, 1859, James B. McPherson Papers, Library of Congress, Washington, DC.

6. Col. Roger Jones to Lewis Cass, February 15, 1836, file A-109 (38), Letters Received by the Secretary of War, Main Series, 1801-70, RG 107, NA, National Archives Microfilm Publication M221, Roll 116.

7. Application files of Lt. James P. Flewellen (Army 47), Lt. James Oakes (Army 123), and Capt. Henry W. Benham (Army 115), Applications for Promotions from Regular Army Officers and for Commissions from Non-Commissioned Officers, 1854-60, RG 107, NA.

8. Blake to Lt. David B. Harris, April 19, 1834, David B. Harris Papers, Duke University Library, Durham, NC.

9. [Lt. Braxton Bragg], "Notes on Our Army," *Southern Literary Messenger* 10 (May 1844): 286. An excellent source of information on intraservice tensions—and on officers' organizational concerns generally—is *Army and Navy Chronicle*, the semiofficial service publication of the 1830s and early 1840s.

10. Col. Henry K. Craig to Charles M. Conrad, December 31, 1851, *A Collection of Annual Reports and Other Important Papers, Relating to the Ordnance Department, Taken from the Records of the Office of the Chief of Ordnance, from Public Documents, and from Other Sources*, comp. Stephen V. Benet, 4 vols. (Washington, DC: U.S. Government Printing Office, 1878-90), 2:414-415.

11. Robert V. Presthus, *The Organizational Society: An Analysis and a Theory* (New York: Vintage Books, 1962), p. 149.

12. Chase to editors of the *National Intelligencer*, March 3, 1838, *Army and Navy Chronical* 6 (Mar. 22, 1838): 178-179; Col. Joseph G. Totten to Franklin Pierce, February 17, 1841; Totten to Chase, April 10, 1841, March 1, 1846, and May 15, 1846; and Totten to Armistead Burt, February 16, 1846, Letters and Reports of Col. Joseph G. Totten, 1803-64, Records of the Office of the Chief of Engineers, RG 77, NA; and Chase to Charles M. Conrad, April 17, 1851, H. Ex. Doc. 5, 32d Cong., 1st sess., pp. 224-234.

13. [Bragg], "Notes on Our Army," *Southern Literary Messenger* 10 (Feb. 1844), 11 (Feb. 1845); [Daniel H. Hill], "The Army in Texas," *Southern Quarterly Review* 9 (Apr. 1846): 434–457; 14 (July 1848): 183–197. Although these articles were published anonymously, their authorship was widely known.

14. William B. Skelton, "Officers and Politicians: The Origins of Army Politics in the United States before the Civil War," *Armed Forces and Society* 6 (Fall 1979): 22–48.

The Army Family:
Myth and Paradoxes

Anton Myrer

A novel is a voyage of discovery—for the writer no less than for the reader. When I decided in the winter of 1965 to attempt a sympathetic portrait in depth of a professional soldier, I first looked at the work of some of my precursors and peers. The cast of characters was not enticing. Mailer's General Cummings reveals himself as a feline exquisite caught in dreams of authoritarian absolutes; Jones's Captain Holmes is a simplistic brute, his wife a vengeful wanton; Marquand's Melville Goodwin is a well-meaning, sentimental soul, his career shrewdly guided by his wife; Heym's and Calmer's divisional commanders are obsessed with macho postures and postwar political schemes; and Gwaltney's Colonel Miles is a spiteful prig. Cozzens's professionals are more sympathetically drawn, but General Beal's adolescent sulks and hijinks reveal a patronizing edge, as does Colonel Mowbray's bungling incompetence—it is the reservist Ross who resolves the bundle of explosive situations on that crowded weekend; and in *Reflections in a Golden Eye* McCullers offers a quintet of grotesques that would have unnerved Krafft-Ebing.[1]

Albert Camus has said somewhere that all crimes are essentially the product of ignorance, and there *is* a fine irony when the novelist—himself a blatant stereotype in the public eye—seizes on so stereotypical a view of the soldier. I must confess that when I began *Once an Eagle* I shared some of this attitude, but 2 years of unceasing research provided a sharp refutation of what might be called the "von Schlieffen syndrome," that specter of a cold, subhuman, certainly sadistic, probably impotent automaton drunk with visions of perpetual war and a military takeover of the republic.

The army has of course had its martinets and bullies, its sycophants and schemers—even, yes, its psychopaths. What profession has not? Still, the long roll of diaries and journals and autobiographies—plus the historical record of objective witnesses—revealed something very different: the mordant wit and introspection of a Joseph Stilwell, the fatherly compassion of a Robert Eichelberger, the steady humility of an Omar Bradley, and the irrepressible vitality of a Red Reeder. I name only a few. Above them all, like some august, benevolent standard, rose the presence of George C. Marshall, one of the few truly superior human beings of our troubled century. Most of these highly personal narratives manifested not arrogance or ruthless ambition but an abiding sense of humanity—shadowed with moments of frustration, resentment, or self-doubt.[2]

In all truth, the civilian observer has often failed to grasp the essential web of contradictions surrounding the warrior's role in our history. For the nation has repeatedly told the soldier:

> Because of our fear of excessive military power—a reality to our forefathers—you will be perpetually distrusted. You will therefore be neglected in time of peace—yet you are not to become embittered. If war comes, you will be the first to be sacrificed, until the awesome might of the country can be brought to bear—yet you should not become cynical. If you survive those bitter, early months of losses and defeats, some of you will be given greater power than Alexander or Caesar ever dreamed of—yet you must not become arrogant in such brief authority. Only after our victorious wars will the most favored among you be fully accepted as leaders in our society—and then usually for the wrong reasons; and with the coming of peace you will be reduced in grade and returned to that atmosphere of neglect and mistrust you knew before.

Such a series of conflicting injunctions would try a saint—and most of us are not saints. But the essential military conundrum bites even deeper: for the soldier, rapid advancement in his profession comes only with war—that world of suffering and desperate choice about which he knows all too painfully—and so, if he is a man of dedication and high moral purpose, he finds himself arduously preparing for an event he must hope will never take place. He is in a very real sense constrained to deny the objective of his vocation, a realization that demands the most selfless dedication of all.

Tensions in the army family seem, then, to have stemmed most often from this inherent conflict between military and civil values.

Captain Bentzoni and family on a carriage ride, Fort Shaw, MT, 1889. *(Source: National Archives)*

Caught between our national preoccupation with quick and unbounded success and the self-abnegatory routine that army life demands, the soldier has been forced either to content himself with quiet satisfaction in a competence not rewarded by society or to superimpose civil aspirations on the military code. Thus two main types of soldier have emerged: the first has accepted the gambit, secure in his conviction that virtue is (indeed *must* be) its own reward; the second has sought to secure advancement through use of civilian techniques—political contacts, the press, the cultivation of personal eccentricities, and self-promotion, divergent paths perhaps most plainly taken in our time by Marshall and MacArthur.

Information about a birth on an army post. Extract dated May 11, 1906, from the Medical History of Fort Robinson, NB. *(Source: National Archives)*

What of the service wife? Her role has been uniquely trying—again and again she is bound to her husband's life without sharing his sense of mission. She must deal with her children's queries or with the often grim inequities of rank in a very personal way. She is all too aware of the swift material achievements of friends "on the outside." Is it worth it, she wonders—all these years of stagnation and sacrifice and hope deferred? I found the diaries and memoirs painfully revealing here. Virtually no one has heard of Margaret Wadelton, but I feel very close to her. She shows herself to be a lively, amusing, intelligent observer of army life—but the wry bitterness, the inverted pride in her husband's exceptional (and unrewarded) talents, gather force with the years. Helen Montgomery's account is less intense, less angry, but the mood of despondency remains.[3] And I came upon other writers, so many others.

For the army wife, too, there was the final, bitterest irony of all: when at last (and unhappily) war does come, and her husband finally achieves authority commensurate with his abilities, he is dispatched to some doomed command at the other end of the earth. The quiet domestic triumph of which she has dreamed through a young lifetime of two-battalion desert and jungle posts is transformed into a far more cruel isolation.

Everywhere the evidence suggests that the army family has been subjected to much greater strain than its civilian counterpart. In view of the pressures of isolation, penury, and even humiliation that it endured, we may well marvel that it held together as much as it did over the years. The adage "Virtue is its own reward" is threadbare and has not been overly honored in a status-avid America during the past half century, but it seems to have stood the army family in good stead.

Notes

1. Norman Mailer, *The Naked and the Dead* (New York: Rinehart & Co., Inc., 1948); James Jones, *From Here to Eternity* (New York: Charles Scribner's Sons, 1951); John P. Marquand, *Melville Goodwin, USA* (Boston: Little, Brown & Co., 1951); Stefan Heym, *The Crusaders* (Boston: Little, Brown & Co., 1948); Ned Calmer, *The Strange Land* (New York: Charles Scribner's Sons, 1950); Francis Irby Gwaltney, *The Day the Century Ended* (New York: Rinehart & Co., 1955); James Gould Cozzens, *Guard of Honor* (New York: Harcourt, Brace & Co. 1948); Carson McCullers, *Reflections in a Golden Eye* (Boston: Houghton Mifflin Co., 1941).

2. Joseph W. Stilwell, *The Stilwell Papers*, ed. Theodore H. White (New York: William Sloane Associates, Inc., 1948); Robert L. Eichelberger, *Our Jungle Road to Tokyo* (New York: Viking Press, 1950); Omar N. Bradley, *A Soldier's Story* (New York: Henry Holt & Co., Inc., 1951); Russell Potter Reeder, *Born at Reveille* (New York: Duell, Sloan and Pearce, 1966).

3. Margaret Wadelton, *Gay, Wild, and Free: From Captain's Wife to Colonel's Lady* (Indianapolis: Bobbs-Merrill Co., 1949); Helen Montgomery, *Colonel's Lady* (New York: Farrar and Rinehart, Inc., 1943).

Commentary on
"The People of the Army"

Edward M. Coffman

When old soldiers, their wives, and children reminisce about their life in the army, the topics generally are the interesting situations they experienced or the characters they knew. To be sure, the men who saw combat talk about that and, if they held important commands, want to analyze as well as describe operations. Although what happened on the battlefield is unquestionably the most crucial element in the history of an army, it is a relatively brief period and rests on an evolution of preparation which took place over years of peacetime. Thus, the historian who makes a thorough study of the Battle of Waterloo should keep in mind the Duke of Wellington's comment that the battle was won on the playing fields of Eton and examine what transpired at Eton prior to 1815. Otherwise he may well never know or may misunderstand what the famed commander believed to have been the essential influence on the British officer corps of the day.

In their papers the panelists briefly sketched the four components of army society—officers, enlisted men (including noncommissioned officers), wives and families. The common note struck by all was that one has to look beyond the myths and stereotypes which befog so much American thinking about their army throughout history. Finlayson pointed out that there was no such thing as a typical army wife and that the changing place of woman in society has affected the traditional position of the army wife as a supportive element of her husband's career. Kohn attacked the adage that the army reflects society by emphasizing the difference between the large wartime armies and the small peacetime establishments. Beyond that he indicated the differences between elite combat units and service troops; between the Indian fighting troops and their contemporaries who spent their enlistments in coastal fortifications. He also called for a more extensive examination of the enlisted men over the years. Fisher promptly answered in his paper on NCOs some of the questions Kohn posed about enlisted men. Skelton then took an exciting new tack by concentrating on one aspect of the ante bellum officer corps. As managers in the nation's largest bureaucracy of the time, officers, he argued, had many of the same attitudes as 20th-century organization men. Finally, Myrer related how his research for his novel *Once an Eagle* had brought out the "abiding sense of humanity" among officers rather than the stereotypical image of men who were arrogant and ruthlessly ambitious.

The papers stimulated an interesting discussion with 12 people contributing either questions or comments. Five of these asked about wives, with several making the point that the situation of the wives of the enlisted men was different from that of officer wives. Skelton's model of the ante bellum officer as organization man provoked one questioner to ask if he was taking a 20th-century theory and applying it out of context. The response was that the historic facts supported his thesis. An army captain then commented that the tradition and sense of history in the military made it difficult to compare to civilian organizations, yet, paradoxically, he then questioned Kohn's point that the military did not really reflect society. Kohn agreed to the extent that society influences the army but he continued to maintain that intrinsically the army remains separate.

Noel Parrish, retired air force brigadier general and history PhD, made the most amusing as well as one of the more interesting comments. In a discussion on the educational level of recruits in the new volunteer army, he introduced the relevant topic of the Depression era army, thus countering the tendency to base judgments on the new volunteer army on the standards of either the World War II or Vietnam conflict armies. He said that when he enlisted in 1930, he hid his education, which included a year's graduate work in history, from his fellow troopers. He added: "The only disappointment was that, although I spent nearly a year with those recruits, not one of them ever suspected that my education was superior."

General Parrish also addressed the crucial problem that historians face—attaining a proper blend of accurate generalization with appropriate human interest detail. In particular he expressed concern that the social science influence had dehumanized history and, if anything, made it more difficult to approach the truth about people and events of the past. He turned to Myrer and asked if historians had to become novelists in order to attain that goal. Myrer did not directly answer the question but did say that he thought: "The novelist is trying for an imaginary world but if he strives hard enough he often can get nearer to the truth than the journalist."

In a sense these papers and the discussion they fostered marked the acceptance of social history by military historians. Just as labor historians in recent years have begun to include studies of the workers, as distinct from institutional studies of the unions or accounts of strikes, military historians have become more cognizant of the possibilities of widening their approach beyond the battlefield. Even in writing about military operations, many historians have begun to follow the advice of John Keegan in *The Face of Battle* to study battles not just from the viewpoint of the commanders but from that of the men who actually fought face to face with the enemy. In doing so, the historian adds the appropriate human detail that both Parrish and Myrer called for as a means of arriving at the truth. Of course, such details can be manipulated, taken out of context, and be as misleading as any faulty generalization. This should not, however, prevent the scholar from using them with proper care. To ignore this essential human element in the study of military affairs is to tell only part of the story and to leave the reader with a distorted image of the past.

Those military historians who explore the possibilities of social history have a significant advantage over their colleagues in other fields. Since the army, as Skelton pointed out, was a large bureaucracy in an era when there were no others of its size, it maintained records which one seldom finds in other areas of society in the 19th century. This means that the researcher can locate more complete information on many individuals whose counterparts in civilian life are virtually lost to history. Aside from the multitude of published War Department reports which are available in many research libraries, there are countless pages of personnel and post records as well as routine correspondence and court-martial files in the National Archives. There are two other large collections that anyone working on any area of army history should also consider: the Special Collections at the U.S. Military Academy Library at West Point and the collection at the U.S. Army Military History Institute, Carlisle Barracks, PA. The former is the smaller and, as one would assume, consists primarily of papers of graduates. The latter has, in addition to an extensive collection of private papers, the voluminous Spanish-American War and World War 1 surveys and a large collection of oral history interviews.

This session in 1979 represented an awareness of the need for expanding the horizons of military history. As the panelists demonstrated, work in the field of the social dimension was already well in progress. Since then, the large number of monographs in this area indicate that it is now generally accepted.

3

THE U.S. ARMY'S IMPACT ON LOCAL COMMUNITIES: Some Explored and Unexplored Pathways

Color lithograph, "Album of Virginia: U.S. Armory at Harpers Ferry ... Jefferson County, VA, 1857." *(Artist Ed. Beyer; lithographed by Rau & Sons, Dresden, Germany; original in Marine Corps Museum, Quantico, VA)*

Two Cultures in Conflict:
Soldiers and Civilians at Harpers Ferry, VA

Merritt Roe Smith

In 1979 I attended a seminar at which a colleague from the Regional Economic History Research Center discussed the initial stages of American technological transfers to Japan.[1] While the paper addressed a number of salient issues that related to the opening of Japanese-American trade during the 1850s, I was intrigued by the speaker's comments about the military underpinnings of these exchanges. Particularly striking was the connection established between the acquisition of American military technology, stemming ironically from Japan's desire to defend its coasts against outside intruders, and the advent of Japanese industrialization. Japan, it appears, was only one of many countries that entered the industrial revolution as a result of strategic needs. France, Germany, China, Romania, the United States, and no doubt many other nations followed similar paths. The resulting socioeconomic configurations reflected the pervasive influence of military thinking.[2]

My present objective is more limited. I propose to address the question of military enterprise and industrialization by considering a technological revolution in the making of arms—frequently called the "American system"—and by assessing its effects on the residents of a 19th-century community. My remarks focus specifically on Harpers Ferry, VA, between 1800 and 1855. The result is a study in contrasts—a clash and partial amalgamation of cultures, if you will—between people

81

steeped in an agrarian-artisan tradition, on the one hand, and, on the other, people who identified with the aims and aspirations of an emerging military bureaucracy.[3] An understanding of these conflicting traditions is of more than just passing interest because, in many ways, they continue to define military-civilian as well as labor-management relations to this day.

Harpers Ferry was the site of one of two national armories sanctioned by Congress in 1794. Nestled among the rocks and mountains of an agrarian hinterland, the village was, to be sure, an unusual spot for a small arms factory. Yet even though other towns possessed better mill facilities, strategic considerations coupled with the personal interests of President George Washington, a native of the Potomac Valley and a large landowner there, ensured the selection of Harpers Ferry.

The village's greatest liability was its frontierlike environment and isolation from other major centers of manufacturing innovation. News traveled slowly. Existing avenues of transportation to major commercial cities such as Baltimore and Philadelphia, moreover, were both expensive and uncertain. All these things greatly complicated the problems of planning and coordinating armory production. Since no churches, schools, or other communal institutions existed at the ferry, everyday life assumed a decidedly rural character in accordance with the agrarian ways of the surrounding countryside. Whether people worked a farm or tended a business establishment, the tempo of life was set by the seasons. Clocked time had little meaning. Like country dwellers in old England, people tended to arrange their daily tasks in accordance with the cycles of nature, frequently punctuating intense bouts of labor with hunting expeditions, barbecues, militia musters, and other festivities. Such diversions served to alleviate the drudgery and isolation of everyday life while reinforcing a romanticized myth of southern leisure.

As part of a large rural culture, the early residents of Harpers Ferry assigned more importance to their own neighborhood, with its agrarian institutions, traditions, and interests, than they did to the nation at large. Given these provincial attachments, they tended to view the U.S. arsenal as a local project sponsored in name only by the federal government. This perspective did not appreciably change once manufacturing operations began in 1802. Indeed, as the years passed, a majority of the town's populace construed the armory's function in even narrower terms. In their eyes, the factory existed not as an efficient producer of military ordnance but as a convenient pork barrel of jobs, contracts, and political patronage for inhabitants of the inner reaches of the Potomac Valley. As late as 1841 the civilian appointees who managed the works clearly mirrored these sentiments. At the same time they deeply resented any attempts by federal officials in Washington to challenge their authority by altering administrative procedures, enforcing common regulations, or changing personnel at the armory.

No group better symbolized Harpers Ferry's commitment to a preindustrial way of life than the armory's early labor force. In 1802 it numbered some 25 men, nearly all of whom had either worked or served apprenticeships in the Pennsylvania-Maryland gun trade and were highly skilled in a wide variety of tasks. The emphasis the "mysteries" of gunsmithing placed on manual dexterity made their methods more artistic than mechanical, more individualistic than organized. To many, the possession of skill represented something more than a means of earning a living. It was a calling, a way of life, a legacy that older artisans could pass on to younger men, especially kin, through the apprentice system and later through "inside contracting." Above all, the craft ethos instilled a sense of workmanship, which served as a source of personal pride, creativity, and satisfaction. Because the element of individuality loomed so large in their lives, the armorers proved to be a fiercely independent breed who balked at any attempt to regulate, systematize, or depersonalize accustomed work procedures at the armory. Such thoroughly inbred work traditions subsequently hindered rather than encouraged innovation at Harpers Ferry.

Until the end of the War of 1812, local interests stood unchallenged at Harpers Ferry mainly because the Secretary of War lacked the administrative staff to coordinate and monitor affairs at the national armories. The situation changed in 1815, however, when Congress passed "an Act for the better regulation of the Ordnance Department." In addition to transferring responsibility for the negotiation and supervision of all arms contracts from the Commissary General of Purchases to the Ordnance Department, the bill placed the national armories at Springfield, MA, and Harpers Ferry under the latter bureau's purview. Equally significant, the legislation empowered the chief of ordnance, Col. Decius Wadsworth, "to draw up a system of regulations . . . for the uniformity of manufacturers of all arms, ordnance, ordnance stores, implements, and apparatus, and for the repairing and better preservation of the same."[4] Wadsworth helped draft this statement, and for the next 40 years its charge became the guiding principle of ordnance policy. Although little noticed at the time, the proviso set the stage for monumental developments in manufacturing technology that eventually shaped the entire American industrial system.

Wadsworth openly espoused the uniformity idea and, as a bachelor with few family obligations, completely devoted himself to its realization. Although he most often thought and spoke of uniformity with regard to improving artillery, certain bureaucratic constraints forced him to aim his policy at parallel developments in the manufacture of small arms. To his credit, he understood that the Ordnance Department could not devise a complex engineering strategy and then simply with-draw to become a passive observer of the undertaking. Success depended on closely monitoring and orchestrating every stage of the plan. Because he was overworked and was beginning to feel pain from a cancerous tumor on his arm, he knew that he had to select a deputy with the necessary skill and determination to oversee the new program and stand firm in the face of opposition. He selected Lt. Col. George Bomford, a West Point graduate and technical specialist who had served as Wadsworth's principal assistant since 1812. To Bomford fell the responsibility of implementing the uniformity system at the national armories. As Wadsworth's designated successor, he would head the Ordnance Department for more than 20 years (1821–42), during which he would witness every important development in the firearms industry. Indeed, from an administrative standpoint, no one would do more to im-plement the new technology than he.

As architects of the uniformity concept, Wadsworth and Bomford pushed relentlessly for order and system at the national armories. In 1816 they announced the adoption of a new model musket explicitly de-signed for serial production with uniform parts. Piecework payments and regularized accounting practices also became the rule, and at the insistence of Wadsworth and Bomford, the armories began to introduce special tools, machinery, and gauging procedures in manufacturing. At Harpers Ferry this strategy received special emphasis in 1819, when a New Englander named John H. Hall was appointed to experiment with novel mechanized methods for producing breechloading rifles with interchangeable parts. Each innovation—and there were many during the 1820s and 1830s—chipped away at valued craft traditions and placed new pressures on the armorers to change their accustomed work habits. An early casualty of the new factory regimen was the apprentice system, a central institution of preindustrial craftsmanship, which was displaced during the 1810s by a method of child labor called "inside con-tracting." The extent of these changes is clearly revealed by the growing division of labor in the armory shops. In 1810 the manufacture of regula-tion smooth-bore muskets was divided into 20 separate occupations. By 1816 the number had risen to 55 and 10 years later it had expanded to 64. Clearly techniques of production were changing, and as a result, armorers were more and more becoming appendages of specialty files and machine tools.

While the new technology gathered momentum, the accompany-ing system of discipline and regimentation was fiercely opposed, and often frustrated, at Harpers Ferry. For years the armory had suffered the reputation of being locally controlled, shamefully abused, and flagrant-ly mismanaged. It also had the doubtful distinction of employing one of the most troublesome labor forces in the country. Attempts to introduce work rules during the 1820s generally went unheeded. "Workmen came and went at any hour they pleased," one officer recalled, "the machinery being in operation whether there were 50 or 10 at work." Along with these practices, armorers claimed the privilege of keeping frequent holidays, transferring jobs at will, drinking whiskey on the premises, and selling their tools "as sort of a fee simple inheritance."[5] They also boasted that anyone who interfered with these rights could expect the same fate as Thomas Dunn, the one civilian superintendent who had attempted to enforce the rules and who was assassinated in 1830 by a disgruntled armorer after only 6 months in office. Everyone knew that the workers determined their own standards of conduct and that they did so with the connivance and support of community leaders and local politicians. "Every way considered," a newly appointed master armorer wrote to a friend, "there are customs and habits so interwoven with the very fibers of things as in some respects to be almost hopelessly remitless."[6] Upon visiting the premises in 1832, Bomford's assistant, Maj. George Talcott, reported that "this armory is far behind the state of manufacture elsewhere and the good quality of their work is effected, at great disadvantage, by manual labor." Contrasting Springfield with Harpers Ferry, he noted, "There is so little machinery at the latter place that no fair comparison of prices can be made." Several years later the same officer detected "a great advance . . . in the introduction of new machinery." "Nevertheless," he added, "much remains to be done to bring it up to the point at which Springfield stood" in 1832.[7]

Committed as they were to the "stability of things and stability of mind" in all undertakings, members of the Ordnance Department deplored the instability that characterized labor practices at Harpers Ferry. As ranking officers in the department, Bomford and Talcott felt especially embarrassed and frustrated about the situation. On numerous occasions during the 1830s they had cautioned civilian superintendents about the lack of internal discipline and had urged them to institute reforms. The calls went unheeded, however. In other respects Bomford and Talcott could do little to enforce the regulations because they resided far from the armories and because the highest officials at Harpers Ferry were civilians who held their appointments through the machinations of the patronage process. Political interests and considerations accordingly informed the actions of civilian managers. Since their local power and support depended on maintaining goodwill in the community, they rarely flaunted their authority or did anything that threatened to jeopardize their relations with the constituents. With regard to work regulations, they left well enough alone.

Thwarted in many attempts to control the civilian superintendents at both armories, ordnance officials had long been looking for an opportunity to initiate sweeping administrative changes at the national armories. The time arrived in 1841 with the inauguration of President William Henry Harrison. When John H. Bell, the newly appointed Secretary of War, announced his intention of introducing thoroughgoing reforms and called upon the chief of ordnance for advice, Bomford recommended replacing civilian superintendents with ordnance officers at the armories. Bell agreed to the plan, and Bomford immediately ordered two of his most experienced subordinates to take command at Springfield and Harpers Ferry. Although spoils-minded politicians felt threatened by the arrangement and roundly denounced it as "fully of mischief in all respects," the secretary nonetheless remained firm in his commitment. The department's "new reign" began April 16, 1841.[8]

During the next 13 years military superintendents exercised exclusive control over the internal operations of both national armories. At their insistence workers abandoned the task-oriented world of the craftsman and reluctantly entered the time-oriented world of industrial capitalism. That the large-scale manufacture of interchangeable firearms paralleled this change was no mere coincidence. From the outset ordnance officers recognized the importance of work rules, clocked days, and regularized procedures in stabilizing the complex human and physical variables present in the workplace. Experience had taught them that there was no alternative—a factory discipline characterized by rigid bureaucratic constraints had to be inculcated and absorbed by all employees. Only in this way could the delicate parameters of the uniform system be maintained.

Such considerations of course gave little solace to the armorers whose work ways were being altered. Time and again pieceworkers and inspectors at Harpers Ferry complained about having to keep regular hours. Time and again they grumbled about the relentless pressures imposed by the new administration as well as about the rigor with which it enforced the rules. While older artisans bemoaned the disappearance of traditional skills, other armorers protested against the lowering of piece rates. All these feelings were reinforced by kinsmen and neighbors who customarily distrusted strangers and resented outside meddling in their local affairs. Since the culprits were military men, politicians from the region continually fanned discontent by publicly attacking the "despotism and oppression" of military rule.[9]

A breaking point came in March 1842, when the entire labor force, led interestingly enough by pieceworkers, walked off the job in protest over the installation of a time clock. The armorers were long accustomed to coming and going from work whenever they pleased. The idea of a clocked day was especially repugnant because it threatened to upset their accustomed work rhythms and to deprive them of control on the shop floor. Since the person primarily responsible for its introduction held the rank of major in the Ordnance Department, the clock reinforced feelings already rife about the pernicious influence of outsiders, particularly military men, at Harpers Ferry. Moreover, its ineluctable cadence served to emphasize the rigorous discipline, regularity, and specialization so often associated with the coming of the machine. In this sense, the clock not only kept time but also symbolically deprived armorers of the freedom of traditional labor. Every minute had to be accounted for, and each accounting fostered further discontent.

The "clock strike" of 1842 represented an emotion-laden response to the consequences of rationalization. The walkout ended when President John Tyler ordered the armorers back to work and promised not to fire the "instigators and fomentors of the outbreak."[10] Nothing, however, had altered their feelings about the system under which they worked. Between 1842 and 1854 mechanization took command at Harpers Ferry, but the armorers maintained a curious aloofness from the forces of change. While they never completely repudiated the new technology, they did not embrace it either. Instead they vacillated between the old and the new, unwilling to break bonds that tied them to a preindustrial past yet unable to dissociate themselves from the gathering momentum of technical creativity.

As much as it sheds light on ante bellum labor unrest, the story of Harpers Ferry is much more than simply a chronicle of resistance to change. Looming ever so large is the decisive role of the state, particularly its military arm, in promoting the new technology and evolving an early form of modern management. Before the 1840s, machine production was much more expensive than handwork. Only government contracts and federal armories could shelter the new technology from the competitive pressures of the marketplace until it matured and spread to large-scale private enterprises such as Colt, Sharps, and the like. Equally significant, the Ordnance Department provided the earliest effective champions of *"Uniformity, Simplicity,* and *Solidarity,"* concepts that formed the very marrow of the new industrial creed and underscored the need for order and system in all undertakings.[11] From the beginning, then, a close association existed between military discipline and industrial discipline.

By midcentury the army's presence had left visible physical and social imprints at Harpers Ferry. In terms of the products themselves, for instance, little evidence remained to remind people that the new Model 1855 rifle and rifle-musket—mainstays of Union and Confederate forces during the Civil War—had evolved from the earlier Model 1803 rifle, a design that clearly reflected the aesthetic tastes and preferences of craftsmen trained in the Pennsylvania-Maryland arms-making tradition. Gone were the simple but elegant embellishments that gave the Model 1803 its distinctive vernacular character. All that remained of the old style was the brass mountings, to be discarded in 1859, and a small patchbox that served little or no functional purpose—faint traces of the past, to be sure.

Like the firearms themselves, the physical plant at Harpers Ferry also reflected the Ordnance Department's utilitarian bent. Between 1845 and 1854, the armory underwent a complete renovation at the hands of its military superintendents. Twenty-five buildings were erected. Unlike the jerry-built structures they replaced, the new shops exhibited careful and consistent planning. As if to underscore the uniformity principle, all of them conformed to the same general style of "factory gothic" architecture and were aligned and landscaped to project a neat orderly appearance. The observer could see how, within the shops, functional design facilitated the flow of work from one stage of production to another. Precision, regularity, and standardization seemed to pervade every aspect of the military enterprise.

Into this environment the Ordnance Department sought to inject a spirit of attentiveness and sobriety by fostering certain social institutions and attacking others. It is no mere happenstance, for example, that the erection of churches (four were built in the 1841–51 period) and the inauguration of the temperance movement coincided with the period of military superintendence at Harpers Ferry. Temperance received special emphasis during the late 1840s when superintendent Maj. John Symington, the local temperance organizer, secured funds to rent a hall for the Sons of Temperance. Soon afterward Symington and his military peers threw their support behind the establishment of free public schools, an issue that was ardently debated in the community. In this question, as in others, the Ordnance Department stood on the side of order and discipline, attempting to break the hold of provincialism at Harpers Ferry and to open the town to a broader cosmopolitan dimension. Such a strategy, of course, involved the military in a prolonged and often bitter struggle with local politicians and their elite patrons.

At issue were questions of power and control: the elimination, for instance, of politics, especially spoils, from armory affairs, the separation of business from pleasure, and the substitution of bureaucratic management for a clannish form of paternalism. No longer could local farmers take orders for the fall slaughter in the armory shops. No longer could stump speakers and evangelists conduct impromptu meetings at the armory gate. No longer could armorers gather in the yard to share a cup of whiskey or to watch a friendly wrestling match. Under military supervision all these practices became relics of the past. The new discipline aimed at curbing idleness and dissipation while promoting diligence and reliability. From the outset an affinity existed between social uplift and social control.

As it turned out, military superintendence of the national armories was short lived. Throughout the 1840s, politicians and constituents from both regions vehemently protested the illegality and repression of military rule. These pressures ultimately prevailed when Congress reversed itself in 1854 and civilian superintendents returned to power. For a short time discipline lapsed and production fell at Harpers Ferry. As much as old traditions fleetingly reasserted themselves, however, the system with its divisions of labor, precision inspections, and self-acting machinery remained intact. By 1860 the die was cast; too much had changed. Too much had been invested to return to the past. Decision makers, including Alfred M. Barbour, the new civilian superintendent, had committed themselves to the new technology and its concomitant bureaucratic control. In so doing, they opened the door to mass production but closed avenues to technological alternatives. Such alternatives would probably have limited the speed and scale of production and would therefore have slowed economic growth. In the "go-ahead" world of 19th-century America, such choices would have been unacceptable.

Notes

1. Eleanor A. Maass, "Early Phases of the Transfer of Technology from America to Japan" (paper presented at the history department hot lunch, University of Delaware, Mar. 14, 1979). Also see Barton C. Hacker, "The Weapons of the West: Military Technology and Modernization in 19th-Century China and Japan," *Technology and Culture* 18 (Jan. 1977): 43–55.

2. See, for example, William H. McNeill, *The Pursuit of Power: Technology, Armed Forces, and Society Since A.D. 1000* (Chicago: University of Chicago Press, 1982); and Merritt Roe Smith, ed., *Military Enterprise and Technological Change: Perspectives on the American Experience* (Cambridge, MA: The MIT Press, 1985). I also am endebted to Dr. Alexandre Herlea of the Conservatoire National des Arts et Métiers for comments and advice on the subject.

3. Since this paper is based on my previous writings, I shall document only direct quotations. For further information, see *Harpers Ferry Armory and the New Technology: The Challenge of Change* (Ithaca, NY: Cornell University Press, 1977); "From Craftsman to Mechanic: The Harpers Ferry Experience, 1798–1854," *Technological Innovation and the Decorative Arts*, eds. I. M. G. Quimby and P. A. Earl (Charlottesville: University Press of Virginia, 1974), pp. 103–139; "Army Ordnance and the 'American System' of Manufacturing, 1815–1861," *Military Enterprise and Technological Change*, pp. 39–86.

4. *U.S. Statutes at Large*, 3:203–205.

5. Maj. John Symington to Capt. William Maynadier, July 12, 1849, and Edward Lucas to Bomford, August 29, 1839, Letters Received by the Chief of Ordnance, Records of the Office of the Chief of Ordnance, Record Group 156, National Archives, Washington, DC. Hereafter records in the National Archives are indicated by the symbol NA, preceded by the record group (RG) number.

6. Benjamin Moor to Maj. Rufus L. Baker, May 5, 1831, Letters Received, Records of the Allegheny Arsenal, RG 156, NA.

7. Maj. George Talcott, Inspection of the Harpers Ferry Armory, December 5, 1832, and July 17–25, 1835, reports of inspections of arsenals and depots (part of the "Special File"), RG 156, NA.

8. William B. Calhoun to John Bell, April 1, 1841, and John Strider to John Tyler, July 4, 1841, Letters Received, RG 156, NA.

9. John H. Strider to Secretary of War, July 26, 1848, and Maj. John Symington to Col. George Talcott, June 29, 1846, August 4 and 12, 1848, May 12, 1849, and May 21, 1851. Letters Received, RG 156, NA; and Benjamin Moor, "Objections to the Military Superintendencies of the National Armories," James H. Burton Papers, Yale University Archives, New Haven, CT.

10. Maj. Henry K. Craig to Col. George Talcott, March 21 and April 1, 1842, and Craig to John C. Spencer, March 28, 1842, Letters Received, RG 156, NA.

11. Col. Decius Wadsworth to Secretary of War, August 8, 1812, Letters Sent to the Secretary of War, RG 156, NA.

Troopers, Taverns, and Taxes:
Fort Robinson, NE, and Its
Municipal Parasite, 1886–1911

Frank N. Schubert

After 1886, when the Nebraska panhandle town of Crawford was found-
ed at the end of track on the Fremont, Elkhorn, and Missouri Valley line,
nearby Fort Robinson provided sustenance for the town economy. This
support took a number of direct and indirect forms, including military
and civilian payrolls and contracts for a variety of goods and services,
such as forage, wood, and construction (see tables 1 and 2 and figure 1).
Crawford did have other sources of income. It was a marketplace for
neighboring farmers, though both Chadron and Alliance became more
important at an early date, and the railroad employed a few men in
town. Neither farming nor the railroad was as important, however, as
the military presence.[1] Fort Robinson had a profound impact: economic
activity in Crawford, as measured by fluctuations in postal receipts (see
figure 2), frequently showed a direct relationship to the army's expenditures for the fort.[2]

   The economic well-being of Crawford merchants, saloon men, and
contractors depended on two military conditions. The fort had to be
heavily garrisoned, and the troops had to have free and convenient access to the town's businesses. Garrison size and construction activity on
post depended on War Department policy and on congressional appropriations. On the other hand, Crawford leaders had much to say about
the terms on which soldiers spent their money in town. The lack of restric-
tions on prostitution, alcohol, narcotics, and gambling represented a
conscious town choice to which there was little opposition. Almost from

TABLE 1
Military Expenditures Available for Local Consumption, 1886–1911
(Thousands of Dollars)

Year	Military Pay	Civilian Pay	Local Contracts	Construction Contracts	Total
1886	41	4	0	3	48
1887	72	4	6	55	137
1888	90	4	3	1	98
1889	94	6	23	12	135
1890	83	8	20	3	114
1891	94	9	27	78	208
1892	82	7	18	1	108
1893	112	6	17	1	136
1894	107	6	29	0	142
1895	94	7	22	3	126
1896	84	6	7	2	99
1897	92	6	10	7	115
1898	42	6	5	0	53
1899	39	10	7	0	56
1900	28	9	11	11	59
1901	31	9	3	26	69
1902	100	9	18	9	136
1903	112	9	17	22	161
1904	119	6	27	24	176
1905	109	NA	23	9	141
1906	86	NA	48	8	142
1907	67	NA	11	194	272
1908	104	NA	14	221	339
1909	157	NA	69	15	241
1910	119	NA	25	12	156
1911	130	NA	34	4	168

Note and Sources: No actual payrolls are available. Estimated annual totals have been developed by multiplying the mean number of officers and enlisted men by the yearly pay of second lieutenants ($1,400) and of privates ($156), respectively. The 1908 increases raised the figures to $1,680 and $218. This method significantly understates the size of the military payroll and thus—to a lesser degree—the importance of all military outlays. The method probably yields figures that satisfactorily reflect changes in the actual payroll, however. Civilian payrolls are based on data in post monthly returns that reported the number of employees, their occupations, and their wages. A revised report form, which went into use in September 1904, did not include this information. Contract data are derived from the 21 volumes of registers of contracts, 1871–1912, Records of the Office of the Quartermaster General, RG 92, NA. All civilian contractors with post office addresses of Crawford or Fort Robinson are considered "local." Locally let construction contracts are included with "Local Contracts" and not with "Construction Contracts."

the outset Crawford systematically exploited these activities for public revenue (see table 3). Levies on saloon owners and prostitutes, which sometimes composed more than one-half of the annual tax collection, supported local schools and paid for law enforcement.

The city council saw the liquor trade's potential for public revenue and levied the first occupational tax on saloonkeepers in the late sum-

TABLE 2
Military Expenditures, 1886–1911 (Thousands of Dollars)

Year	Local	Dawes County	Three County	Northwestern Nebraska	Nebraska	Other	Total
1886	48	6	0	0	16	1	71
1887	137	20	0	2	14	0	173
1888	98	12	0	0	0	23	133
1889	135	2	0	0	2	12	151
1890	114	0	0	0	15	6	135
1891	208	4	0	0	8	12	232
1892	108	2	0	18	10	20	158
1893	136	0	0	5	22	11	174
1894	142	1	2	0	7	10	162
1895	126	6	0	0	16	0	148
1896	99	0	0	15	6	1	121
1897	115	1	0	3	24	3	146
1898	53	5	0	2	3	3	66
1899	56	0	1	5	17	12	91
1900	59	0	1	0	25	0	85
1901	69	0	0	0	9	0	78
1902	136	0	0	2	54	7	199
1903	161	0	0	9	59	3	232
1904	176	0	2	0	53	0	231
1905	141	0	0	10	32	0	183
1906	142	0	1	7	31	0	181
1907	272	0	1	7	35	0	315
1908	339	0	0	0	72	0	411
1909	241	0	0	4	77	0	322
1910	156	0	1	21	63	0	241
1911	168	0	2	17	11	0	198

Note and Sources: For sources, see table 1. "Local" expenditures are defined just as they were in table 1: military payrolls, civilian payrolls, local contracts, and all construction contracts. The "Three-County" area is the northwestern corner of the state: Box Butte, Sheridan, and Sioux counties. Dawes County is listed separately. "Northwestern Nebraska" is roughly the northwestern quarter of the state minus the four counties in the corner. Counties included in this column are Cherry, Thomas, Hooker, Grant, Logan, McPherson, Arthur, Morrill, Scottsbluff, and Banner.

mer of 1886.[3] In addition, a saloon license fee, also authorized by state law, was collected by the town fathers.[4] Over the next three decades, until statewide prohibition in 1916, the small municipality extracted a large portion of its revenue from taxes on saloons. From the outset, the lucrative military market promised substantial public revenue through support of local taverns. The U.S. government had already lent a hand in 1881 by prohibiting the sale of spirits on army posts.[5]

The $30 occupation tax of 1886, enacted in midyear just after the town was founded, was supplemented by an additional $500 license levy in 1888. Moreover, the enactment explicitly designated the license fee to support "the common school of the school district of the village of

Figure 1. Local Army Expenditures, 1889–1905

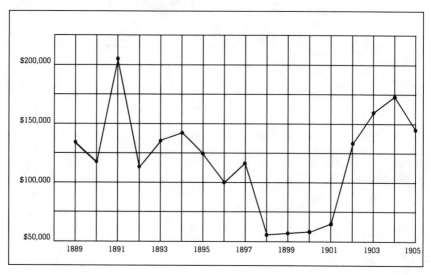

Figure 2. Crawford Post Office Receipts, 1891–1905

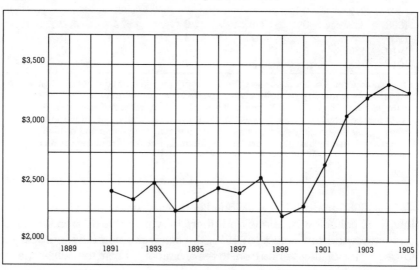

94

TABLE 3
The Size of the Garrison and Saloon Revenues

Year	Mean Garrison Size	License Fees ($)	Occupation Taxes ($)	Total Revenues ($)
1887	321	0	115.00	115.00
1888	401	1,833.00	110.00	1,943.00
1889	430	3,416.70	207.50	3,624.30
1890	381	3,000.00	180.00	3,180.00
1891	452	3,000.00	144.00	3,144.00
1892	353	2,684.00	140.00	2,824.00
1893	517	2,000.00	2,000.00	4,000.00
1894	476	2,500.00	1,250.00	3,750.00
1895	412	2,000.00	500.00	2,500.00
1896	367	2,500.00	625.00	3,125.00
1897	421	2,335.00	586.75	2,921.25
1898	205	2,000.00	500.00	2,500.00
1899	212	2,000.00	500.00	2,500.00
1900	155	1,500.00	375.00	1,875.00
1901	159	1,200.00	682.50	1,882.50
1902	495	2,500.00	1,375.00	3,875.00
1903	537	2,000.00	1,400.00	3,400.00
1904	563	2,000.00	1,400.00	3,400.00
1905	508	2,000.00	1,400.00	3,400.00
1906	408	2,500.00	1,750.00	4,250.00
1907	302	3,000.00	2,100.00	5,100.00
1908	411	2,605.49	2,605.49	5,210.98
1909	568	2,416.67	2,416.67	4,833.34
1910	425	2,000.00	4,000.00	6,000.00
1911	487	2,000.00	4,000.00	6,000.00
1912	567	1,500.00	3,000.00	4,500.00

Source: City ordinances and city council minutes.

Crawford."[6] The town plainly intended to make the soldiers who frequented local taverns pay for the school. This tax remained at $500 through 1912 and brought more than $56,000 into the city treasury. The occupation tax, which rose to $1,000 in 1910, brought an additional $33,000 into the general fund. The annual collection varied considerably but was usually adequate. In fact, the yearly sum collected for the school district at times exceeded the need. City fathers then used the money for other purposes, such as the purchase of a hook and ladder truck for the fire department.[7]

The tie between saloon revenues and the size of the garrison grew to be fairly explicit. Generally, the size of municipal receipts increased with troop strength. During the period of the Spanish-American War and Filipino Insurrection, the city took in $2,900 in 1897, the last full year of the 9th Calvary's tour of duty at Robinson, and $3,800 in 1902, the year the

10th Cavalry arrived. In the intervening years, when war led to drastic cuts in the garrison, revenue declined to $1,800.

There were several exceptions to this rule between 1887 and 1912, some of which can be tentatively explained. From 1888 to 1889 tax receipts almost doubled, while the garrison remained nearly unchanged. The unusual increase was probably due to the closing of Col. Edward Hatch's post canteen, which had operated for 5 months during 1888. Before the War Department ordered Hatch to close the facility, it provided a convenient alternative to town saloons and probably cut into their business.[8]

Changes in the racial composition of the garrison may have caused some of the more substantial deviations from the direct relationship between the size of the garrison and saloon revenues. Black soldiers, generally known to be more temperate than whites, may not have patronized the bars in equal numbers.[9] In 1897–98 the decline in revenues was much smaller than the reduction in troops might have warranted, perhaps because early in 1898 units of the white 6th joined the black cavalrymen of the 9th and the white 1st replaced both later in the year. Similarly, the replacement of the black 10th Cavalry by a smaller number of men from the 8th Cavalry in 1907 was accompanied by an increase in saloon revenues.[10]

Local tax revenues and the profits of saloon men were enhanced by successful temperance drives in some nearby towns. Gordon, about 60 miles east of Crawford, voted for prohibition in 1889. When Rushville and Hay Springs followed in 1906, all of nearby Sheridan County went dry. Alliance also banned intoxicants for some years but reversed itself in 1909. Chadron and Crawford, the largest towns in Dawes County, rejected prohibition in the same year. Nevertheless, the *Crawford Tribune* said in 1816 that statewide prohibition was favored by an "overwhelming majority" except in Omaha, the largest and consequently most sinful community in Nebraska. John Barleycorn may have died "without much fuss or formality," but his quick demise probably depended on fortuitous circumstances. In 1913 troops from the post went to Colorado to break a strike. Shortly afterward, the whole garrison transferred to the Mexican border, where the men remained until American entry into World War I. Meanwhile, the city's property tax rate rose sharply from 31 to 48 mills in 1912–16.[11] Therefore the financial adjustments necessitated by the loss of saloon revenues were made when the troops pulled out, not when Nebraska went dry.

Crawford had a temperance movement of its own that was never strong enough to exert substantial political pressure. The only recorded Women's Christian Temperance Union activity before 1910 was the establishment of a reading room. A chapter of the Anti-Saloon League also operated for at least a short time in the early 20th century. These organizations remained outside the municipal consensus. Even some ministers of the local Methodist Church were soft on "Demon Rum" although occasional acts of terrorism perpetrated by saloon men and their allies appear to have influenced the clergy and other citizens.[12]

Until 1907 town policy also systematized, exploited, and encouraged prostitution. In December 1886, prostitutes were classified as vagrants and were made liable to a fine. In March 1887, the city council instructed Marshal N. S. Jackson to compile a list of all "sporting women," collect 5 dollars every month from each, and pay the money into the city treasury. From the outset, the town made the vagrancy ordinance the basis for regular collections from the prostitutes. The fines authorized by Ordinance 6 amounted to a "whore tax" rather than a penalty for criminality.[13]

Funds accumulated in this manner were ultimately put to good use. School Superintendent Jeanette Meredith made a bid for the money in 1894, but there is no indication that the council approved her request. A December 1895 resolution directing the marshal to "pay himself by collecting donations from the prostitutes" died on council for lack of a second. A month later, however, just such an arrangement was approved: the "donations" would go into a special fund from which the city would pay the law officer.[14]

In some years the whore tax yielded substantial amounts for the city (see table 4). The available evidence on collections indicates that the town tapped a source of revenue less lucrative than the saloons but still significant. If collected every month, the tax doubtless represented a major part of total receipts. In 1906 the large collection combined with $4,250 in tavern fees to yield nearly $6,000 for the city. Total receipts for the year were only $9,515, so saloons and prostitutes accounted for more than 60 percent of local revenue for the year.[15]

TABLE 4
The Whore Tax, 1888–1907

Year	Amount ($)	
1888	$90	(4)
1890	50	(2)
1897	102	(5)
1899	32	(2)
1902	226	(unk)
1903	326	(unk)
1904	425	(12)
1905	772	(6)
1906	1,633	(11)
1907	1,038	(6)

Note: Figures in parentheses are numbers of months for which data are available. Where no parenthetical figures appear, the number of months was unknown.

Source: Reports of collections in city council minutes and local newspapers.

Efforts to control prostitution centered on keeping the women out of residential areas and saloons. The motive for the periodic harassment of prostitutes was clearly stated in a petition signed by "numerous citizens." They asked the council to force all "lewd women" into residences in the same section of town, where they would not be "an annoyance to respectable families."[16] Efforts to create a discrete red light district apparently succeeded. By the last months of the 10th Cavalry's tour on post, an area in the west end was identified as a center of prostitution and other vices.[17] This part of town was convenient to the post and occupied undesirable real estate near the railroad tracks.

Pressure from Fort Robinson in 1902 forced Crawford to alter its relationship with the prostitutes. Capt. Charles Grierson, alarmed by the number of venereal infections on post, threatened a military boycott of local businesses if corrective measures were not taken. The town responded with a program of physical examinations for the women, which was enforced by the marshal. This arrangement escalated the town's involvement in the enterprise and stimulated business. Arrests surpassed previous records as the number of whores increased.[18] The city created boom conditions by removing the fear of venereal disease from the minds of potential patrons.

The boom ended after the 10th Cavalry had departed. The city council banned prostitution on July 16, 1907. In the autumn the mayor and county attorney jointly notified keepers and residents of bawdy houses of their intention to enforce the new morality. Thereafter, arrests decreased as prostitution either declined temporarily or went underground.[19]

Community decisions on attracting soldiers through institutionalized vice appear to have been based largely on judgments concerning exploitation of a black garrison. The evidence in support of this claim is tenuous and circumstantial but suggestive. In the first place, the only public protest against saloon policy occurred not only in a period of declining troop strength but shortly after replacement of the black 9th by white cavalrymen. This abortive effort to impose a new morality was not followed by another until 1907, the year the black 10th ended a 5-year tour of duty on post. A month after the 10th left and the white 8th arrived, the *Tribune* discerned a "new order of things . . . both at Crawford and Fort Robinson." The "new order" on post resulted from the arrival of the white regiment. It began to manifest itself in town a month later when the town council approved a citizens' petition for the abolition of prostitution, but it did not crystallize until 1910, when the town lost its bid for a new state normal school. In addition, a series of prosecutions for gambling, the first since the ban on games of chance in 1903, began in the fall of 1907. Even saloonkeeper and city councilman John Bruer paid a $10 fine after pleading guilty to a gambling charge. Some of the penalties meted out in 1910 reached $100 and court costs. Prohibition of prostitution and

Fort Robinson, NB, circa 1893. *(Source: National Archives)*

punishment of gambling infractions may have taken place only coincidentally after departure of the black troops, but I can adduce no other
reasons for these steps' having been taken in 1907.[20]

By 1909 violations of the law had become common knowledge. The
Tribune reminded its readers that whorehouses were still plentiful, and it
demanded a prompt end to the business. Almost a year later, Fort
Robinson Surgeon James Church counted six cases of venereal ailments
in 2 months. More significantly, Church claimed that the city physician
still examined and certified prostitutes. Thus, 3 years after prostitution
had been outlawed, city officials maintained—perhaps surreptitious-
ly—the old system of supervised prostitution.[21] The ban amounted
merely to a victory for individuals who wished to hide prostitution from
the respectable citizenry.

Until 1910, vice did not generate visible tensions. Taxes were low,
and everyone probably knew why, although no public resolutions of
thanks were ever tendered to whores, saloonkeepers, and soldiers. The
Tribune and occasional competitors for the town's small readership devoted their energy to boosting rather than to muckraking. The city
council also systematically excluded evidence of bickering from its records. An informal but effective policy kept records of debates on
citizens' petitions for closure of saloons off the books. Indeed there may
have been little strain to hide. In most years municipal elections were
tranquil affairs involving as few as 40 voters.[22]

In 1910 Crawford experienced a major political upheaval after it lost its bid to become the site of a state normal school. Crawford competed with Valentine and three panhandle towns, Alliance, Chadron, and Scottsbluff, in boasting of ideal locations and moral purity. While the state normal board inspected the towns, Crawford leaders supplemented newspaper publicity by sending saloon men John Bruer and Paris Cooper, shortly to be elected mayor, to lobby for the school in Lincoln. The *Tribune* recited Crawford's many advantages: railroad connections, White River fishing, scenery, and the town park and described Crawford as a "town of churches, which would furnish moral tone to those so inclined." Troubled by a Lincoln paper's allegation that vice still flourished in Crawford, the editor of the *Tribune* said that public morality had improved considerably in recent years and that Crawford was a "wide-awake, progressive town." In fact, rejection of Crawford because of the proximity of Fort Robinson would be foolish. Crawford's rivals, all railroad towns, were even wilder. Moreover, said the editor, discovering a new municipal asset, students at a Crawford normal school would derive extra benefits through observation of military life and tactics at the post.[23]

When Chadron won the school, the *Tribune* initially attributed the defeat to poor leadership. Other observers considered the proximity of the post to have been the vital factor. Crawford's problem, however was more complex. An old-time resident recalled, "Chadron had the railroad men and they were just as rough as the soldiers."[24] To this citizen, the big difference was Crawford's substantial black population, which resulted from many years of black garrisons at Robinson. Another problem, the one about which nobody yet talked, was Crawford's long history of actively encouraging prostitution and other vices.

Loss of the normal school ruined any hope the town might have had for growth beyond village status. Reflections on this bitter defeat and Crawford's persistent reputation as "the stink pot of Northwest Nebraska" brought on a crusade against vice that ended the long-standing political consensus and generated deep divisions in the town. Soon after the announcement of the school decision, the county sheriff arrested owners of 12 brothels, and Mayor Cooper himself was charged with ownership of one house as well as with accepting bribes to protect tavernkeepers from the law. Members of city council were also arrested for taking bribes to allow bawdy houses to remain open. The habitual tranquillity of local politics was shattered, and two parties began to develop.[25]

The elections of 1910 and 1911 focused the community's attention on problems that had developed from the long dependence on Fort Robinson. Public decisions regarding exploitation of the trade of largely Afro-American garrisons had tied municipal revenues to the size of the garrison and had committed the town to semipublic prostitution. These developments had grave consequences when the normal school was established. Loss of the institution doomed Crawford to village status, marked the beginning of a period of explosive political divisions, and heightened voter interest as the community wrestled with decisions regarding its social and economic structure.[26] Although the statewide ban on prostitution in 1911, the decline of the garrison on post, and prohibition in Nebraska all diminished the importance of the political struggles of 1910 and 1911, the debates were very important when they took place. They showed then, as they show now, that the ways of dealing with Fort Robinson that had developed with time had failed and that these same arrangements doomed Crawford's one opportunity to lure a stable and respectable institution to replace or supplement Fort Robinson.

Notes

1. *Crawford Tribune*, June 28, 1901, and June 26, 1903; *Corn Belt: A Journal Illustrating the Agricultural Section of the United States West of the Mississippi* 2 (July 1896):14, 6 (April 1898):5; *The Great Northwest: Its Marvelous Growth and Wealth* (Omaha: n.p., 1889), pp. 3, 14.

2. Citizens and postmasters general as well as local boosters considered postal receipts an important economic indicator. In 1883 postmasters' salaries were tied to postal revenue by law, and Postmaster General William Gresham observed that pay in his department would therefore depend "largely upon the condition of the business interests of the country." The data in table R139–145 of U.S. Bureau of the Census, *The Statistical History of the United States from Colonial Times to 1957* (Washington, DC: U.S. GPO, 1960), pp. 496–497, show that receipts throughout the nation did react to overall economic change. *Annual Report of the Postmaster General of the United States, 1883* (Washington, DC: U.S. GPO, 1893), p. 10; Report of the First Assistant Postmaster General, in *Annual Report of the Postmaster General of the United States, 1893* (Washington, DC: U.S. GPO, 1893), pp. 75–77; *Annual Reports of the Post Office Department, 1902* (Washington, DC: U.S. GPO, 1902), and *Crawford Tribune*, March 28, August 1, and October 3, 1902.

3. Minutes of the meetings of the Crawford City Council, vol. 1: September 15, 1886. Council minutes, ordinances, and police court records are located in the city hall at Crawford, NE.

4. *The Compiled Statutes of the State of Nebraska, 1881, 2d ed., with Amendments 1882, 1883, and 1885* (Omaha: Gibson, Miller, and Richardson, 1885), pp. 135, 142; J. E. Cobbey, *Consolidated Statutes of Nebraska, 1891* (Lincoln: State Journal Company, 1891), p. 66.

5. Monthly post return from Fort Robinson for March 1881, Records of the Office of the Adjutant General, 1780's–1917, Record Group 94, National Archives Microfilm Publication M617, Roll 1028, Washington, DC. Hereafter, records in the National Archives are indicated by the symbol NA, preceded by the record group (RG) number. Report of the Adjutant General, in *Annual Report of the Secretary of War, 1881*, 4 vols. (Washington, DC: U.S. GPO, 1881), 1:45; Report of the Inspector General, in *Annual Report of the Secretary of War, 1882*, 4 vols. (Washington, DC: U.S. GPO, 1882), 2:71.

6. Ordinance 22, June 1888, Crawford, NE. In 1901 the allocation of occupational taxes on saloon men to local schools became a statewide practice (*Crawford Tribune*, May 24, 1901).

7. Minutes, Crawford City Council, vol. 1: December 5, 1892, April 3, 1893, and March 20, 1895; and vol. 2: November 23, 1897.

8. *Army and Navy Journal* 25 (June 16, 1888):963; 25 (June 30, 1888):975; and 26 (December 22, 1888):321; *Crawford Tribune*, April 6, 1906.

9. Report of the Chief Surgeon, Department of the Platte, quoted in *Annual Report of the Secretary of War, 1896*, 10 vols. (Washington, DC: U.S. GPO, 1896), 1:473; report of inspection, Fort Robinson, August 21, 1893, Reports of Inspection, Department of the Platte, vol. 2, Records of U.S. Army Continental Commands, 1821–1920, RG 393, NA. See Frank N. Schubert, "The Suggs Affray: The Black Cavalry in the Johnson County War," *Western Historical Quarterly* 4 (Jan. 1973):66, for court-martial and desertion data and officers' comments indicating the greater reliability and temperance of black troops.

10. Data for years in which nearly equal numbers of white and black troops on post yield similar results. In 1904, when Fort Robinson was occupied by 563 black soldiers, saloon revenues were $3,400. In 1909 and 1912, a similar number of white cavalrymen resided on post, and saloon revenues were $4,833 and $4,500, respectively. It is also possible that the pay increase of 1908 was responsible for the upsurge of spending in local taverns during the 8th Cavalry's tour of duty.

11. Mari Sandoz, *Old Jules* (Lincoln: University of Nebraska Press, 1971), p. 117; and *Crawford Tribune*, April 9, 1909, November 10, 1916, and May 4, 1917. Property tax levies are specified in city ordinances passed annually in the spring.

12. Typescript historical sketch of the First Methodist Church, Crawford, NE, Nebraska State Historical Society, Lincoln, pp. 2–3; *Souvenir Book: Crawford, Nebraska, 75th Year, 1886–1961* (Crawford: n.p., 1961), p. 68; *Crawford Clipper*, January 29, 1892; and *Crawford Tribune*, August 4, 1905.

13. Ordinance 6, December 6, 1886; Minutes, Crawford City Council, vol. 1: March 7 and May 2, 1887. Other towns near military posts put prostitution to similar uses. See Carl Coke Rister, *Fort Griffin on the Texas Frontier* (Norman: University of Oklahoma Press, 1956), p. 134; David K. Strate, *Sentinel to the Cimarron: The Frontier Experience of Fort Dodge, Kansas* (Dodge City: Cultural Heritage and Arts Center, 1970), p. 99.

14. Minutes, Crawford City Council, vol. 1: January 8, 1894, December 17, 1895, and January 6, 1896.

15. Ibid., vol. 2: May 1907. Total city expenditures and revenues were reported as erratically as the whore tax, so a systematic summary of their relationship is impossible.

16. Ibid., vol. 1: May 9, 1887, January 2, 1888, June 11 and September 2, 1889, and May 2, 1894; and vol. 2: July 27, 1899.

17. Clarissa Lindemann Narrall, "The Night Three Men Were Shot," *Old Timers' Tales*, 2, pt. 1 (Chadron, NE: Crazy Horse Cultural Center, 1971), p. 171.

18. Commanding Officer, Fort Robinson, to Chairman, Village Board of Trustees, June 1902, Letters Sent, Fort Robinson, RG 393, NA; Chairman, Village Board of Trustees, to Capt. Charles H. Grierson, July 17, 1902, Register of Correspondence, Post Surgeon, Fort Robinson, RG 393, NA; Minutes, Crawford City Council, vol. 2: April 3, 1902; and Crawford Police Court Docket.

19. *Crawford Tribune*, October 4, 1907; and Crawford Police Court Docket.

20. *Crawford Tribune*, June 14, 1907, and June 24, 1910; Minutes, Crawford City Council, vol. 2: July 10 and 16, 1907; and Ordinance 114, July 17, 1907.

21. *Crawford Tribune*, June 18, 1909, and April 21, 1911; monthly sanitary report of Fort Robinson for April 1910, Records of Fort Robinson, RG 393, NA.

22. Minutes, Crawford City Council, vol. 1: April 2, 1894; *Crawford Tribune*, April 9 and 30, 1897; March 25 and April 8, 1898; April 7, 1899; and April 6, 1900.

23. Minnie Alice Rhoads, *A Stream Called Deadhorse* (Chadron, NE: n.p., 1957), pp. 50–51; *Crawford Tribune*, February 12, March 5, April 6 and 23, September 3, and December 24, 1909.

24. Ibid., January 14, 1910; *Souvenir Book*, p. 12; Donald Danker, taped interview with Miss [Clarissa ?] Lindeman, n.d., Nebraska State Historical Society, Lincoln, NE.

25. *Crawford Tribune*, January 28, February 11, and March 4, 1910; Minutes, Crawford City Council, vol. 2: March 10, 1910; and "Historical Sketch of the First Methodist Church," p. 5.

26. *Crawford Tribune*, March 25, April 1, 8, 15, and 22, and May 27, 1910, and March 10, 17, 24, and 31, and April 7, 1911; Minutes, Crawford City Council, vol. 2: April 8, and May 3, 6, and 27, 1910, and April 8 and May 2, 1911. Crawford's decisions regarding vice and the town's relationship to the post parallel developments in Kansas cattle towns in several ways. See Robert F. Dykstra, *The Cattle Towns* (New York: Atheneum, 1968), pp. 74, 85, 100–105, 125–126, 239. The most interesting similarity appears in the area of political participation. In the cattle towns, numerous factional splits stimulated widespread involvement in public issues. In Crawford, which maintained at least the appearance of a broad consensus for many years, the normal school disaster and related disputes over vice generated the factions that made public policy and elections of councilmen matters of general concern.

Red, Black, and White:
The U.S. Army at Columbus, GA

Elaine C. Everly

One of the major purposes of the series of National Archives conferences of which this is the 19th is the stimulation of research through a greater utilization of the records of the U.S. Government that are in this building and in our regional branches. At each conference at least one member of the National Archives staff gives a paper discussing research possibilities in a specific body of records or on a general topic, such as the impact of the military on local areas, the subject now under discussion. Rather than do so, however, I am hoping to encourage future research by sharing with you my observations, made almost entirely from federal records in this building, regarding the military's impact on one very small part of our country, the area near Columbus, GA, on the Chattahoochie River during three periods of military involvement, which I have called the red, black and white periods.

I believe that the U.S. Army's relationship with Columbus is especially interesting because it illustrates several of the roles that the army has played in American history and the varying nature of its impact on the same locale at different periods of time. Still, Columbus is by no means unique in this respect; other areas of the United States have been affected in similar ways.

White expansion into Indian territory gave rise to the first military involvement in the Columbus area. At the end of the colonial period, the country drained by the Chattahoochie River was inhabited mainly by the Creeks, a tribe of the southern confederacy. During the Creek War of 1813, Georgia militia erected a post on the west bank of the Chattahoochie River about 10 miles below the present city of Columbus, calling it Fort Mitchell. Here Brig. Gen. John Floyd and his Georgia militia repaired in late November 1813 after destroying the Creeks at the village of Auttose on the Tallapoosa River in Alabama.[1] At this first Fort Mitchell, Lafayette reputedly crossed the Chattahoochie during his visit to Alabama in 1824.[2]

The U.S. Army first came to the area in August 1825 to establish a "new" Fort Mitchell on or near the old site in order to keep peace in the Creek Nation until the Indians had been transported west of the Mississippi as part of the federal government's policy of Indian removal. In response to Georgia Governor George M. Troup's reports of disturbances among the Creeks regarding the recently negotiated treaty to cede their lands, Gen. Edmund Pendleton Gaines received orders to go to Milledgeville, to survey the situation and to station troops at the Creek agency "where you may think it best calculated to provide the object of the executive."[3] For the next 12 years regular army troops, although never numbering more than 250 men and sometimes as few as 25, garrisoned the fort, which, as the surviving records indicate, was usually in a bad state of repair.[4]

While there would probably have been a city at the falls of the Chattahoochie had the two Fort Mitchells never existed, Columbus was in fact laid out in 1828, just 3 years after Fort Mitchell had been reestablished. In addition to the post and its garrison, the army presence in the area was further manifested by the quartermaster officer, who from his office in Columbus was supplying the nearby fort and troops fighting the Seminoles in Florida, was depositing his funds in a local bank, was acquiring supplies from local farmers, and was storing goods in the city.[5]

Although the presence of the U.S. Army had a substantial economic impact on the Columbus area, the major consequences were social. The garrison served to preserve peace by restricting white settlement on Indian lands, and the U.S. Marshal of Alabama did not hesitate to call on the federal troops to assist him in removing white intruders. Consequently troops and settlers frequently clashed. The stormy relationship between the military and the local citizenry grew intense in October 1833, when the superior court of Russell County, AL, found the post commander in contempt for refusing to turn over to civil authorities the enlisted men who had killed a white intruder.[6] For their part, the post officers looked upon the local whites with disdain. Realizing the impossibility of removing the whites who were establishing permanent settlements on Creek lands and aware of the need for more troops to protect the Indians, one commander reported: "There is hardly a white man

HEADQUARTERS THIRD MILITARY DISTRICT,

(DEPARTMENT OF GEORGIA, FLORIDA & ALABAMA,)

ATLANTA, GEORGIA, *May* 25, 1868.

SPECIAL ORDERS }
No. 112. }

I.—The following named municipal officers of the City of Columbus, State of Georgia, are hereby removed from office :

F. G. WILKINS—Mayor.

ALDERMEN.

1st Ward—LOUIS HAIMAN, THOMAS FELL.
2d Ward—J. C. PORTER, J. W. SAPPINGTON.
3d Ward—JAMES M. DENSON, J. M. ESTES.
4th Ward—JOHN MCILHENNEY, JAMES A. BRADFORD.
5th Ward—J. A. FRAZER, L. W. WALL.
6th Ward—WILLIAM H. WILLIAMS, JOHN S. CARGILL.
MATHEW MURPHY—City Marshal.
ROBERT WOODS—Deputy City Marshal.

II.—Captain WILLIAM MILLS, 16th U. S. Infantry, is hereby appointed Mayor of the City of Columbus, State of Georgia, to fill a vacancy.

III.—The following appointments are hereby made to fill vacancies in the Board of Aldermen for the City of Columbus, State of Georgia :

1st Ward—JOSEPH E. WEBSTER.
2d Ward—GEORGE HUNGERFORD.
3d Ward—THOMAS M. HOGAN.
4th Ward—WALTER H. JOHNSON.
5th Ward—JOHN W. DUER.

IV.—THOMAS GRIER is hereby appointed Deputy City Marshal for the City of Columbus, State of Georgia, to fill a vacancy.

V.—Acting Assistant Surgeon RUFUS CHOATE, U. S. Army, having reported at these Headquarters, will proceed to Montgomery, Alabama, and report to the Commanding officer sub-District of Alabama, for duty at Greenville, in that State. The Quartermaster's Department will furnish the necessary transportation.

VI.—LEROY M. WILLSON is hereby appointed Treasurer of Morgan County, State of Georgia, to fill a vacancy.

VII.—WILLIAM H. BURR is hereby appointed Tax Collector for Morgan County, State of Georgia, to fill a vacancy.

VIII.—F. M. ADAMS is hereby appointed Mayor of the City of St. Mary's, Georgia, to fill a vacancy.

IX.—THOMAS A. RAMSEY is hereby appointed Judge of Probate for the County of St. Clair, State of Alabama, to fill a vacancy.

X.—Upon the recommendation of the Commanding officer sub-District of Alabama, the following municipal officers of the City of Tuscaloosa, State of Alabama, are hereby removed from office :

Mayor—HENRY McGOWAN.
Marshal— —GARDNER.
ALDERMEN.
1st Ward—T. F. SAMUELS.
2d Ward—O. BERRY.
3d Ward—R. RABBITT.

The climax of U.S. military intervention into the civil affairs of Columbus, GA, came on May 25, 1868 when the military district commander named the local post commander at Columbus mayor of the city. (*Source: National Archives*)

XI.—The following appointments are hereby made to fill vacancies in the municipal offices of the City of Tuscaloosa, State of Alabama :

Mayor—DAVID WOODRUFF.
Marshal—JOHN PURCELL.
ALDERMEN.
1st Ward—T. P. LEWIS.
2d Ward—MORRIS ROBERTS.
3d Ward—JOHN BURNES.
5th Ward—A. LYNCH.

XII.—J. W. MARTIN is hereby appointed a Justice of the Peace in the City of Tuscaloosa, State of Alabama, to fill a vacancy.

BY ORDER OF MAJOR GENERAL MEADE :

R. C. DRUM,
Assistant Adjutant General.

OFFICIAL :

Assistant Adjutant General.

Adjutant General.

U. S. Army.

to be found in this section of country, that is not looking out and waiting for the time when he expects to be able to swindle an Indian out of a good touch of land."[7]

In 1836 the U.S. Army's role in the area suddenly and drastically reversed itself, changing from that of protector of the Indians to that of defender of the white settlers. The post commander at Mitchell informed the War Department in May that "the warwhoop is now sounding throughout the [Creek] nation."[8] Several weeks later he reported that the Indians had murdered whites, destroyed property, and burned the village of Roanoke, GA, killing 15 to 20 people.[9] Soon, 1,000 to 1,500 militia gathered at Columbus to oppose 1,200 to 1,500 Indians. Thanks to the military, by November the Indian insurrection was over, and reports from Fort Mitchell told of the capture of fugitive Creeks who were trying to make their way to the Cherokee Nation.[10]

The insurrection ended and the Indians removed from the area. The settlers then clamored for the military to withdraw and, to hasten their withdrawal, literally began to move Fort Mitchell out from under the garrison. Whereas the post commander complained in general terms to the War Department that the settlers had invaded the military reserve and were stealing as much government property as they could, the assistant surgeon at Mitchell was more specific. He reported that the local citizens had destroyed the post hospital, breaking and stealing the windows, taking the doors from their hinges, and tearing up and carrying off the floor.[11] In November 1837 Fort Mitchell was abandoned, and the following June the land that had been reserved for military purposes was restored to the jurisdiction of the General Land Office. The red period had ended, and for the next quarter century there was no military presence at Columbus.

If the red man had brought about the first military involvement in the Columbus area, the black man caused the second. At the time Fort Sumter fell, Columbus was a small manufacturing town of 12,000 situated in the midst of a fertile agricultural area worked by slave labor. Ante bellum Columbus was an important supply center, with flour, paper, and cotton mills, and an ironworks. As early as 1862, the Confederates recognized the strategic and commercial importance of the city and began to plan for its defense. Among other things their plans resulted in the establishment of a small navy yard and a military hospital in the town. Confederate forces maintained control of Columbus throughout the war, but on April 16, 1865, 7 days after Lee had surrendered, the city fell to Union troops commanded by Gen. Emory Upton. About 4,000 dismounted men assaulted the breastworks of the city, capturing 52 field guns and taking 1,200 prisoners.[12] For the next 6 years, U.S. Army troops occupied the Columbus area.

As the status of the black man in American society was the cause of the Civil War, so his place in the reconstructed South was one of the main reasons for the military occupation. During 1865 and 1866 parts of several regiments, including two companies of the 103d U.S. Colored Infantry, were quartered in Columbus. At this time white officers were reporting that they had heard a "great many remarks" about what the southern whites were going to do with the "damned Nigger troops" and unsubstantiated complaints that black troops had robbed and insulted white women were widespread. Racial tensions reached a climax on February 13, 1866, when Pvt. James Gant of Company F was shot on the streets of Columbus by a white man who was subsequently released by the local authorities, thereby nearly setting off a riot among the black troops who wanted to avenge the assault. Within a year all black troops had been withdrawn.[13]

The departure of the 103d U.S. Colored Infantry did not end the military occupation of Columbus. From April 1867 to July 1868 there was a military post at Columbus, garrisoned by Company G of the 16th U.S. Infantry.[14] During this period the army assumed many functions of the local government. From his Macon headquarters the military district commander promulgated regulations concerning the registration of voters and the treatment of blacks. He appointed the registrar for the county of Muscogee, in which Columbus is located, selected the members of the city council, and on May 25, 1868, as the climax of all the political activity, named the post commander at Columbus mayor of the city.[15] In addition, district provost marshals preserved law and order and supported the Freedmen's Bureau officials, who were responsible for all affairs relating to blacks in the Columbus area.

The Freedmen's Bureau, an agency of the War Department that was staffed by army officers, volunteer officers mustered out of service, and a few civilian agents, concerned itself mainly with educational and social programs for the blacks, even though it was frequently criticized for actions taken by the occupation troops. In operation from the summer of 1865 through December 1868, the office of the assistant commissioner for Georgia designated Columbus as the headquarters for one of the several subdistricts into which the state was divided, making the officer at Columbus responsible for the work of the agents in Muscogee and neighboring counties.

The officials of the Freedmen's Bureau in the Columbus area performed many tasks undertaken by modern social workers. They distributed food and clothing to destitute people, operated a hospital, assisted the teachers of the newly established schools for blacks, and investigated charges that former slaves, particularly minors, were still being held in bondage. Equally important, they witnessed the contracts that returned the freedmen to the plantations under the new system of contract labor, contracts that stipulated the obligations of employers and employees in an often futile attempt to preserve the fruits of emancipation and the southern agricultural system as well.[16] Considering

Georgia fully restored to the Union after the congressional elections of 1870, the federal government in early 1871 ended the military's special relation with Georgia, and the black period at Columbus came to a close.

Joyful at the withdrawal of U.S. troops from the Columbus area in the early 1870s, the civic leaders of Columbus were actively lobbying for the return of U.S. Army troops less than 30 years later. War with Spain being first a possibility and then a reality, the city fathers pushed for the establishment of a temporary or permanent military camp in the vicinity. Although some troops were at Columbus during the winter of 1898-99,[17] not until World War I did their efforts succeed, with the establishment of Camp Benning, ironically named for Confederate Brig. Gen. Henry L. Benning.

The white period of army involvement at Columbus is the story of Fort Benning, the site of by far the longest and the most significant military presence in the Columbus area. Selected as the location of the Infantry School of Arms several months before the armistice, Camp Benning, as it was known until February 1922, initially consisted of a reservation of 98,000 acres in Muscogee and Chattahoochie counties, GA. According to official War Department records, the 1918 decision to establish the camp was based on military considerations alone: the reserve had almost every conceivable form of terrain, and it was large enough to stage a complete day's operation of infantry in action. Furthermore, the climate was mild enough to permit technical and tactical training throughout the year, and Columbus was an important railroad center.[18] Nonetheless, Benning certainly had not been forced on an unwilling Columbus. The Columbus Chamber of Commerce and the Georgia delegation in Congress lobbied for its establishment and, having succeeded, continued to push for the expansion of its facilities.[19]

In the interwar period, Benning became one of the major posts of the IV Corps Area and the site of many maneuvers, which as early as 1920 included air service troops. Between the armistice with Germany and the Japanese attack on Pearl Harbor, from 5,000 to 7,000 troops supported the infantry school and several companies of the 24th and 29th Infantry Regiments were regularly stationed at the post.[20] Such luminaries in American military history as Stilwell, Bradley, and Marshall as young men served on the staff of the infantry school or attended its classes.

During World War II Fort Benning grew enormously in size and importance, becoming one of the largest training and reception centers in the United States. The opening of a parachutist school early in the war expanded the reservation into Russell County, AL, on the opposite side of the Chattahoochie River. Later in the war the post received one of the first contingents of members of the Women's Army Corps, and it was one of the army installations that held Italian and German prisoners of war. Its wartime facilities and activities are too numerous to mention. The magnitude and importance of the activities carried on at Benning during World War II are illustrated, however, by the prodigious number of 66,000 second lieutenants who graduated from the post's officer candidate school between July 1941 and September 1946.[21] Fort Benning suffered little from postwar retrenchment and during the Korean conflict served as one of the major army training centers in the United States. It remains one of the major military installations in the country.

The impact of Fort Benning on the growth and development of Columbus could in itself be the subject of a lengthy dissertation. Fort Benning occupies a reservation of 285 square miles, employs thousands of military and civilian personnel, and expends millions of dollars annually. Thousands of local citizens derive their income, directly or indirectly, from activities performed at the post. The economic impact of the third and latest military presence in the Columbus area can perhaps best be understood by an examination of the city's growth in population during the five decades following the establishment of Fort Benning. In 1920, shortly after Benning was established, Columbus had a population of more than 20,000. By 1970, Columbus had become the second largest city in Georgia, with a population of more than 162,000 despite the fact that the city had never attained the prominence predicted for it as a major manufacturing city.

While the presence of a large military installation is usually economically advantageous to a community, the social effects are frequently mixed. During World War I soldiers from camps at Macon, GA, and Montgomery, AL, were attracted to Columbus because it was a "wide open" city where servicemen were welcomed in saloons and in houses of prostitution. By 1921 Benning was reporting the highest rate of new cases of venereal disease per 1,000 men of all commands in the army.[22] During World War II the many bars, brothels, and roadhouses in Columbus and nearby Phoenix City, AL, "accommodated" the military personnel. Most of these public houses were designated by name in post orders declaring them off limits to military personnel. Fort Benning General Order No. 43, dated August 1, 1942, also declared off limits a lengthy list of establishments in Chattahoochie, Muscogee, and Russell counties where clairvoyance, mindreadings, voodoo, magic, and other forms of fortune-telling or placing and removing of "spells" were practiced.[23]

Jurisdiction over such matters as the arrest of disorderly military personnel, collection of debts incurred by military personnel, claims arising from automobile accidents involving servicemen, the cost of off-post housing, and the use of the military reservation have all been subjects of dispute or discussion at one time or another between Columbus authorities and the military post. In 1930, for example, the army was questioned about blacks who were reportedly moving into the camp zone and squatting on the land. The commander at Benning replied that 45 families had permission to occupy shacks and to cultivate designated pieces of land, a right they had assumed prior to the establishment of the reservation.[24]

Any subject dealing with blacks was and remains a sensitive issue at Fort Benning. In the interwar years about 20 percent of the command was black. Segregation, common to Georgia at that time, was practiced at the post, where there were separate, if not always equal, facilities for the blacks. During World War II many of the special investigations of conditions at Benning by the inspector general's office had to do with race relations.

Indians, blacks, and whites brought about the military presence at Columbus at three different periods, and each presence has left a lasting mark on the area. The first secured the area for white settlement; the second attempted, with some success, to bring the black man out of legal bondage; and the third, more than any other single factor, made Columbus the city that it is today.

The history of the multifaceted relationships between Columbus, GA, and the U.S. Army can best be gleaned from the holdings of the War Department in this building: the monthly post and unit strength returns, the correspondence of the Secretary of War, the Adjutant General, and the Quartermaster General; the voluminous records of army geographical and tactical commands; the numerous and varied reports of the Freedmen's Bureau; and the general courts-martial proceedings of the Judge Advocate General all attest to the military's profound and lasting impact on Columbus.

Notes

1. Benson J. Lossing, *The Pictorial Field Book of the War of 1812* (New York: Harper & Brothers Publishers, 1868), pp. 768–769.

2. Slips of papers indicating that the Adjutant General's office obtained information from C. W. Brewer's *History of Alabama* (1872), p. 511; Reservation Files, "Fort Mitchell, AL," Records of the Office of the Adjutant General, 1780's–1917, Record Group 94, National Archives, Washington, DC. Hereafter, records in the National Archives are indicated by the symbol NA, preceded by the record group (RG) number.

3. James Barbour to E. P. Gaines, May 20, 1825, Letters Sent by the Secretary of War Relating to Military Affairs, 1800–89, vol. 12, pp. 155–156; Records of the Office of the Secretary of War, RG 107, NA, National Archives Microfilm Publication M6, roll 12.

4. Monthly returns from Fort Mitchell, AL, August, 1825–April 1840, Returns from U.S. Military Posts, 1800–1916, RG 94, NA, National Archives Microfilm Publication, M617, roll 785.

5. Consolidated Correspondence File "Fort Mitchell," Records of the Office of the Quartermaster General, RG 92, NA.

6. J. S. McIntosh to Adjutant General, September 9, 1833, File M215, Adjutant General's office (hereafter AGO) 1833, Letters Received by the Office of the Adjutant General, Main Series, 1822–1860, RG 94, NA, National Archives Microfilm Publication M567, roll 86.

7. Philip Wager to Adjutant General, September 9, 1832, File W137, AGO 1832, Letters Received by the Office of the Adjutant General, Main Series, 1822–60, RG 94, NA, National Archives Microfilm Publication M567, roll 77.

8. J. S. McIntosh to Adjutant General, May 9, 1836, File M138 AGO 1836, Letters Received by the Office of the Adjutant General, Main Series, 1822–60, RG 94, NA, National Archives Microfilm Publication M567, roll 127.

9. J. S. McIntosh to Adjutant General, May 24, 1836, File M162 AGO 1836, Letters Received by the Office of the Adjutant General, Main Series, 1822–60, RG 94, NA, National Archives Microfilm Publication M567, roll 127.

10. J. W. Washington to Adjutant General, November 14, 1836, File W309 AGO 1836, Letters Received by the Office of the Adjutant General, Main Series, 1822–60, RG 94, NA, National Archives Microfilm Publication M567, roll 134.

11. Madison Mills to Surgeon General, November 6, 1835, "Fort Mitchell," Quartermaster Consolidated File, RG 92, NA.

12. Bvt. Maj. Gen. J. M. Wilson to Brig. Gen. William D. Whipple, June 29, 1865, and "Itinerary of the Cavalry Corps of the Military Division of the Mississippi," *The War of the Rebellion: A Compilation of Official Records of the Union and Confederate Armies*, ser. 1, vol. 49 (Washington, DC: U.S. GPO, 1897), pp. 371–372 and 384.

13. Lt. Col. John A. Bogert to Bvt. Col. S. B. Mee, February 22, 1866, File C 36 DG 1866, Letters Received by the Department of Georgia, Records of U.S. Army Continental Commands, 1821–1920, RG 393, NA.

14. Monthly returns from the Post of Columbus, GA, April 1867–July 1868, Returns from U.S. Military Posts, 1800–1916, RG 94, NA, National Archives Microfilm Publication M617, roll 1504.

15. Special Orders No. 112, May 25, 1868, Headquarters, 3d Military District, and Orders and Circulars, vol. 584, RG 94, NA.

16. Letters Sent, April 1866–January 1869, vols. 222 and 223, and Letters Received, February 1867–December 1868, by the Subassistant Commissioner at Columbus, GA, Records of the Bureau of Refugees, Freedmen, and Abandoned Lands, RG 105, NA.

17. Index cards entitled "U.S. Forces, Columbus, GA," Index to General Correspondence of the Adjutant General's Office, 1890–1917, RG 94, NA, National Archives Microfilm Publication M698, roll 250.

18. "Facts Relative to Camp Benning and the Infantry School," n.d., File 7-51.3, Camp Benning, GA, Records of the Historical Section Relating to the History of the War Department, 1900–41, Records of the War Department General and Special Staffs, RG 165, NA.

19. See Camp Benning Project Files, especially decimal file 680.1, General Correspondence of the Adjutant General's Office, 1917–25, Records of the Adjutant General's Office, 1917–25, RG 407, NA.

20. Monthly Returns of Fort Benning, GA, 1917–39, RG 407, NA.

21. John H. Thompson, *This Is Your Army* (1952), reprinted from the *Chicago Tribune* publication located among records relating to Fort Benning, GA, in the custody of the U.S. Army Center of Military History, Washington, DC.

22. Col. E. D. Anderson, memorandum to the Adjutant General, May 31, 1921, decimal file 726.1, Camp Benning Project Files, General Correspondence of the Adjutant General's Office, 1917–25, RG 407, NA.

23. General Orders, No. 43, August 1, 1942, Headquarters, Fort Benning, GA, Records of Fort Benning, GA, Records of U.S. Army Commands, 1942– , RG 338, NA.

24. Report of Campbell King, February 22, 1930, to Adjutant General, decimal file 291.21, Camp Benning Project Files, General Correspondence of the Adjutant General's Office, 1926–39, RG 407, NA.

4

THE U.S. ARMY AS AGENT OF SOCIAL CHANGE AND AS INSTRUMENT OF SOCIAL CONTROL

Camp Scene at Warrenton, VA, November 1862 (*Source: Alexander Gardiner Collection, National Archives*)

Not North of Dixie's Line: The Social Limitations and Political Implications of the Wartime Emancipation Process

Armstead L. Robinson

The Civil War era is a very useful period for researchers interested in a deeper understanding of the roles played by the U.S. Army in encouraging and controlling domestic social change. Obviously, such roles raise fundamental questions about the place of the military in a democratic society. The politicization of military power usually assumes one of two dominant forms. Either an army takes upon itself the task of shaping society through military control of the processes of social change, or an army becomes the pliant tool of elite civilian groups. In either case, politicized military power works to the detriment of democracy.[1] During the Civil War, Lincoln made unprecedented use of his powers as commander in chief, employing martial law in wide areas of the North and ruling by decree when he felt the occasion warranted.[2] Yet despite the often dreary prognoses for northern victory, the Union army remained under civilian control, forswearing an opportunity to take advantage of a national emergency in which the very survival of the federal republic hung in the balance. Thus, if the Civil War–era army became a force in domestic social change, it had to have done so as a pliant agent of the President's will.

The army's relationship with Afro-American slaves probably formed the most critical arena in which Lincoln sought to influence domestic social change. During the Civil War, the army served as the implementary agency for one of the major social revolutions in 19th-

117

century American life. Chattel slavery had existed in America since the 17th century. During the Civil War, the army became the instrument that Lincoln chose for the implementation of his emancipation policy. By working to destroy the institution of slavery, the Civil War army not only helped to crush the Confederacy but also accomplished the sudden transformation of Afro-Americans from chattel slaves into potential citizens.[3] The success of wartime emancipation ensured that the Civil War and Reconstruction era would witness a broad national debate over the whole question of race relations in America.

From the obvious success of wartime emancipation, it would be all too easy to conclude that the army performed quite efficiently as an agent of social change during the Civil War era. Nothing, however, could be farther from the truth. Rather than acting smoothly to implement the racial policies of the Lincoln administration, the Union army became part of the energetic national debate over the social consequences of emancipation. Precisely because wartime emancipation raised the profound question of the future status of former slaves, the evolution of federal racial policy opened a Pandora's box of social and political dilemmas. Were the freed people to be allowed to move about as they pleased? What would be the consequences if several million southern blacks seized upon emancipation as an excuse to abandon the South in favor of permanent residence in the North? In short, wartime emancipation raised the fundamental question of the kinds of social and political status that freedmen were to possess in the postwar world.

In the absence of a national consensus about the proper status of former slaves, we should not be too surprised to discover that a Union army that represented the diversity of America's peoples performed fitfully as an agent of federal racial policy. Lincoln's indecisiveness contributed significantly to the army's difficulty in implementing federal racial policies. In fact, the President failed to articulate a consistent stance. The Lincoln administration launched into the Civil War loudly insisting that emancipation was the antithesis of federal policy. Yet as the war progressed, the pressure of military necessity gradually forced Lincoln to contravene his earlier position. He ended the war proclaiming emancipation as the measure essential to the defeat of the Confederacy.[4] Lincoln persisted in denying that emancipation would become a northern war aim right up to the moment when he issued the preliminary emancipation proclamation, so that it is easy to see why an army of citizen soldiers found it difficult to enforce his racial policies consistently.

The vagaries of federal policy notwithstanding, we cannot fully comprehend the army's fitful performance solely on the basis of the President's decision to reverse his initial opposition to emancipation. Indeed, Union soldiers found it difficult to take a position precisely because emancipation raised social and political issues of the first magnitude. George Fredrickson and Joel Williamson are persuasive when they argue that the nation as a whole was not yet ready to extend to former slaves the full range of social and political rights that white Americans believed to be their own birthright.[5] Yet Mary Berry is equally persuasive when she asserts that Lincoln's decision to use Afro-American troops in defense of the Union raised the insoluble problem of how to deny citizenship to men who had fought to defend the nation.[6] With public opinion divided sharply over the issue of Afro-American rights, the Union army soon discovered its vulnerability to the social and political force at work within American society. To the extent that the army both reflected and molded public opinion on racial issues, we shall find in the story of wartime emancipation significant insight into the relationship between the will of the people, on the one hand, and, on the other, the interests of the civilian wielders of the people's military power.

This perspective calls into question viewpoints that see the U.S. Army as a compliant monolith, willing to enforce without question the socially coercive orders of civilian authorities. The *prospect* of emancipation proved so controversial that the Union army found itself ensnarled in sharp internal debates over the propriety of enforcing Lincoln's orders. Furthermore, the *reality* of emancipation provoked a similar response because the army mirrored the nation's deeply divided will. In each instance, significant segments of the army objected to Lincoln's orders. Both officers and men voiced their objections first to the President's orders not to interfere with slavery and subsequently to his decree that they work diligently to emancipate the slaves. To the extent that Lincoln and the general staff found themselves compelled to expend considerable energy seeking to obtain compliance within the army, I believe we may well have uncovered one of the major social mechanisms that helped to transform the war to save the Union by protecting slavery into a war to save the Union by destroying slavery.[7] An army whose officers and men helped to shape federal racial policy through willful disobedience ought not to be regarded as an effective agent of social control.

Implicit within my position is a strong objection to arguments that the army's hierarchical structure transforms its members, ipso facto, into pliant agents of the wishes of elite groups within American society.[8] During the last two decades, we have learned far too much from studies of the master/slave relationship ever again to believe that the conscious actions of subordinates can be inferred from knowledge merely of what their superordinates wish that behavior to be.[9] I believe that military historians could profit from the emphasis among the new social historians on viewing history "from the bottom up."[10] Instead of simply assuming monolithic compliance with presidential directives, students of the U.S. Army must search for evidence of the extent to which soldiers followed their orders. Inevitably, this search will yield a divided record. How sharply divided that record is may tell us a great deal about the army's effectiveness in enforcing different types of orders. Indeed, this search will surely lead to analyses of the social factors that explain the degrees of compliance revealed in different situations.

During the Civil War, the Union army showed itself vulnerable to the very social conflicts that created the necessity for its intervention in domestic affairs. For as we shall see, both officers and men took it upon themselves to decide whether they agreed with the shifting goals of Lincoln's racial policies. These disagreements within the military mirrored the fiercely partisan debates then raging within the larger society over these very policies. By conceptualizing the U.S. Army as a living social institution, we shall be able to illuminate more fully the connections between broad changes in the character of American life and the internal history of the American military.

I

The first 18 months of the Civil War encompassed the period during which Lincoln insisted steadfastly that emancipation was the antithesis of northern war policy. The President's first inaugural address, delivered on March 4, 1861, included the following blunt statement: "I have no purpose, directly or indirectly, to interfere with the institution of slavery in the States where it exists. I believe I have no lawful right to do so and I have no inclination to do so."[11] Lincoln suited his actions to his words. Not only did his general in chief and Secretary of War order northern armies to avoid interference with slavery, but Lincoln also moved decisively against generals who disobeyed his orders.[12] Lincoln maintained this staunch public opposition to emancipation right up through September 1862. While doing this, Lincoln absorbed severe criticism from elements within his own party for his opposition to emancipation. In fact, Horace Greeley, in an editorial titled "The Prayer of Twenty Millions," lambasted Lincoln for failing to take the high ground of emancipation in the struggle to save the Union. Lincoln replied as follows:

> My paramount object in this struggle is to save the Union, and it is not either to save or destroy slavery. If I could save the Union without freeing any slave, I would do it and if I could save it by freeing all the slaves I would do it; and if I could save it by freeing some and leaving others alone I would also do that. What I do about slavery and the colored race, I do because I believe it helps save the Union; and what I forbear I forbear because I do not believe it would help save the union.[13]

This position remained federal policy until late September 1862, when the President suddenly reversed his public posture. Seizing upon the opportunity presented by the stalemate at Antietam, Lincoln promulgated the preliminary Emancipation Proclamation. This proclamation threatened to free all of the slaves in the Confederacy unless the war ended by January 1, 1863.[14] So sharp is the contrast between Lincoln's two positions on emancipation that we are compelled to ask how northern soldiers reacted to such a rapid shift. The evidence suggests that Lincoln's change in policy followed the trend of opinion within the army rather than leading it. Long before September 1862, troops driven by the immanent logic of war against a slaveholding enemy began increasingly to refuse to enforce the initial policy of avoiding interference with slavery. As the army faced what amounted to an open revolt in the ranks, Lincoln saved face and saved the Union by beating a hasty retreat from sustaining slavery toward the new policy of emancipation.

This theory of the military origins of emancipation places great emphasis on viewing the Civil War from the perspective of front-line participants, both officers and common soldiers. It was they who, as in any war, bore the brunt of enforcing the President's orders. The troops soon discovered that the slaves posed a major problem. Wherever the army went, blacks hoping to escape from slavery ran toward it. No matter what the generals or the line officers tried to do, slaves kept running toward the freedom they believed lay in the northern army's camps. By running toward the Union army at every opportunity, fugitive slaves forced men at the front lines to decide again and again whether they intended to obey the President's directives.[15] As the war progressed, an increasing number of volunteer officers and men found the returning of fugitive slaves morally repugnant. That they refused to continue enforcing Lincoln's orders ought to caution scholars who see the army as a pliant tool of social coercion. Unless the orders given to American soldiers conform to what they believe to be right, the Civil War experience suggests, unquestioning obedience will be difficult to obtain.

II

Was there a sustained conflict within the Union army with regard to the enforcement of Lincoln's early war policy opposing interference with the slaves? We might suspect that the regular army would tend to hew more closely to the President's policies than would short-term volunteers. And the evidence from military records supports this hypothesis. The West Point–trained general staff adopted a strict "law and order" approach. Grant best exemplified the regular army's attitude toward the problem posed by fugitive slaves. "I have tried studiously to prevent the running off of negroes from all outside places," insisted General Grant, "as I have tried to prevent other marauding and plundering. So long as I hold a commission in the Army I have no views of my own to carry out. Whatever may be the orders of my superiors and the law shall be carried out. . . . When Congress enacts anything too odious for me to execute, I shall resign."[16] If conflict existed within the northern army regarding enforcement of Lincoln's noninterference with slavery edicts, we would not expect to find systematic disobedience among officers of the regular army.

Lincoln could count on the professional officer corps to attempt rigid enforcement of his fugitive slave policy, a policy based on the 1850 Fugitive Slave Law. Two days before the First Battle of Bull Run, General in Chief Winfield Scott directed officers along the Potomac River to allow Virginia slaveholders to cross over into Maryland in order to recover fugitive slaves suspected of hiding in army camps.[17] Gen. George McClellan commanded the Ohio River segment of the northern lines in the spring of 1861. McClellan issued a circular to the people of western Virginia and eastern Kentucky, promising, "Not only will we abstain from all . . . interference [with your slaves] but we will on the contrary, with an iron hand crush any attempt at insurrection."[18] Even the Connecticut-born Gen. Nathaniel Lyon attempted to reassure slaveholders in Missouri. "I do hereby give notice to all the people of this State," asserted the soon-to-be-martyred Lyon, "that I shall scrupulously avoid all interference with the business, rights and property of every description recognized by the laws of this State and belonging to law abiding citizens."[19]

Cracks appeared very quickly in this apparently united front. While commanding at Fortress Monroe, VA, in May 1861, Gen. Benjamin Butler found cause to refuse to return three fugitive slaves who had sought refuge within northern lines. Butler defended his actions by citing the doctrine in the international laws of war that allowed belligerents to deny their opponents access to articles of war. Butler, one of the many "political generals" with whom Lincoln had to contend, decreed that able-bodied male slaves who had been given over voluntarily to the Confederacy were functioning as instruments of war against the United States of America. Although Lincoln desired desperately to separate the army from any involvement with the slavery issue, the President found Butler's designation of such male escapees as "contrabands of war" easier to accept in silence than to fight publicly.[20]

Gen. John C. Fremont took this precedent to heart and tried to adapt Butler's policy to the situation in Missouri. During the summer of 1861, Fremont faced a multifront partisan struggle in which Union and Confederate supporters took turns despoiling each other's property. Despairing of his ability to impose order in his war-wracked state, Fremont assumed administrative control of Missouri on August 31, 1861, by issuing a decree imposing martial law:

Its disordered condition, the helplessness of the civil authority, the total insecurity of life, and the devastation of property by hands of murderers and marauders, who infest every county of the State, and avail themselves of the public misfortunes and the vicinity of the hostile foe to gratify private and neighborhood vengeance, and who find an enemy wherever they find plunder, finally demand the severest measures to repress the daily increasing crimes and outrages which are driving off the inhabitants and ruining the State.

Fremont followed Butler's lead, believing that threatening the property of Confederate sympathizers might reduce partisan violence. Accordingly he decreed that the slaves of persons found in open rebellion against the government of the United States "are hereby declared freemen."[21] However, failing to acknowledge the distinction between slaves willingly turned over to serve Confederate forces and slaves belonging to persons who sympathized with the Confederacy, Fremont violated the lawyerly caution that undergirded Butler's position at Fortress Monroe. In the process, Fremont set himself on a collision course with the President.

Lincoln responded immediately to Fremont's challenge. News such as that presented by Col. Robert Anderson compelled the President to act quickly. Anderson warned Lincoln about Fremont's proclamation: "if not immediately disowned and annuled Kentucky will be lost to the Union—I have already heard that on reception of the news from Missouri a company which was ready to be sworn into the Service, disbanded."[22] Lincoln gently urged Fremont to redraft the proclamation so as to conform to national policy. The President wrote Fremont about his fears that the decree would "alarm our Southern Unionist friends and turn them against us; perhaps ruin our fair prospects for Kentucky."[23]

Fremont insisted on marching to the tune of the northern antislavery radicals who assured him that Lincoln dare not countermand his Missouri proclamation for fear of political retaliation in the North. The general adamantly refused to consider any amendments to his decree. In reply Lincoln not only revoked Fremont's decree but soon removed the truculent general from command of the Department of the Missouri.[24]

Few other generals proved willing to contest matters with Lincoln in so direct a fashion. Nonetheless, a number of volunteer officers came increasingly to rely upon their intuitive sense of the strategies likely to bring the Confederacy to its knees. While serving under McClellan in July 1861, Ohio-born Col. John Beatty expressed the sentiments of numerous northern soldiers, particularly those raised in staunchly Republican areas:

I am not convinced of a speedy termination of the war. . . . I believe the war will run into a war of emancipation, and when it ends, African slavery will have ended also. It would not, perhaps, be politic to

> say so, but if I had the Army in my own hands, I would take a short cut
> to what I am sure will be the end result—commence the work of
> emancipation at once and leave every foot of soil free behind us.[25]

Col. Hugh Ewing did not share Beatty's taste for immediate emancipation, but his position could hardly be described as one tending to the
support of slavery; "I think and find most agree with me that slavery
should be abolished and a system of peonage instituted."[26]

Junior officers and common soldiers often carried these proposi-
tions to their logical conclusions. An incident that occurred near
Camelton, VA, in September 1861 clearly showed the drift of behavior
among men at the front. General Rosecrans followed Lincoln's lead and
issued stringent orders forbidding soldiers in his command from interfering with either civilians or their property. Reacting to these directives,
the superintendent of the crude oil works dispatched a blistering complaint that Union troops occupying his area kept firing at civilians
working in their own cornfields. The superintendent also warned that
soldiers were tampering with local slaves: "I find that your officers and
men are constantly encouraging our negroes to invent all sorts of stories
and at least one officer, said to be a captain of the Cavalry, said to one of
our negroes, 'We are fighting for you! And when we ask of you information you must tell us the truth.'" General Rosecrans responded by
reassuring the superintendent of the army's "intention to protect your
works as long as we remain in the valley."[27] The series of similar complaints that dot Rosecrans's files, however, attest to the general's
inability to compel his soldiers to abstain from interfering with slavery.

Generals could order, but individual soldiers had to obey, and
many soldiers could not bring themselves to enforce the Fugitive Slave
Law. A soldier from Wisconsin who claimed to be an abolitionist, said
that his father gave him the following advice as he departed to fight to
save the Union: "Be true to your country my boy, and be true to the flag.
But before the country or the flag, be true to the slave."[28] Other, less ideo-
logically motivated soldiers nonetheless found reason to ignore orders
from the general staff about their interaction with runaway slaves. Pvt.
John Handley, for example, served in a company under General Rosecrans; his company mess hired several "sable cooks" they knew to be
fugitive slaves because camp servants lightened the drudgery of military life.[29]

To no avail did General Rosecrans struggle to halt what were
called personal emancipations. Although he reminded his men that only
authorized persons should be allowed to enter their camps, the general
found it necessary to repeat his orders on the subject of fugitive slaves.
He ordered General Cox, for example, to allow a slaveholder to search
Cox's camp for a particular fugitive. "The colored boy referred to is sup-

Black Laborers at Work Near the James River, Virginia (*Source: Mathew Brady Collection, National Archives*)

posed to be in the employment of some one in your Brigade. Please see to it that Col. Smith gets him."[30] Yet, what could the staff do about the following incident? An Indianapolis soldier found a slave child wandering about after the Battle of Cheat River. When the soldier's 90-day enlistment expired, he took the child home with him.[31] As long as the soldiers involved in personal emancipation proved willing to swear falsely that the former slave in their custody had accompanied them on their journey into the war zone, General Rosecrans's orders would remain the object of willful and flagrant disobedience.

In the west, Gen. Henry Halleck fought a similarly prolonged and frustrating battle against personal emancipation. Halleck succeeded Fremont as commander of the Department of the Missouri. Taking accurate cues from Fremont's denouement, Halleck moved quickly to disassociate himself from the taint of emancipationism. Accordingly, in November 1861, Halleck issued General Order No. 3, a departmental directive that ordered northern soldiers to avoid all contact with the slaves.[32] Halleck soon discovered what Rosecrans already knew: orders from the general commanding could neither prevent personal contact between slaves and the troops nor halt personal emancipation. Many of the troops simply refused to obey Halleck's orders. As a result, General

Halleck issued and reissued orders seeking to stop the emancipation of camp servants. Typical of his efforts was the following letter: "I am determined to put a stop to such things. Every regiment will be examined as soon as it reaches St. Charles [a suburb of St. Louis] and fugitives turned out. I will also arrest every officer who permits his men to violate General Order No. 3."[33]

The problem simply refused to disappear. Several weeks later Halleck interjected a strenuous objection to the practice of personal emancipation. "It is *not* right and proper for federal officers to take negroes from Union men and I hope you will put a stop to such practices in your command."[34] That similar difficulties frustrated the efforts of Generals Grant, Sherman, Butler, and McClernan attests to the ubiquity of Halleck's dilemma.[35] Each one of these officers discovered what McClellan, Rosecrans, and Halleck had already learned: northern soldiers could not be compelled to enforce socially coercive orders with which they disagreed. When whole regiments began concealing blacks as a means of liberating them, the general staff found itself confronting an incipient revolt.

Letters from common soldiers best expressed the viewpoint taken by many front-line troops about orders that they respect the property rights of slaveholders. Sylvester Bishop wrote his mother in July 1862:

> I have learned a great deal since coming south. I used to think all we had to do was treat the Secesh well to gain them to the Union. Experience has taught me better. . . . The very men whose persons and property we are forced to guard . . . would if they had a fair chance shoot us. While I do not intend to molest their property myself . . . , yet my sympathies are not so tender for Secesh who lose a little property as they were a few months ago.[36]

Pvt. Elias Brady explained why so many volunteers refused to obey Lincoln's orders that they respect slaveholders' property rights:

> It does us good to distroy the greesey bellys property when some of the boys git holt of any property of any kind belonging to the rebels they distroy it as fast as they can and say dam him he was the coss of bringing us here that is sow if they will not come back and restore peace again as long as we half to be away from our friends at home we calculate to live as fat as we can and aim to live off them all we can I think the more we distroy the sooner we can whip them.[37]

This philosophy of total war emerged first among troops raised in Kansas, troops who came to be known as the Jayhawkers for the violence of their assaults upon the property of slaveholders. Capt. John Brown, Jr., captured the flavor of Civil War, Kansas style, in a July 1862 letter:

Deprive the rebels of every means by which they had successfully carried on the war against the United States. Their wagons were loaded with household stuff such as would be especially needed to set up their slaves in housekeeping in Kansas. . . . Of the property seized, the principal part was turned over to the United States Quartermaster. . . . Before our regiment left Missouri more than two thousand slaves were by us restored to the possession of themselves, were "Jayhawked" into freedom. This especially secured for us the title of "Jayhawkers" which ever since we have borne without blushing. The chief difficulty we had to confront from first to last has been the persistent effort of those in higher authority to make us yield to the demands of slavery.[38]

Refusal to "yield to the demands of slavery" aptly conveyed the sense of mission increasingly prevalent among northern soldiers during the summer of 1862.

Although Gen. William Sherman gained great fame for his scorched earth policy during the campaigns of 1864 and 1865, the avidity with which northern soldiers pillaged slaveholders shocked Sherman in 1862. Sherman tried to explain to Secretary of War Stanton the behavior of a particularly malcreant volunteer regiment: "They are lawless and violent and like all our volunteers have for years been taught that the people, the masses, the majority are 'King' and can do no wrong. They are no worse than the other volunteers, all of whom came to us filled with the popular idea that they must exact war, that they must clear out the Secesh, must destroy and not protect their property, must burn, waste and destroy."[39] By the summer of 1862, large segments of the Union army simply refused to protect either slavery or the property of slaveholders, despite Lincoln's orders to the contrary. Indeed, Lincoln knew of the difficulties being experienced in the field. The President told a delegation of Congressmen representing border slave states in the spring of 1862, "If the war continues, slavery in your States will be extinguished by mere friction and abrasion—by the mere incidents of war."[40] Lincoln knew that he faced a widespread and deep current of opposition to the return of fugitive slaves. The breadth and depth of this resistance to the rendition of runaway slaves suggests the acuity of James G. Blaines' observation: "In the presence of arms the Fugitive Slave Law became null and void and the Dred Scott Decision was trampled beneath the iron hoof of war."[41]

III

Lincoln's decision to proclaim emancipation did not end the sharp national debate over the evolution of federal racial policy. In fact, the President's new stance further fueled the debates by transforming issues about Afro-American citizenship and rights from theoretical concerns into the stuff of fierce partisan politics. Illinois Senator Trumbull cogently articulated the social and political complications when he pointedly asked what the government intended to do with recently freed former slaves. "We do not want them set free to come among us," asserted Trumbull. "We know it is wrong that the rebels should have the benefit of their services to fight us; but what do you propose to do with them?"[42] Samuel Cox of Ohio employed even more direct language when he asked the House of Representatives: "Is there a member here who dares to say that Ohio troops will fight successfully or fight at all, if the result shall be the flight of the black race by millions northward?"[43] An English observer best described the social limitations and the political implications of wartime emancipation when he said, "The working men in the northern states, though they have neither sympathy nor fellow feeling for the colored race, make no objection to their emancipation, providing they remain south of Dixie's Line."[44]

Herein lay the major challenge facing Lincoln's attempt to employ the Union army as an agent of social change. Few northerners were prepared to countenance the massive resettlement of former slaves. Yet how was such a movement to be prevented once the blacks had been given their freedom, particularly in light of the obvious dangers posed by living within a war zone? To his credit, Lincoln understood these social and political dilemmas as clearly as anyone. In his December 1862 annual message, for example, the President offered a number of assurances that emancipation would not become the pretext for the wholesale northward flight of freed people into the "free" states.[45] Lincoln favored the colonization of the freedmen as an expedient solution to the tangled question of civil rights for blacks within American society. Wartime colonization proved a disaster, both because of resistance among blacks and also because of the failure of experimental efforts in Haiti and Chiriqui.[46] Trimming his sails to meet the drift of northern public opinion, Lincoln found himself compelled to depend upon the northern army to control the effects of the social changes its disobedience of his earlier orders had helped to initiate.

The prospect of serving as agents of emancipation proved as objectionable to some Union soldiers as the obligation to enforce the Fugitive Slave Law had been unacceptable to soldiers with abolitionist backgrounds. Particularly in the border slave states of Missouri, Kentucky, and Maryland, Lincoln's decision to couple emancipation with a policy of arming black troops meant that recruitment and emancipation became synonymous. Men who had sided with the North in order to preserve slavery found themselves in the ironic and uncomfortable position of having to fight to destroy the institution of slavery. Inevitably, such a compromising situation produced resistance within the Union army.

Witness, for example, the bitter complaint of a Missouri Unionist who discovered that his reward for supporting the North became the necessity of enforcing emancipation. At his court-martial the colonel insisted that "he wished to God that at the beginning of the present war he had gone South."[47]

Nowhere did these protests reach the crescendo that they achieved in Kentucky. In November 1862, Colonel McHenry, a Kentucky Unionist, ordered the men under his command to treat blacks seeking emancipation as runaway slaves; McHenry could not obey the orders of a northern government that would turn to Afro-Americans in order to defend itself. Leslie Rowland's ongoing study of the emancipation experience in Kentucky is persuasive when it asserts that the conjunction of enlistment with emancipation became the most controversial issue in Kentucky during the final 2 years of the Civil War. Like their fellow pro-Union slaveholders in Missouri and Maryland, Kentuckians protested vehemently against an emancipation policy that resulted in freeing not only their prime male hands but also large numbers of black dependents as well. The numerous incidents of abusive conduct toward blacks that occurred in the border slave states measured the resistance many proslavery Unionists felt toward the idea of wartime emancipation.[48]

As troubling as these problems were, the most serious dilemmas arose when the army tried to cope with the hundreds of thousands of women, children, and elderly persons who had accompanied able-bodied male slaves on flights toward freedom. Sherman was particularly pensive. "If the runaway negroes are encouraged we will be overwhelmed with them. They would soon eat us out, encumber our march and give ground to the assertion that we came South to steal negroes."[49] Pressing for an answer to his concern, Sherman asked the provost marshal for guidance as the winter of 1862–63 approached. "I foresee much trouble as the winter comes to the women and children. Does Congress intend to free and call for all negroes? Is this not a task too great to be undertaken? Will it not overburden our commissary by attempting too much?"[50] Grant put the matter best when he asked Halleck almost plaintively: "What am I to do with the surplus negroes?"[51]

The crush of Afro-American dependents proved more of a challenge than the Civil War army could master. An institution designed to cope with able-bodied males found it impossible to deal adequately with the waves of freed people of all ages, sexes, and physical conditions who willingly risked their lives to emancipate themselves. Lincoln recognized the dimensions of the problem and dispatched Adjutant General Lorenzo Thomas to the Mississippi valley in the spring of 1863. Thomas soon understood that emancipation could not be made to work unless the dependents of male slaves could be provided for adequately. The Adjutant General also understood that hostile reactions in the Midwest and the Northeast precluded the obvious solution of removing black dependents from the war zone. Recognizing that provisions had to be made for these dependents, but that neither the army nor the northern states seemed willing to assume such a burden, Thomas concluded, "These people must in great measure remain in the Southern States now in rebellion, and in the rear of our lines as our armies advance until a new home beyond our boundaries can be found."[52]

Thomas proposed the establishment of refugee camps on plantations abandoned by Confederates fleeing from the northern army. Yet even before Lincoln accepted Thomas's suggestions, the army had begun moving to divest itself of a responsibility it could not discharge effectively. On the South Carolina Sea Islands, for example, the army welcomed the services of northern civilians who volunteered to supervise the care of slaves emancipated by northern military victories.[53] In the Mississippi valley, Grant gladly shifted the burden of caring for black dependents upon Chaplain John Eaton and a corps of northern civilian volunteers. Grant's offhand comment upon first meeting Eaton suggested his awareness of the dilemmas involved. Eaton recalled Grant's greeting as follows: "Oh you are the man who has all those darkies on his shoulders."[54]

Chaplain Eaton's impressions during his first days with "all those darkies on his shoulders" offer a moralizing but graphic account of the reasons why the Union army failed as an agent of social control. The wartime advent of freedom left Afro-Americans in a variety of conditions:

> Coming garbed in rags or silks, with feet shod or bleeding, individually or in families or in large groups. . . . Their condition was appalling. There were men, women and children in every state of disease and decrepitude, often nearly naked, with flesh torn by the terrible experiences of their escape. Sometimes they were intelligent and eager to help themselves; often they were bewildered or stupid or possessed by the wildest notions of what liberty might mean. . . . A few had profited from the misfortunes of their masters and stood in lurid contrast to the grimmer aspects of tragedy—women in travail, the helplessness of childhood and old age, the horrors of sickness and frequent death.[55]

Advance preparations for so large a task could not be made. As a result, the army often revealed itself to be grossly insensitive to the feelings and needs of the Afro-American dependents whom emancipation thrust in its path. When a staunch Michigan abolitionist went to Cairo, IL., to assist in caring for slave dependents, she encountered a stark example of the fundamental incongruity of family sensibilities and military necessity in an active war zone. Mrs. Laura Haviland came across a black

woman who refused to board a steamer for transportation to another refugee camp while her mortally ill 8-year-old son remained alive. The
slave mother refused to abandon her son even after he died, explaining
to Mrs. Haviland: "Oh Missus, it 'pears like I can't leave him so; they'll
leave him out here tonight an' dese whorf-rats are awful. De eat one
chile's face all one side off, an' one of its feets was all gnawed off. I don't
want to leave my child on dis bear ground." When Mrs. Haviland tried to
intercede with the officer in command of transporting the refugees, he
brushed her concerns aside with a brutally frank reminder of war's bitter
realities: "You won't allow such things as these to break your heart after
being in the army a little while and seeing our soldiers buried in a ditch,
with no other coffin than the soldier's dress. For the time being, we bury
hundreds in that way. . . . If we can get a piece of board to lay them on
when we put them in their graves we do well."[56] Although Mrs. Haviland
succeeded in having this particular child buried properly, her experience graphically illustrated the Union army's fundamental dilemma
when called upon to provide custodial care for black dependents freed
by emancipation. Operating within his normal assumptions, the officer
found little cause for exceptional grief in the slave woman's plight. Yet
the woman refused to obey military orders until she discharged her
sense of familial obligation. The difficulties inherent in meeting and resolving these conflicts explain the army's failure as an agent of social
control.

Details of the story of the abandoned plantations, the abortive 40-
acres-and-a-mule experiment, the Freedmen's Bureau, and the failures
of Radical Reconstruction go far beyond the scope of my efforts here.
Suffice it to say that American society found it easier to proclaim emancipation as a measure essential to saving the Union than to cope with the
social and political consequences of the end of slavery. The record of the
failures of the First Reconstruction is writ too large to require much elab-
oration.[57] The army's formal participation in these matters ended with
the conclusion of the Civil War. Many former soldiers served with distinction in the Freedmen's Bureau, while others showered themselves
with ignominy. Because of rapid postwar demobilization, however, and
also because neither President Johnson nor President Grant favored military intervention in domestic racial conflicts, the army played little
further role in resolving the social and political dilemmas its wartime
function as an agent of social change had helped to create.

As we complete our examination of that wartime role, we are compelled to conclude that the Civil War army showed its weakness as an
agency for either encouraging or controlling domestic social change. In-
asmuch as nonmilitary personnel had to be called in to assume the
burden of caring for the Afro-American dependents freed by emancipation, we see that the army was ill suited for successful intervention in

domestic social issues, and it often is. Indeed, the Civil War army found itself ensnarled in the very political and social debates that it had hoped to quell. A largely volunteer army acting in hotly disputed domestic issues is unlikely to isolate itself from domestic politics. Because Civil War volunteers and draftees reflected the divided will of the American people on the proper course of national racial policy, we must conclude that the army did not function effectively as an agency either to encourage or to control domestic social change. Its utility as a pliant tool of elite civilian interest groups seems open to serious question. Perhaps this reluctant role touches the essence of the place of the military in a democratic society. The will of the people, as reflected in the behavior of its soldiers, often does act as the final constraint on the actions of the people's armed forces.

Notes

This essay results from a project generously funded by UCLA's Center for Afro-American Studies.

1. Barrington Moore, *The Social Origins of Dictatorship and Democracy: Lord and Peasant in the Making of the Modern World* (Boston: Beacon Press, 1966), pp. 304–308, and 447–451.

2. James G. Randall, *Constitutional Problems Under Lincoln* (Urbana: University of Illinois Press, 1951).

3. Eugene D. Genovese, *The Political Economy of Slavery: Studies in the Economy and Society of the Slave South* (New York: Pantheon Books, 1965); Ira Berlin, et al., eds., *The Destruction of Slavery, Series I, Volume I* of *Freedom: A Documentary History of Emancipation, 1861–1867* (New York: Cambridge University Press, 1985); Mary Francis Berry, *Military Necessity and Civil Rights Policy: Black Citizenship and the Constitution, 1861–1868* (Port Washington, NY: Kennikat Press, 1977), pp. ix–x.

4. John Hope Franklin, *The Emancipation Proclamation* (Garden City, NY: Doubleday, 1971), pp. 129–146.

5. George M. Frederickson, *The Black Image in the White Mind: The Debate on Afro-American Character and Destiny, 1817–1914* (New York: Harper and Row, 1971), pp. 165–197; Joel Williamson, *The Crucible of Race: Black-White Relations in the American South Since Emancipation* (New York: Oxford University Press, 1984).

6. Berry, *Military Necessity and Civil Rights*, pp. 75–84; Harold M. Hyman, *A More Perfect Union: The Impact of the Civil War and Reconstruction on the Constitution* (New York: Alfred A. Knopf, 1973.

7. Armstead Robinson, "Day of Jubilo: Civil War and the Demise of Slavery in the Mississippi Valley, 1861–1865" (Ph.D. diss., University of Rochester, 1976), pp. 347–436.

8. Jerry M. Cooper, "The Army as Strikebreaker: The Railroad Strikes of 1877 and 1894," *Labor History* 18 (Spring 1977):179–196.

9. Eugene D. Genovese, *Roll, Jordan, Roll: The World the Slaves Made* (New York: Pantheon, 1974).

10. Jesse Lemisch and J. K. Alexander, "White Oaks, Jack Tar, and the Concept of the Inarticulate," *William and Mary Quarterly*, 3d ser., 29 (Jan. 1972):109–134.

11. Abraham Lincoln, "First Inaugural Address, March 4, 1861," *Messages and Papers of the Presidents*, ed. James D. Richardson, 20 vols. (Washington, DC: U.S. GPO, 1897), 7:3206–3213.

12. Louis S. Gerteis, *From Contraband to Freedman: Federal Policy Toward Southern Blacks, 1861–1865* (Westport, CT: Greenwood Press, 1973), pp. 11–32.

13. Franklin, *The Emancipation Proclamation*, pp. 25–26.

14. Ibid., pp. 55–88.

15. Fred A. Shannon, *The Organization and Administration of the Union Army, 1861–1865*, 2 vols. (Cleveland: The Arthur H. Clark Co., 1928), 2:148–168.

16. U. S. Grant to Elisha Washburne, February 11, 1862, in *General Grant's Letters to a Friend*, ed. James Grant Wilson (New York: T. Y. Crowell and Co., 1897), pp. 3–5.

17. Gen. Winfield Scott, Order No. 12, July 19, 1861, *The War of the Rebellion: A Compilation of the Official Records of the Union and Confederate Armies*, 128 vols. (Washington, DC: U.S. GPO, 1880–1901), 2d ser., 1:760. Hereafter this compilation is cited as *OR*.

18. Gen. George McClellan, "To the People of Western Virginia," May 26, 1861, *OR*, 1st ser., 2:48.

19. Gen. Nathaniel Lyon, "Proclamation to the People of Missouri," Confederate States of America, War Department, "Papers Found on the Body of Nathaniel Lyon," June 18, 1861, Collection of Miscellaneous Confederate Papers, War Department Collection of Confederate Records, Record Group 109, National Archives, Washington, DC. Hereafter records in the National Archives are indicated by the symbol NA, preceded by the record group (RG) number.

20. Gen. Benjamin F. Butler to Gen. Winfield Scott, May 24 and 27, 1861, in *Private and Official Correspondence of General Benajamin F. Butler During the Period of the Civil War* (Norwood, MA: Plimpton Press, 1917), pp. 104–108 and 112–114.

21. Gen. John C. Fremont, "Proclamation," August 30, 1861, *OR*, 1st serv., 3:466–467.

22. Col. Robert Anderson to President Abraham Lincoln, September 13, 1861, Anderson Collection, The Filson Club, Louisville, KY.

23. Lincoln to Fremont, September 2, 1861, *OR*, 1st ser., 3:469–70.

24. Fremont to Lincoln, September 8, 1861, and Lincoln to Fremont, September 11, 1861, *OR*, 1st ser., 3:477–478 and 395–496; Allan Nevins, *Fremont, the West's Greatest Adventurer*, 2 vols. (New York: Harper & Bros., 1928), 2:574.

25. John Beatty diary, entry for July 9, 1861, *Memoirs of a Volunteer, 1861–1863*, ed. Harvey S. Ford (New York: W. W. Norton and Co., 1946), p. 24.

26. Hugh Ewing diary, entry for September 28, 1862, Ewing Papers, Ohio Historical Society, Columbus, OH.

27. Thomas N. Ayers to General Cox, September 11, 1861, Letters Received, Kanawha Brigade, Army of West Virginia; and Joseph Darr, Jr., Acting Assistant Adjutant General to Thomas N. Ayres, November 1, 1861, Letters Sent, Headquarters Department of Western Virginia, Records of U.S. Army Continental Commands, 1821–1920, RG 393, NA.

28. Bell Irvin Wiley, *The Life of Billy Yank: The Common Soldier of the Union* (Garden City, NY: Doubleday, 1952), pp. 40–41.

29. James I. Robertson, ed., "An Indiana Soldier in Love and War: The Civil War Letters of John V. Hadley," *Indiana Magazine of History*, 59 (September 1963):215.

30. Joseph Darr, Jr., Acting Assistant Adjutant General to Brig. Gen. Jacob D. Cox, November 18, 1861, Letters Sent, Headquarters, Army of Western Virginia, RG 393, NA.

31. Emma Lou Thornbough, *The Negro in Indiana before 1900* (Indianapolis: Indiana Historical Bureau, 1957), p. 167.

32. Gen. Henry Halleck, General Orders, No. 3, November 20, 1861 (vol. 50/77) Department of the Missouri [hereafter DMO], RG 393, NA.

33. Halleck to William Sweitzler, Columbia, MO, February 12, 1862, Letters Sent, DMO (vol. 10 DMO), and General Orders No. 37, February 14, 1862, (vol. 50/77 DMO), DMO, RG 393, NA.

34. Halleck to Col. A. G. Nugent, Harrisonville, MO, January 25, 1862, Letters Sent, Headquarters, DMO (vol. 10 DMO), RG 393, NA.

35. Robinson, "Day of Jubilo," pp. 373–386.

36. Sylvester Bishop to Mother, July 21, 1862, Bishop Papers, Indiana Historical Society, Indianapolis, IN.

37. Elias Brady to Wife, November 24, 1862, Brady Papers, Southern Historical Collection, Chapel Hill, NC.

38. John Brown, Jr., to Parker Pillsbury, July 18, 1862, in "Letters of Daniel R. Anthony, 1857–1862," ed. Edgar Lansdorf, *Kansas Quarterly* 24 (Fall 1958):352.

39. Gen. William Sherman to Secretary of War Edwin Stanton, January 25, 1863, Letter Book 22, Generals' Papers, Records of the Office of the Adjutant General, 1780's–1917, RG 94, NA.

40. James Ford Rhodes, *History of the Civil War* (New York: Macmillan, 1919), p. 151.

41. James G. Blaine, *Twenty Years of Congress from Lincoln to Garfield*, 2 vols. (Norwich, CT: Henry Bibb, 1884), 1:369.

42. Jacque Voegeli, "The Northwest and the Race Issue, 1861–1862," *Journal of American History* 50 (September 1962):240–241.

43. Wood Gray, *The Hidden Civil War: The Story of the Copperheads* (New York: Viking Press, 1942), p. 109.

44. James D. Burns, *Three Years Among the Working Classes in the United States During the War* (London: Smith, Elder, and Co., 1865), p. xii.

45. Abraham Lincoln, "Second Annual Message," December 1, 1862, in *Messages and Papers. . .* , ed. Richardson, 8:3327–3343.

46. Charles H. Wesley, "Lincoln's Plan for Colonizing the Emancipated Negroes," *Journal of Negro History* 4 (Jan. 1919):7–21; and Paul J. Scheips, "Lincoln and the Chiriqui Colonization Project," *Journal of Negro History* 37 (Oct. 1952):418–453.

47. Gen. Stephen Hurlbut, General Court-Martial Order No. 87 (vol. 17/25 16AC) 16th Army Corps, RG 393, NA.

48. ___. Leslie S. Rowland, "Recruitment in the Border States: Maryland, Missouri and Kentucky," in Ira Berlin, Joseph P. Reidy, and Leslie S. Rowland, eds., *The Black Military Experience, Series II* of *Freedom: A Documentary History of Emancipation* (New York: Cambridge University Press, 1982): 183–278; Barbara J. Fields, *Slavery and Freedom on the Middle Ground: Maryland in the Nineteenth Century* (New Haven: Yale University Press); Robinson, "Day of Jubilo," pp. 437–521; and Charles L. Wagandt, *The Mighty Revolution: Negro Emancipation in Maryland, 1862–1864* (Baltimore: Johns Hopkins University Press, 1964). The draft riots of 1863 were sparked in part by popular opposition to emancipation. See the following: Williston Lofton, "Northern Labor and the Negro During the Civil War," *Journal of Negro History* 34 (July 1949):251–273; Forrest Wood, *Black Scare: The Racist Response to Emancipation and Reconstruction* (Berkeley: University of California Press, 1968); and V. Jacque Voegeli, *Free but Not Equal: The Midwest and the Negro During the Civil War* (Chicago: University of Chicago Press, 1967).

49. Gen. William Sherman to Worthington, July 11, 1862, 5th Division, District of West Tennessee. Copy in General Sherman's Letter Books, vol. 2, Generals' Papers, RG 94, NA.

50. Sherman to Gault, November 11, 1862, ibid.

51. Grant to Halleck, November 11, 1862, in *The Papers of Ulysses S. Grant, September 1–December 8, 1862*, ed. John Y. Simon, 8 vols. to date (Carbondale: Southern Illinois University Press, 1977–), 6:315.

52. Adjutant General Lorenzo Thomas to Secretary of War Stanton, April 1, 1863, Thomas Orders and Letters, Generals' Papers, RG 94, NA; Herbert G. Gutman, *The Black Family in Slavery and Freedom, 1750–1925* (New York: Pantheon Books, 1977), pp. 461–475.

53. Willie Lee Rose, *Rehearsal for Reconstruction: The Port Royal Experiment* (Indianapolis: Bobbs-Merrill, 1964), pp. 199–241.

54. John Eaton, *Grant, Lincoln, and the Freedmen* (London: Longmans, Green, and Co., 1907), p. 9.

55. Ibid., pp. 2–3.

56. Laura Haviland, *A Woman's Life Work* (Chicago: C. V. Waite, 1887), pp. 246–248.

57. C. Vann Woodward, "Seeds of Failure in Radical Race Policy," in *American Counterpoint: Slavery and Racism in the North-South Dialogue* (Boston: Little, Brown and Co., 1971), pp. 163–183.

The Army
and Industrial Workers:
Strikebreaking in the
Late 19th Century

Jerry M. Cooper

During the years 1877 to 1900, the U.S. Army served in the field 11 times to aid civil authorities in suppressing industrial disorders. The nature of these interventions varied considerably. In the railroad disorders of 1877 and 1894, federal troops intervened to suppress what amounted to general strikes. Three times during the 1890s the army moved into the turbulent Coeur d'Alene mining region of northern Idaho for lengthy occupations of Shoshone County that led to the ultimate destruction of the miners' unions. In less-known interventions—at Omaha, NE in 1882, during anti-Chinese disorders led by organized labor in Seattle, Washington Territory, in 1885 and 1886, or during the coal strike in the Indian Territory in April–June 1894—the mere appearance of federal troops ensured an end to labor strikes and disorders.[1]

The President could send federal troops to aid civil authorities in suppressing domestic disorder in response to an appeal from a state or territorial legislature or from the governor when the legislature was not in session and could not easily be convened. The legislature or governor was obligated by precedent to attest that state and local governments had exhausted all efforts to restore order and, having failed, required federal assistance. The President was authorized as well to use federalized militia, the army, and the navy to enforce federal law or to prevent the loss of constitutional rights if domestic disorder thwarted civilian federal officials from doing so. In the latter case state governments played

136

no part in bringing federal troops to field service or in facilitating their relief.[2]

The army did not seek this duty, nor did it plan or train for it. On rare occasions general officers in command of geographic departments— Major Generals John M. Schofield and Oliver O. Howard, to name two—conducted discreet inquiries as to the likelihood of labor troubles within their commands and sketched probable responses to civil disorder. They never prepared fully developed mobilization plans for industrial riot duty, however. It was not in the institutional nature of the late 19th-century army to plan in detail for future action of any sort. This condition was only partly the service's fault, for it generally lacked policy guidance from its civilian superiors. Certainly there was a paucity of federal guidelines for military intervention in industrial disorders. Here policy was so poorly developed during the Gilded Age that when presidents, cabinet members, federal judges, and generals confronted a call for federal military assistance, they were forced to respond on an ad hoc basis.[3]

By 1877, law and precedent had made clear enough the means *by which* federal troops could be committed to the aid of civil authorities, but the nature of industrial disorders and the lack of well-conceived federal policy relating to them did not make at all clear the purposes *for which* troops were to be used. The army served in labor upheavals ostensibly simply to restore order and to allow civilian state or federal officers to enforce the law and court orders and to arrest people who broke the law or defied the courts. Disorders in strikes, however, usually came when employers attempted to resume railroad, factory, or mining operations under police or military protection. Consequently, the restoration of law and order, that is, the restoration of the employer's right to use his property, inevitably led to strikebreaking. Perhaps it did so unavoidably, in view of the late 19th-century tenor of the law and public and private attitudes concerning property rights and the unfettered movement of the individual in the economic system.[4]

Despite certain inevitable aspects of the law, deliberate strikebreaking was rarely the result of presidential intent. Only the Cleveland administration could be charged with a conscious attempt to use federal troops as strikebreakers—in the 1894 Pullman Strike. The Pullman Strike was extraordinary, however, involving all the major trunk lines operating to the West out of Chicago. Most of these lines were designated military roads by law; a number of them as well were in federal receivership and were hence under the protection of federal courts; all carried U.S. mail and were involved in interstate commerce. President Grover Cleveland and Attorney General Richard Olney set out to break the strike because they saw Eugene Debs's tactic of a general strike through an industrial union, the American Railway Union (ARU), as a direct challenge to federal authority. Cleveland and Olney, by using the U.S. Army, succeeded overwhelmingly in breaking the strike, in coincidentally destroying the ARU, and in temporarily eliminating Debs as an effective leader of industrial workers. The Pullman Strike was extraordinary as well because it was the only instance in the late 19th century when federal troops intervened in a major labor-capital conflict as a result of federal initiative.[5]

Federal troops most commonly intervened in industrial disorders upon the appeal of a state or territorial governor. Under these circumstances, the lack of a well-defined federal strike policy tended to enmesh the army in deliberate attempts to break strikes, and sometimes to break unions as well, regardless of the intent of the President who approved federal assistance to state officials. The army's intervention in the bitter labor-capital conflict in the Coeur d'Alene lead and silver mining region of northern Idaho ended in this manner.

Geographically isolated from the more populous southern portion of the state, Shoshone County, ID, in the 1890s endured an acrimonious economic and political struggle between increasingly militant miners and iron-willed employers. Mining was the only significant economic activity in the county, an activity controlled by absentee owners and dominated by a single firm, the Bunker Hill and Sullivan Mining Company. The miners controlled political affairs in Shoshone County during the decade through a Democratic-Populist party coalition, while Republicans closely affiliated with the mine owners dominated state government. Despite the use of private armed guards, infiltration of the unions by private detectives, and attempts to gain injunctions from state and federal courts, the owners could not break the power of the Western Federation of Miners (WFM). The WFM managed to organize most of the miners but failed to intimidate the private guards or to force mine owners to accept collective bargaining, union recognition, and binding contracts.

Violence often attended the struggle for power in the Coeur d'Alene in the 1890s. Both miners and nonunion employees of the mines went about the region heavily armed. Both sides relied upon physical intimidation in efforts to force their opponents out of the valley. Twice before 1899 the level of violence reached a point where state officials called for federal troops, in 1892 and 1894. In both instances, the state of Idaho and the mine owners sought to use the presence of federal troops as an opportunity to rid the Coeur d'Alene of organized labor. Insisting that the WFM was a criminal conspiracy bent on destroying state authority and imposing union rule by terror, mine owners unsuccessfully sought to persuade the federal government to establish a permanent military subpost in the region. The army did occupy the area for 4 months after the 1892 intervention, but even with state cooperation, the owners failed to break the WFM's power.[6]

The nearly 10-year struggle between miners and mine owners came to an end in 1899. By then the union had organized every mine in Shoshone County except the one that counted most, the Bunker Hill and Sullivan Mining Company, which adamantly refused to recognize or bargain with the union. After an armed stalemate that lasted for weeks, the two antagonists finally went to war. The federal government, through the U.S. Army, provided the necessary power to give the owners ultimate victory.

On April 29, 1899, between 800 and 1,000 armed miners attacked the Bunker Hill and Sullivan mine and mill at Wardner, driving off the private guards, killing two nonunion men, and dynamiting the Bunker Hill and Sullivan plant. The miners then returned to their homes, and the next day the other mines in the Coeur d'Alene were fully manned and working. Governor Frank Steunenberg and his auditor general, Bartlett Sinclair, immediately set about obtaining federal troops. With the Idaho National Guard still in the Philippines, federal troops were probably needed in the Coeur d'Alene. The miners' political domination of Shoshone County and the union's ability to mobilize 1,000 armed men foredoomed any local or state effort to identify and arrest the men responsible for the destruction and murder on April 29. Steunenberg and Sinclair, however, were less concerned about arresting lawbreakers than they were in destroying the WFM as a power in Idaho.[7]

President William McKinley quickly acceded to Steunenberg's request for troops. On May 2, the first elements of the 24th Infantry, Capt. Joseph B. Batchelor commanding, arrived at Wardner. Under Bartlett Sinclair's direction, federal troops imposed martial control on the Coeur d'Alene. Governor Steunenberg officially declared martial law in the area on May 3. Regulars took control of the single railroad line in the district, preventing any civilian travel in or out of the area. Army officers restricted civilian use of the telegraph as well. Troops systematically searched all public and private buildings for arms and ammunition, then arrested and incarcerated every male adult in the Coeur d'Alene, regardless of occupation or union affiliation. Throughout the roundup, the state made no effort to obtain search or arrest warrants. Sinclair used the power of martial law to remove all Shoshone County officials from office and named Dr. Hugh France, an employee of the Bunker Hill and Sullivan firm, as county sheriff. He also appointed a number of nonunion Bunker Hill and Sullivan employees as deputy sheriffs.[8]

Throughout the first days of army occupation, the military commander of the Department of the Colorado, Brig. Gen. Henry C. Merriam, acquiesced in the state effort to crush the WFM. After conferring with Governor Steunenberg at Boise on May 1, General Merriam went on to Wardner to supervise the troops under his command and to work directly with Bartlett Sinclair. Sinclair issued a state proclamation requiring all mine owners to employ miners who held a state work per-

Newspaper Coverage by the Spokane, WA *Spokesman-Review* of the Bunker Hill Strike *(Source: Miners' Riot Scrapbook, Department of the Columbia, Records of U.S. Army Continental Commands, National Archives)*

mit. Miners could obtain a permit only after denying participation in the destruction of the Bunker Hill and Sullivan plant, declaring the WFM as the perpetrator of that destruction and renouncing union membership. Merriam thoughtlessly signed the proclamation, which the state published with the general's signature prominently displayed. Indeed, Merriam's single attempt to modify or temper the state campaign against the union was to urge Sinclair to provide a better prison for the incarcerated miners.⁹

General Merriam also supported Steunenberg's intent to keep federal troops in Idaho for an indefinite time. The army had had no difficulty in establishing or maintaining order. The miners had wisely made no effort to resist federal occupation of the area, had meekly submitted to the mass arrests, and had accepted, however sullenly, martial rule. Nonetheless, Merriam and Steunenberg believed it essential to maintain martial law for some time to come. Merriam's chief concern was the miners' reaction to the work permit system, which went into effect on May 18. State officials feared that miners would resist the system with violence. They did not but nonetheless resolutely refused to obtain state permits. Since employers could hire only men holding state work permits, the mines closed down, leaving, as Merriam reported, "a large number of idle and sullen men in the mining centers of Wallace, Burke, and Mullan."¹⁰ The general and the governor agreed that a substantial force of regulars should remain to watch idle miners, to guard the temporary state prison at Wardner, now dubbed the "bull pen," and to protect mines and mine property.¹¹

For much of 1899, the army's major task was to provide security for the "bull pen." On May 7, nearly 1,000 men were imprisoned at Wardner. The state slowly reduced the number of prisoners throughout May, but there were still 350 on May 25. Not until October 31, when 24 prisoners remained in custody, did the state finally assume control of the prison. At that time, the War Department reduced the federal force in Idaho, which had totaled 800 in late May, to 100 cavalrymen. Steunenberg continued martial law for the rest of his tenure, and his successor finally restored civil rule in Shoshone County on April 11, 1901, nearly 2 years after the original federal intervention. At least a company of regulars remained on duty in the Coeur d'Alene throughout the period of martial law.¹²

The army's 2-year occupation allowed Idaho and the mine owners to realize their goal of destroying the WFM. State officials made no secret of their intent. State Attorney General Samuel H. Hays stated early in May 1899, "We have the monster by the throat and we are going to choke the life out of it. . . . It is a plain case of the state or union winning."¹³ Idaho representatives continued to assert that the union was criminal in its intent and methods. They explained the turbulence of the preceding 10 years as wholly the fault of the union. Much of the mining community not directly connected to the WFM was depicted as morally guilty for tolerating the existence of the conspiracy. Consequently, Steunenberg and his associates argued, federal troops had to be kept in Idaho until the perpetrators of evil were permanently expunged.¹⁴

Bartlett Sinclair wrote to General Merriam in mid-August 1899 that troops would be needed for at least another 6 months, for despite the apparent quiet, "the Western Federation has by no means ceased its efforts to incite the Dynamiters to revolt in opposition to the State laws. I do not think the State could maintain order twenty-four hours without the presence of the troops."[15] Steunenberg used similar arguments in persuading Secretary of War Elihu Root to retain regulars in Idaho. Above all, the governor stressed, "A section or community given over for years to terrorism and crime cannot be purged in three months or five months."[16] The state sought and achieved a purge. Of the 1,000 men arrested in early May, only 14 ever went to trial; 11 of them were convicted, though none for murder. On the other hand, in February 1900, when the mines were once again in full operation, 7,000 miners, most of whom had been imported from the East, were at work under the permit system. A mere 130 of them had once belonged to the Western Federation of Miners.[17]

As noted earlier, the army did not seek this duty, nor did it advocate a policy of strikebreaking and union busting. Nonetheless, as had been the case in other late 19th-centruy federal military interventions to aid state officials, the service proved to be a remarkably pliant tool in 1899. President McKinley was partially responsible for allowing a state government so closely allied with management to use the army as a union buster. From the very beginning of the episode, presidential supervision of the intervention was slight. Whatever the excesses of the miners' tactics, the struggle in Idaho was more than a simple question of law and order. It was a complex economic-political contest of wills of a fundamental nature, a fact McKinley ignored or one of which he was unaware. Consequently, the President allowed Steunenberg to determine the need for federal troops, to define the upheaval as an insurrection and meet it with martial law, and to use federal troops to violate the civil and political rights of union and nonunion citizens in Shosone County. Either it never occurred to McKinley that the governor was intent on destroying the WFM or he did not disagree with the policy.[18]

The administration took a direct interest in the affair only after the Western Federation of Miners and other labor groups mounted an editorial campaign of protest. As a result of the WFM appeal, organized labor deluged the White House with petitions that charged General Merriam with union busting and demanded withdrawal of federal troops from Idaho. The McKinley administration's response to the protests, which continued through the summer of 1899, was essentially a public relations effort. Secretary of War Russell A. Alger at first merely denied the army's involvement in the maintenance of the bull pen and enforcement of the work permit system. Further protests led the President to ask for an explanation from the War Department.

Adjutant General Henry C. Corbin queried Merriam on the union charges, but the general denied any role in the state program. Finally, in light of the unrelenting union press and petition campaign, Alger in effect reprimanded Merriam by ordering him to adhere to his "original instructions. The Army must have nothing whatever to do with enforcing rules for the government of miners and Miners Union."[19] The Secretary of War released the telegram to the press and included a copy of it in his replies to all petitions. Alger plainly did not contemplate relieving Merriam or, after discovering the nature of the state use of the army, go beyond Merriam and Steunenberg for information regarding conditions in the Coeur d'Alene.[20]

The petitions and letters of protest continued to arrive in Washington during July and August. Adjutant General Corbin now handled War Department responses to criticism of the army. In face of the "Floods of Labor Union telegrams," Corbin suggested: "It seems to me that a polite suggestion to these men that the matter rests with the Governor of Idaho would meet the situation and *let them feel* that their telegrams have at least received attention."[21] His standard reply to all protests was that the army was not responsible for the actions of the state of Idaho and that all appeals for a change should go to Steunenberg. When President McKinley requested an inquiry into union charges that regulars had brutalized imprisoned miners, Corbin asked Merriam and Steunenberg to carry out the probe. Not surprisingly, both men denied any wrongdoing. Corbin and McKinley accepted their explanations without question.[22]

The union protest was of sufficient strength to move Congress to action. In February of 1900 the House Military Affairs Committee, with a Republican majority, traveled to Idaho to investigate the federal occupation and to hold hearings. The committee's majority report absolved the administration, the army, General Merriam, and Governor Steunenberg. Accepting the governor's contention that the WFM was a criminally conspiratorial group, the majority report concluded: "Brig. Gen. H. C. Merriam and the officers and men under him are to be commended for their wisdom, prudence, and soldierly behavior during the turbulent days of riot and insurrection in Idaho, and the result of this investigation is a complete exoneration of their conduct."[23]

Guided by presidential action and inaction, civilian and military officials of the War Department deferred consistently to Idaho officials, particularly when the question of relieving federal troops arose. Merriam, Corbin, and Elihu Root, Alger's replacement as Secretary of War, did not want federal troops to remain in Idaho for a long time. The army was severely pressed for manpower in 1899, and there were no adequate winter quarters in the Coeur d'Alene for the men of the 6th Cavalry. Above all, Root disliked the use of regulars to guard the bull pen. "I do not wish in any way to make any suggestion relating to the administration of justice in your state," he wrote Steunenberg in late September,". . . but I am much disinclined to have the troops . . . continued longer in the attitude of retaining custody of the citizens of a State who have remained so long without being tried."[24] Despite his disinclination, Root deferred to the governor's wishes and allowed a military guard to be kept over the bull pen for another month. The federal deference to Steunenberg's definition of insurrection of course allowed some federal force to be retained in the state until 1901.[25]

McKinley and his civilian and military advisers read article IV, section 4, of the Constitution and the applicable revised statutes too literally. The Constitution and federal law obliged the federal government to aid a state in suppressing domestic disorder that the state could not control. Whatever the political realities of an age that demanded careful federal treatment of the states, however, the Constitution and practice did not compel the President to turn over control of the army to a state official until he saw fit to do so. Once McKinley conceded the point that Steunenberg could determine when federal troops were needed and when they could be released, it followed naturally that he would provide little supervision as to how they were used. In the early 20th century, Presidents Theodore Roosevelt and Woodrow Wilson exercised much greater care in committing federal forces to the aid of state officials and maintained direct presidential control of regulars when on duty in states.[26]

The orders that sent General Merriam to the Coeur d'Alene reflected the McKinley administration's lack of attention to proper supervision of federal troops. With both McKinley and Alger out of Washington on April 29, Adjutant General Corbin wrote the order sending regulars to Idaho. Corbin's telegram to Merriam merely told him to "repair at once to the capital of the State and after conference with the authorities thence you go to the seat of action."[27] These were the original instructions to which the general had been admonished by Alger but they were of the vaguest sort and were hardly a guide for the conduct of a military commander in the field. General Merriam took them to mean that he was to act as state officials requested, and he behaved accordingly.

Federal law and army regulations provided some guidelines for officers aiding civil officials. The key federal statute was the 1878 *posse comitatus* act, passed by a Democratic Congress to curb perceived abuse of federal military power during Reconstruction. The law prohibited use of the army as a posse without the explicit command of the President and required that federal military aid to civilians be conducted within the chain of command. Army Regulations, section 490, as clarified by a series of general orders issued by the commanding general, Maj. Gen. John M. Schofield, in 1894, stated:

> In the enforcement of the laws, troops are employed as a part of the military power of the United States, and act under the orders of the

President as Commander-in-Chief. They cannot be directed to act under the orders of any civil officer. The commanding officers of troops so employed are directly responsible to their military superiors. Any unlawful or unauthorized act on their part would not be excusable on the ground of an order or request received by them from a marshal or other civil officer.[28]

President McKinley violated federal law by giving Steunenberg command of a part of the army and in effect compelled army officers to violate army regulations by placing them under his orders. Steunenberg went one step further by delegating that command to Bartlett Sinclair. Neither officers in the field nor their superiors within the chain of command questioned this arrangement or challenged the ways in which Sinclair used the troops. When asked about the relationship between the auditor general and Merriam, A. J. Forney of the Idaho attorney general's office testified, "I think Mr. Sinclair had absolute control, and General Merriam rendered his assistance."[29] Sinclair affirmed this relationship: "There was no order that I have made that General Merriam has not carried out. I know of no public act of his wherein he has failed to carry out any request that I have made of him."[30]

General Schofield's interpretation of the posse comitatus law, as incorporated in army regulations, held that the army was simply to provide the force necessary to quell disorder and to prevent riotous assemblages from hindering civil officials from carrying out any duties of a public nature. Regulars were to interpose themselves between the disorderly and civil officials, but the onus of law enforcement fell on the latter. Officers perforce had to confer with the civilians they were to assist, but in Schofield's interpretation, the army was an independent force beholden only to its superior officers and to the president, not to civil officers outside the chain of command.[31]

Merriam was obviously unaware of the strictures of army regulations. No one in the military chain of command called him to account for his ignorance. In 1894, General Schofield insisted that officers serving during the Pullman Strike refuse to take orders from civilians. He carefully and continually supervised the conduct of a strike duty to ensure compliance with his orders. There was little inclination, and probably little time, within the War Department to provide General Merriam with specific instructions or supervision. The demands of the Filipino Insurrection and the occupation of Cuba and Puerto Rico absorbed much of the department's time and energy. With Secretary of War Alger in disrepute and Commanding Gen. Nelson A. Miles ignored by the President, the War Department's high command was in disarray. Until Elihu Root took the post of Secretary of War, Adjutant General Corbin served as

McKinley's key military adviser. No one in Washington, as is evident from Miles's absence from the entire affair, monitored Merriam's conduct in Idaho.[32]

The general also faced several demands on his time beyond his assignment to the Coeur d'Alene. The shortage of general officers because of overseas commitments left Merriam in command of two military departments, the Department of the Colorado, with headquarters in Denver, and the Department of the Missouri, with offices in Omaha, NE. Together with his dual departmental responsibilities, he confronted the tasks of mustering out Spanish-American War volunteers, recruiting the new federal volunteer force, and preparing stateside regular regiments for duty in the Philippines. Merriam lacked the time, energy, and intellect to meet these responsibilities and simultaneously to administer the Idaho intervention. His desire to be rid of the job as quickly as possible was most evident in his communications with Corbin in mid and late May.[33]

The lack of a well-defined federal industrial relations policy, administrative neglect on the part of the McKinley administration, and the chaos within the military bureaucracy in 1899 contributed significantly to the Coeur d'Alene abuses. More fundamental, however, was the fact that the administration did not question the legitimacy of Steunenberg's methods or goals. Although Republicans on the House Military Affairs Committee, which investigated the intervention, went to great lengths to exculpate McKinley and the army from any wrongdoing, holding Idaho responsible for all policies dealing with the WFM, it nonetheless found Steunenberg's approach "heroic," praised him for his "courage and fearlessness," and concluded that he had the authority to "employ whatever men and means he deemed necessary, under the emergency of martial law, to suppress the insurrection in Shoshone County."[34]

General Merriam revealed a basic sympathy with Steunenberg's policies as well. Bereft of any direction from Washington, ignorant of the requirements of section 490 of the army regulations, and lacking a defined federal policy on strike duty, Merriam naturally followed his own instincts. He informed Corbin: "The Governor's course appears to me judicious and his prompt support necessary to arrest lawlessness and crime which has obtained in this county for several years. With troops well placed, order will be preserved. . . . Well disposed miners will return to work and the turbulent element gradually disappear."[35]

Despite later denials that he had anything to do with the work permit system, Merriam personally authored the passages in the state proclamation that required miners seeking work permits to deny that they had participated in the April 29 uprising and "to deny or renounce membership in any society which has incited, encouraged, or approved of said riots."[36] Several times he indicated a strong dislike for unions in general, not just the turbulent element of the WFM, a dislike shared by many of his fellow officers in the late 19th century. Early in the intervention he told a correspondent of the *Idaho Daily Statesman* that unions were largely responsible for the troubles in the Coeur d'Alene and that it might be best to have a law "making the formation of such unions or kindred societies a crime."[37]

The general's subordinates as well believed that federal troops were needed to control the miners. Lt. Henry G. Lyon testified "that the miners, particularly at Burke, were a fearless devilish lot; that they loved nothing better than a fight," and hence needed careful surveillance from soldiers.[38] Capt. B. W. Leavell reported to the Adjutant General that, while he had been on duty in Idaho for nearly a month and had yet to witness any violence, still "I am convinced only the presence of Federal troops prevents bloodshed, arson and other acts of violence."[39] Lt. Col. William E. Dougherty, the senior officer commanding in Idaho in June 1900, accepted as well the state's contention that the WFM was a violent criminal conspiracy that could be suppressed only by regulars. Dougherty reported that "About 80 per cent of the dupes of these men [W.F.M. organizers] are foreigners, most ignorant of our laws and institutions." He believed it "necessary to maintain in this district a representation of the power of the Federal government." Steunenberg's imposition of martial law, supported by the army, was necessary, and if continued "this plague spot of incivism and anarchy will be obliterated."[40]

The minority report of the House Military Affairs Committee investigation of the Coeur d'Alene intervention charged that Gen. Henry C. Merriam too easily acceded to the demands of Idaho officials. Minority committeemen asserted that Merriam was not obligated to obey any of Bartlett Sinclair's requests, and "it was equally his duty to refuse to grant any requests of the governor himself unless they were valid and legal requests."[41] It is highly unlikely that Henry Merriam ever seriously considered refusing the demands of Sinclair, let alone those of Frank Steunenberg. His superiors had ordered him to Idaho to cooperate with state officials in the suppression of disorder; in his opinion, he met the spirit as well as the letter of his orders. Herein lies the irony of federal intervention in the Coeur d'Alene conflict of 1899, an irony present in all the army's service in industrial disorders during the late 19th century. The army perhaps served its civilian leaders too well.

Merriam and his subordinate officers made no effort to have their orders modified, whether they emanated from Washington or Boise. These men did not urge a strong whiff of grapeshot, but they did not suggest a closer adherence to the niceties of due process either. There simply was no jarring clash of values between officers and civilians when the army moved quickly and efficiently to implement the state's plan to crush organized miners. Merriam, indeed, was almost slavish in his willingness to meet the demands of Governor Steunenberg. Civilian control of the army, including military deference to elected state officials, was so complete that the officer corps carried out its orders in Idaho without question.

The conduct of the U.S. army in industrial upheavals in the 19th century reveals a congruence of certain military and civilian values. Officers were not only imbued with the concept of civilian control but also were in fundamental agreement with their elite civilian counterparts in business, industry, academia, and government regarding the need to control a turbulent and disruptive industrial work force. The army's relations with industrial workers were shaped by these shared perceptions. Soldiers disliked the disorder that attended industrialization in the United States. Military men viewed the motives and methods of organized labor with suspicion. The extralegal, direct action tactics of the Western Federation of Miners were more than violations of the law—they were potential threats to the nation as a whole. The fears that an uncontrolled industrial proletariat might sunder society, which underlay so much of Progressive era reform, were felt along officers' row as often as in the boardroom. Containment of disorder might mean the salvation of society. On this elemental point the officers who served to suppress industrial disorders completely agreed with the civilians who ordered them out and with the civilians who directed them at the state level.[42]

Notes

1. See Jerry M. Cooper, *The Army and Civil Disorder: Federal Military Intervention in American Labor Disputes, 1877-1900* (Westport, CT: Greenwood Press, Inc., 1980). Also see Jerry M. Cooper, "The Army as Strikebreaker: The Railroad Strikes of 1877 and 1894," *Labor History* 18 (Spring 1977):179-196.

2. The relevant sections of the Constitution and Revised Statutes governing federal military assistance to civil authorities are discussed in Frederick T. Wilson, "Federal Aid in Domestic Disturbances, 1787-1922," S. Doc. 263, 67th Cong., 2d sess. (Washington, DC: U.S. GPO, 1922), pp. 5-12; and Bennett M. Rich, *The Presidents and Civil Disorder* (Washington, DC: Brookings Institution, 1941), pp. 189-206.

3. The best discussion of federal labor policy in the late 19th century is Gerald G. Eggert, *Railroad Labor Disputes: The Beginnings of Federal Strike Policy* (Ann Arbor: University of Michigan Press, 1967), pp. 19-22, 224-232. On Schofield's preliminary planning, see Capt. J. P. Sanger to Schofield, November 11, 1884; January 15 and 24, 1885, in Letters Received, 1876-1888, ser. 2 John M. Schofield Papers, Library of Congress, Washington, DC, and John M. Schofield, *Forty-Six Years in the Army* (New York: Century Co., 1897), pp. 454-455. Howard's actions were reported in his 1893 annual report as commander of the Department of the East, in *Annual Report of the Secretary of War for 1893*, 4 vols. (Washington, DC: U.S. GPO, 1893), 1:107.

4. On the legal options open to organized labor in the late 19th century, consult Frederic J. Stimson, *Labor and Its Relation to Law* (New York: Scribner and Sons, 1895), pp. 47-51 and passim; T. M. Cooley, "Labor and Capital Before the Law," *North American Review* 139:

337 (Dec. 1884):503–516; Arnold M. Paul, *Conservative Crisis and the Rule of Law: Attitudes of Bar and Bench, 1887–1895* (Ithaca, NY: Cornell University Press, 1960), pp. 6–18, 105–107; and Herbert G. Gutman, "Work, Culture, and Society in Industrial America, 1815–1919," *American Historical Review* 78:3 (June 1973):569–576, 581–585.

5. Eggert, *Railroad Labor Disputes*, pp. 153–175.

6. Background on the labor disputes in the Coeur d'Alene for the 1890s is given in Lt. George E. French, 4th Infantry U.S.A., "The Coeur d'Alene Riots," *Overland Monthly*, 26:2d ser. (July 1895):32–49; Samuel H. Hays, Idaho State Attorney General, *Report to the Governor on the Insurrection in Shoshone County Idaho, Commencing on April 29, 1899* (n.p., n.d.); D. E. Livingston-Little, "An Economic History of North Idaho: Part V, Discovery and Development of the Coeur d'Alene Mines," *Journal of the West* 3 (July 1964):325–335; Melvyn Dubofsky, *We Shall Be All: A History of the Industrial Workers of the World* (Chicago: Quadrangle Books, 1969), chaps. 2 and 3; Vernon H. Jensen, *Heritage of Conflict: Labor Relations in the Nonferrous Metals Industry up to 1930* (Ithaca, NY: Cornell University Press, 1950), pp. 74–80; and Robert W. Smith, *The Coeur d'Alene Mining War of 1892* (Corvallis, OR: Oregon State College, 1961). The army's role in the 1892 and 1894 interventions is discussed in Cooper, *The Army and Civil Disorder*, chap. 7.

7. The April 29 outbreak is described in "Report of Brig. Gen. H. C. Merriam, U.S.A., on Miners' Riot in the State of Idaho," S. Doc. 24, 56th Cong., 1st sess. (Washington, DC: U.S. GPO, 1900), pp. 15–20 (hereafter referred to as "Miners' Riot in Idaho"). Hays, *Report to the Governor of Idaho*, pp. 10–11; U.S. Industrial Commission, "Report on the Relations and Conditions of Capital and Labor in the Mining Industry," H. Doc. 181, 57th Cong., 2d sess. (Washington, DC: U.S. GPO, 1901), p. xvii (hereafter cited as "Report on the Mining Industry"). The press in the Northwest gave extensive coverage to the upheaval, as seen in the April 29–May 5, 1899, issues of the *Idaho Daily Statesman* (Boise), *Spokesman-Review* (Spokane, WA.), and the *Rocky Mountain News* (Denver).

8. The principal source for following the military decisions and actions in the 1899 Idaho intervention is file 231071, Adjutant General's Office (AGO) Document File, 1890–1917, Records of the Office of the Adjutant General, 1780's–1917, Record Group 94, National Archives, Washington, DC. Hereafter records in the National Archives are indicated by the symbol NA, preceded by the record group (RG) number. File 231071, a large consolidation of records arranged chronologically, contains correspondence from the initial request for troops on April 29, 1899, through mid-1900. The orders for military aid to Idaho and the early movements of troops to the mining region may be followed in a series of telegrams exchanged between Gen. Henry C. Merriam and Adj. Gen. Henry C. Corbin dated April 30 to May 6, 1899, in this same file. Portions of this correspondence, along with some of the general's observations, were published in Merriam's special report "Miners' Riot in Idaho." Other segments were included in his "Report of Brig. Gen. H. C. Merriam, U.S.A., Commanding Department of the Colorado," in *Annual Reports of the War Department for Fiscal Year 1899*, 3 vols. (Washington, DC: U.S. GPO, 1899) (hereafter cited as "Report of Dept. of Colorado"). Merriam's report appears in part 3 of volume 1. Two other sources of importance contain evidence and testimony on the army's role in the Coeur d'Alene. They are: U.S. Industrial Commission, "Report on the Mining Industry"; and U.S., Congress, House, Committee on Military Affairs, "Coeur d'Alene Labor Troubles," H. Rept. 1999, 56th Cong., 1st sess. (Washington, DC: U.S. GPO, 1900). For the activities of the 24th Infantry, see May and June 1899 returns of the regiment, Returns from Regular Army Infantry Regiments, June 1821–December 1916, RG 94, NA, National Archives Microfilm Publication M665, roll 249. The mass arrests and imposition of martial law are detailed in Merriam, "Report on Miners' Riot in Idaho," pp. 2–7, and "Report of Dept. of Colorado," pp. 52–54; and in U.S. Industrial Commission, "Report on the Mining Industry," pp. 421, 430, 436–437. The decision to commit troops to Idaho may be followed in a series of telegrams, Steunenberg to McKinley, George B. Cortelyou, McKinley's private secretary, and to Adjutant General

Corbin; Benjamin F. Montgomery to McKinley, all dated April 29; and Secretary of War Russell A. Alger to Corbin; Corbin to Alger, May 1, 1899. All wires are in series 1, microfilm reel 6, William McKinley Papers, Library of Congress, Washington, DC.

9. Merriam's conference with Steunenberg is reported in "Miners' Riot in Idaho," pp. 2–3. The general's role in the adoption of the permit system is somewhat murky, but he clearly approved of it, as seen in pp. 8–10 of "Miners' Riot in Idaho" and in "Report of Dept. of Colorado," pp. 55–56. See as well Merriam to Corbin, May 30, 1899, in AGO Document File, 1890–1917, File 231071, RG 94, NA. Nonetheless, he disavowed any responsibility for the policy in the manuscript copy of his special report, AGO Document File, 1890–1917, File 268947, RG 94, NA. Merriam's attempts to improve the prison are noted in "Miners' Riot in Idaho," p. 7, and Merriam to Corbin, June 12, 1899, AGO Document File, 1890–1917, File 231071, RG 94, NA.

10. To Corbin, May 17, 1899, AGO Document File, 1890–1917, File 231071, RG 94, NA.

11. See Merriam to Corbin May 12 and 16, June 1, and October 8 and 11, 1899, AGO Document File, 1890–1917, File 231071, RG 94, NA. His comments in "Miners' Riot in Idaho," pp. 10–15, and "Report of Dept. of Colorado," pp. 56–61, also supported keeping troops in Idaho. Regarding the miners' rejection of the permit system, see reports in the *Spokesman-Review*, May 13, 15, 18, and 19, 1899.

12. The number of men in the bull pen and the regulars' duty as prison guards are recounted for various dates in Merriam, "Miners' Riot in Idaho" and in "Report of Dept. of Colorado." The gradual reduction of troops in the region and their removal as guards at the prison are noted in Merriam to Corbin, November 4, 1899; Corbin to Merriam, November 13, 1899; Steunenberg to Secretary of War Elihu Root, November 29, 1899; Root to Steunenberg, December 9, 1899; and Merriam to Corbin, December 6, 1899, all in AGO Document File, 1890–1917, File 231071, RG 94, NA.

13. *Idaho Daily Statesman*, May 9, 1899.

14. The state's intent to eliminate the WFM is explained in detail in a 22-page letter Governor Steunenberg sent to Root, October 10, 1899, AGO Document File, 1890–1917, File 231071, RG 94, NA. The union was depicted as a criminal conspiracy by F. W. Bradley, president, Bunker Hill and Sullivan Mining Company, in speaking to Senator George L. Shoup of Idaho, May 9, 1899; also see Senator Shoup to President McKinley, July 23, 1899; Bartlett Sinclair to General Merriam, August 18, 1899, AGO Document File, 1890–1917, File 231071, RG 94, NA. Also see Sinclair's testimony to U.S. Industrial Commission, "Report on the Mining Industry," pp. xviii–xxi and 544–546; and Hays, *Report to the Governor of Idaho*, passim.

15. August 18, 1899, AGO Document File, 1890–1917, File 231071, RG 94, NA.

16. Ibid. Steunenberg to Root, October 10, 1899.

17. On the trials, see Idaho, Executive, *Biennial Report of the Governor of Idaho 1901* (Boise: Idaho State Printer, n.d.), pp. 11–12, in a statement by Governor Frank W. Hunt, Steunenberg's successor. On the impact of the permit system, see Committes on Military Affairs, "Coeur d'Alene Labor Troubles," p. 114.

18. It is evident from the absence of presidential correspondence in AGO File 231071 and the McKinley Papers on microfilm at the Library of Congress that the president rarely took official action in the Coeur d'Alene episode.

19. May 31, 1899, AGO Document File, 1890–1917, File 231071, RG 94, NA.

20. A copy of the WFM appeal to labor is in the May 9, 1899, material, ser. 1, reel 6, McKinley Papers, Library of Congress, Washington, DC. A large number of labor journals reprinted the appeal as part of their editorial efforts to protest the army's presence in Idaho. As examples chosen from among many, see the *Omaha Western Laborer*, May 20, 1899, and *Pueblo (CO) Courier*, May 26, 1899. In AGO File 231071 there are well over 100 labor

petitions addressed to the President or to the Secretary of War. Many came from WFM lo-
cals in the Rocky Mountain states, but just as large a number are from nonmining labor
groups. The Galveston, TX, Labor Council; Hoboken, NJ, Typographical Union; San Francisco Building Trades Council; United Labor League of Philadelphia; American Flint
Glass Workers' Union, Muncie, IN; Cigar Makers' Local No. 174, Joliet, IL; and the Coopers'
International Union, Cincinnati, were among many nonmining union groups sending protests. The early War Department response is seen in Corbin to Pueblo (CO) Trades and
Labor Assembly, May 25, 1899, and Alger to McKinley, May 29, 1899, in AGO Document
File, File 231071, RG 94, NA; Alger to Ernest Bohin, Corresponding Secretary, Central Fed-
erated Union, New York City, May 22, 1899, Semi-Official Letters, vol. 18: 421, Russell A.
Alger Papers, William L. Clements Library, University of Michigan, Ann Arbor, MI. Also
see Merriam, "Miners' Riot in Idaho," pp. 11–12, and "Report of Dept. of Colorado," pp. 55–
58. The President's first interest in the labor protest was indicated in George B. Corbin to
Alger, May 26, 1899, AGO Document File, 1890–1917, File 231071, RG 94, NA. Merriam's
denial of the charges followed in a series of telegrams between him and Corbin, May 26 to
May 30, 1899, ibid. On the release of Alger's May 31 reprimand to the press, see Merriam to
Corbin, June 6 and 21, 1899, ibid.

21. To George B. Cortelyou, July 28, 1899, AGO Document File, 1890–1917, File 231071, RG
94, NA. Emphasis added.

22. Corbin's policy of referring labor protestors to Governor Steunenberg is evident in his
telegram to William Hagerty, Butte Miners' Union, August 4, 1899. For a similar response,
see Secretary of War Root to George W. Cromer, Member of Congress, 8th Congressional
District, IN, October 30, 1899. McKinley's request for a review of the army's conduct in Idaho is seen in Cortelyou to Corbin, July 17, 1899, with enclosures. All three communications
appear in the AGO Document File, 1890–1917, File 231071, RG 94, NA. The request then
went to General Miles, who forwarded it to General Merriam, who sent it to Maj. Allen
Smith, commanding federal forces at Wardner. Smith added some comments and sent it to
Merriam with the observation that all charges were false. The document then traveled
back to Washington, with accompanying endorsements, through the chain of command.
Finally, on August 31, McKinley received the entire report.

23. Committee on Military Affairs, "Coeur d'Alene Labor Troubles," p. 125. The committee
took testimony from all principal state and military officials and interviewed a number of
miners, nonunion people who had been arrested, and union officers. For the committee's
overall conclusions, see pp. 1–3.

24. September 28, 1899, AGO Document File, 1890–1917, File 231071, RG 94, NA.

25. The concern with relieving troops in Idaho or at least with finding decent winter quarters for them is indicated in Merriam to Corbin, September 7 and 20, 1899; C. H. Fischer,
acting assistant surgeon, Department of the Colorado, to Surgeon General of the Army,
September 22, 1899; Merriam to Corbin, November 4, 1899; Capt. F. A. Edwards, commanding troops in the Coeur d'Alene, to Merriam, November 17, 1899; Merriam to Corbin,
December 6, 1899; Corbin to Merriam, December 6, 1899; Root to Steunenberg, September
28, 1899; Root to Attorney General of the United States, October 12, 1899, and Steunenberg
to Root, October 10 and 12, 1899. All of these documents are in the AGO Document File,
1890–1917, File 231071, RG 94, NA. Articles in the Idaho Daily Statesman, October 24 and
27, and November 8, and in the Spokesman-Review, October 22 and 24, November 2 and 3,
1899, relate to the question of relieving troops in Idaho.

26. Wilson, "Federal Aid in Domestic Disturbances, 1787–1922," pp. 310–315, provides a
brief overview of Roosevelt's and Wilson's methods of sending regulars to aid the states.
President Rutherford B. Hayes allowed governors to dictate troop withdrawals after the
1877 disorders had subsided. They too used regulars for strikebreaking purposes. See Cooper, The Army and Civil Disorder, pp. 64–65, 75–82.

27. April 30, 1899, in AGO Document File, 1890–1917, File 231071, RG 94, NA.

28. U.S., Executive, War Department, *Regulations of the Army of the United States, 1895* (Washington, DC: U.S. GPO, 1895), p. 69. On the origins of the posse comitatus law and Schofield's clarifying general orders, see Cooper, *The Army and Civil Disorder*, pp. 83–84, 104–105, and 112–113.

29. Forney's comment quoted by Congressman John J. Lentz (Democrat, OH) in U.S., Congress, House, *Congressional Record*, 56th Cong., 1st sess., 33, pt. 8:475.

30. In testimony included in U.S. Industrial Commission, "Report on the Mining Industry," p. 554.

31. Cooper, *The Army and Civil Disorder*, pp. 104–105.

32. Russell F. Weigley, *History of the United States Army* (New York: Macmillan, 1967), pp. 305–312, and Graham A. Cosmas, *An Army for Empire: The United States Army in the Spanish-American War* (Columbia: University of Missouri Press, 1971), chaps. 2 and 3, discuss the general condition of the service in 1898 and 1899. Miles's relationship with McKinley, Alger, and Corbin is analyzed in Edward Ranson, "Nelson A. Miles as Commanding General, 1895–1903," *Military Affairs* 29:(Winter 1965–66):179–200.

33. Merriam's departmental responsibilities are discussed in his "Report of Dept. of Colorado," pp. 25–27, and in "Report of Brig. Gen. H. C. Merriam, commanding the Department of the Missouri," *Annual Reports of the War Department for Fiscal Year 1899* (Washington, DC: U.S. GPO, 1899), 1, pt. 3:14–17.

34. Committee on Military Affairs, "Coeur d'Alene Labor Troubles," pp. 110, 128, and 58.

35. May 17, 1899, AGO Document File, 1890–1917, File 231071, RG 94, NA.

36. "Miners' Riot in Idaho," p. 9.

37. *Idaho Daily Statesman*, May 7, 1899. See similar comments in *Rocky Mountain News*, May 30, 1899 and the *Spokesman-Review*, May 10 and 11, 1899. Also see Merriam to Corbin, June 5, 1899, AGO Document File 1890–1917, File 231071, RG 94, NA. Merriam to Corbin, letter marked "personal," August 18, 1899, in ser. 1, reel 7, McKinley Papers, Library of Congress, Washington, DC. Merriam's comments in "Miners' Riot in Idaho," p. 10, and "Report of Dept. of Colorado," p. 57.

38. Committee on Military Affairs, "Coeur d'Alene Labor Troubles," p. 117.

39. To Corbin, June 3, 1899, AGO Document File, 1890–1917, File 231071, RG 94, NA. In the same file see also Leavell to Merriam, June 13, 1899.

40. To Corbin, June 9, 1900, also in the same file.

41. Committee on Military Affairs, "Coeur d'Alene Labor Troubles," p. 129.

42. The impact of industrial disorder upon the officer corps in the late 19th century is examined in Cooper, *The Army and Civil Disorder*, chap. 9. On the congruence of values between army officers and some civilians in the 1890s and during the Progressive era, see the suggestive remarks of Russell F. Weigley, "The Elihu Root Reforms and the Progressive Era," in *Command and Commanders in Modern Warfare: Proceedings of the Second Military History Symposium, United States Air Force Academy*, ed. William Geffen, 2d ed. (Washington, DC: U.S. GPO, 1971), pp. 15–17, and Allan R. Millett, *Military Professionalism and Officership in America*, Mershon Center Briefing Paper (Columbus: Ohio State University, Mershon Center, 1977), pp. 15, 19–21.

The Army and Domestic
Surveillance on Campus

Joan M. Jensen

I shall describe one aspect of civilian-military relations, the impact of military surveillance on civilian politics, in one institutional setting, that of American campuses. My time period is 1920 to 1970, with emphasis on the interwar period of the 1920s and 1930s but including a comparison of the situation then with that existing in the late 1960s. Involved in these campus civilian-military relations were two parts of the army bureaucracy: army intelligence (known as G-2 during the interwar years) and the Reserve Officers Training Corps (ROTC). Campus administrators, students, and faculty were naturally all deeply involved in the policy concerning military training, but radical and pacifist groups as well as patriotic groups also became involved in defining military training policy. I shall focus on the interactions of these civilian and military groups during 50 years of American history.

Although wartime surveillance of civilians by the army dates back to the Revolutionary War, military intelligence lacked a formal bureaucratic structure until the early 20th century. Army commanders used covert or secret surveillance on an ad hoc basis during Indian wars and in labor strikes, but not until 1893 did the War Department publicly announce its intention of gathering information scientifically about its enemies. With this commitment to intelligence, domestic surveillance began to expand. Domestic surveillance remained minimal during the Spanish-American War, but the army watched Cuban immigrants and

153

used several hundred civilian volunteers to watch citizens suspected of opposing the war effort. During the occupation of the Philippines from 1898 to 1904, the army developed a bureaucratic structure to conduct domestic surveillance, and during the Mexican border troubles of 1914, the War Department installed this system along the southwestern border. Shortly after America entered the European war in 1917, the War Department established the Military Intelligence Division (MID), which had offices throughout the United States.[1]

Domestic military surveillance greatly expanded during World War I. The words of Col. James H. Reeves, head of military intelligence during the 1920s, best explain how army intelligence officers felt about this expansion:

> Many of the duties performed by the Military Intelligence Division during the war appeared to belong to certain civil bureaus of the government and should not have been taken over by a military bureau; but, due to the unwillingness on the part of civilian bureaus to assume the burden—or more probably to their inability to expand sufficiently rapidly to meet the needs—this Division assumed the load. So the Military Intelligence Division became involved in espionage and counter-espionage not confined to the military service, but for the greater part among the civilian population of the country, with passport control, fraud and graft protection, protection of munition plants, and many other subjects of a similar nature.[2]

Some officers within the MID, such as Col. Ralph Van Deman, then director of MID, saw this need as an opportunity to establish the value of intelligence in the eyes of skeptical line officers. Because Allied intelligence forces gave the American MID little role in Europe, domestic surveillance became the major work of MID during the war. By the end of the war almost 300 MID officers were on duty in Washington and were scattered around the United States. Several hundred thousand civilian volunteers, most of them organized in patriotic groups, worked with them to watch the home front from 1917 to 1919.[3]

After the war, the War Department cut back the Military Intelligence Division drastically, partly because of lack of funds and partly because of criticism of military surveillance of civilians. The bureaucratic structure, expanded during the war, remained essentially the same, however. It consisted of a central office located within the army general staff in Washington, DC, variously called MID or G-2, and regional offices in the headquarters of each of nine corps area commands. By 1925, appropriations for G-2 had decreased from $2.5 million in 1919 to $65,000. Officers feared that continued public criticism of counterespionage activities among the civilian population might further reduce their budget. Washington officers thus spent much time in the 1920s lecturing corps area intelligence officers on their proper functions. Col. Reeves summed up the problem in 1927: "These activities [wartime domestic counterespionage] brought G-2 a certain unfavorable notoriety, as they were the functions by which G-2 became known generally to the rank and file of the army, as well as to the layman. This general opinion is one which unfortunately still exists. One of our daily problems is to live down our evil reputation and convince our own people in the army, as well as in civil life, what G-2 really is and what it does."[4]

Although Washington officers continually lectured both intelligence officers and other officers regarding the legitimate peacetime work of the G-2, this work itself was never clearly defined. G-2 still considered part of its legitimate work the study of radical groups in the United States in order to be able to forecast domestic disturbances. The problem was how to carry out this task, given MID fear of public criticism and severe funding limitations.[5]

The main concern of MID was its obligation to provide current domestic intelligence for war plan WHITE. War plan WHITE, developed by the Army War College during the red scare of 1919 for use in domestic disturbances, called for current estimates of the strength and activities of both conservative and radical groups. These plans were to be developed at each corps area headquarters and were to be kept current by intelligence officers who had the job of collecting information for them. Fearing criticism by the public, however, the War Department ordered intelligence officers to collect all this information indirectly through civilian agencies or private patriotic groups. Thus an informal, decentralized, ad hoc information-gathering structure became attached to the bureaucratic skeleton of the peacetime G-2. This network between G-2, civilian intelligence agencies, and conservative patriotic groups funneled information on civilian political activity to regional corps area headquarters so that they could maintain their secret war plan WHITE in readiness should a major domestic disturbance occur. By 1927, G-2 officers believed that student groups, together with women, farmers, labor and religious groups, posed the greatest danger to internal security because radicals were making attempts to infiltrate them.[6]

As long as MID considered the investigation of radical politics a legitimate response to the need to forecast domestic disturbance, some involvement on its part was inevitable. The extent of involvement was limited during the 1920s and 1930s by public groups that criticized the division's active involvement. At the same time, growing student involvement in radical issues also made it inevitable that MID would become concerned about campus dissent. American students had traditionally supported wars enthusiastically. Exceptions to the general political conformity among students were small groups of Asian Indian students on the campuses of the University of California at Berkeley and at New York University who had worked for independence from Great Britain. In 1917 and 1918, military intelligence agents cooperated with the Justice Department and British military intelligence in confiscating the property of Asian Indian students, in interrogating them, and in helping to collect evidence to prosecute them under the Espionage Act. Indians and their few American political allies thus became the first students to come under military surveillance.[7] Generally, however, there was no need for G-2 to watch students before criticism of campus ROTC programs developed in the 1920s and 1930s.

War Department involvement on American campuses dated back to the establishment of land grant colleges under the Morrill Land Grant Act of 1862, which required that colleges offer instruction in military tactics. Land grant college administrators developed a variety of policies in response to their Morrill Act obligation to provide military instruction. They found officers wherever they could to give instruction on military tactics: one college had a former Austrian officer; others had National Guard officers; yet others might have an officer near retirement who had been assigned by the War Department. At first the War Department assigned officers to colleges only when it could spare them. In 1893, however, Congress set a limit of 110 officers who could be detailed to colleges. From that time onward, the War Department assigned regular officers to all land grant colleges.[8]

None of these officers engaged in covert activities on campus. On occasion, they even became the object of citizen watching, as when Lt. Richard Rowan, one of America's first military intelligence officers and a hero of the Spanish-American War, was spied upon by members of the Women's Christian Temperance Union. The WCTU reported to the President of Kansas State Agricultural College that Rowan had been going on drinking binges, thus providing a bad example for students. The college president complained to President Theodore Roosevelt, who removed Rowan immediately. The War Department then transferred Rowan to a remote barracks in the state of Washington.[9]

While an incident such as that involving Lieutenant Rowan might cut short an officer's tenure on campus, these appointments sometimes stretched into long-term assignments. No officer's tenure was more important than that of Maj. George L. Converse, who was attached to Ohio State University for more than 14 years. Converse's long tenure at Ohio State University allowed him to work with Ohio administrators and alumni to develop what was known as the "Ohio plan" to unite land grant colleges and the War Department in a new relationship. This plan culminated in the establishment of the ROTC in all land grant institutions. By 1917 every land grant college required at least 2 years of ROTC for its male students. ROTC would soon become part of non–land grant college education programs as well.[10]

Despite enthusiastic support for ROTC at land grant colleges, the War Department bypassed campuses to set up separate officer training camps at the beginning of World War I. When decreasing enrollments drove educators to protest the lack of use of colleges by the War Department, the War Department set up the Student Army Training Corps (SATC) in response. Administrators then virtually turned over their institutions to military officers. Four hundred colleges and 140,000 students were soon involved in this SATC program. Enrollments shot up, but so too did military-civilian tensions on campus. At the University of Michigan, officers told students to ignore faculty rules or face court-martial. Other officers threatened faculty members with court-martial for violating army rules. Academic communities seemed relieved when the War Department discontinued the program in December 1918, following the armistice. Nevertheless, the presence of the military on campus increased in the years after the war. As the War Department demobilized, it began to look to the colleges as a primary source of peacetime officer recruits. Public demand for disarmament also encouraged a military retreat to campuses where administrators still welcomed ROTC as a valuable source of discipline.[11]

Support by administrators for military discipline dated back to the late 19th century. Administrators considered such discipline a way to buttress their authority over an expanding student body expecting to be upwardly mobile in an urbanizing and industrializing society. Higher education was then evolving from a narrow, elite religious program to a broader-based secular one that culminated in the establishment of the land grant college system. University administration in the first two decades of the 20th century has been called "paternalistic self-government" by C. Michael Otten. Self-government usually meant that administrators encouraged students to discipline themselves according to narrow rules established by the administration and faculty but cloaked in an ideology of loyalty to the "fostering mother" (the alma mater). Many administrators saw military discipline as an equally important element in ensuring loyalty to the university, and this ideology was best expressed by Edward Orton, Jr., Dean of the College of Engineering at Ohio State University, who collaborated with Major Converse in integrating college military programs into the National Defense Act of 1916 as the ROTC.[12]

In a famous speech delivered before a joint meeting of the engineering and agricultural college associations in Washington in 1913, Orton explained why military instruction was of disciplinary value. Obedience, he argued, came from the knowledge of power and authority. While intellectual conviction must be used to its limit in securing obedience, said Orton, "there must always be the shadow of the big stick in the background, whether one deals with savages, or boys; or college professors."[13] Orton was so eager to dignify military work on campus that he suggested the faculty recognize salutes and return them to military officers. The Orton "big stick" speech proved a great success. Gen. Leonard Wood enthusiastically endorsed it, and it became the ideological basis for the ROTC program. Orton, along with President W. O. Thompson and Ralph D. Mershon, a wealthy alumnus of Ohio State, lobbied for the ROTC program. They elicited the backing of Ohio congressmen, called for support from engineers and land grant administrators, and themselves endorsed it before Congress.[14]

Student response to military discipline is more difficult to gauge than administrative support. According to William T. Harris, U.S. Commissioner of Education in 1891, no department of instruction was subject to more criticism and adverse comment than military science. At the University of Illinois student officers struck in 1870 and again in 1891 against compulsory drill, successfully reducing the university requirement to 1 year of drill. According to the *New York Times*, University of California students rioted against campus military programs in 1905. Elsewhere, however, students apparently acquiesced to university requirements, and the overwhelming public support for an expanding national military program made it unlikely that students would disagree with or challenge administrative requirements for mandatory drill. Moreover, before World War I, interpretations of their responsibility varied from college to college. Of 49 land grant colleges established before 1917, 20 percent had optional military training during some years. Rutgers University required only science students to take military training. Other institutions, such as the University of California at Berkeley, required 3 hours a week of all male freshmen and sophomores. Texas Agricultural and Mechanical College imposed complete military discipline on male students at all times. Young men at Texas A & M spent 16½ hours a week at military instruction and had to secure a pass to leave the campus.[15]

After World War I, the number of students increased dramatically, and since ROTC was compulsory at all land grant colleges as well as at a number of non–land grant colleges, the number of army officers on campus also increased. When the University of Illinois student strike against military drill occurred in 1891, 1 in every 33 young people, or 157,000 youths between the age of 18 and 21, attended college. By 1920, almost 600,000, or 1 in 12, crowded the campuses. By 1928, 1 in every 8, more than 1 million young people, went to college. A large majority were young men. The coonskin coat may be remembered as the garb of the college student of the 1920s, but for thousands of first- and second-year male students, an ROTC uniform was far more common.[16]

Before 1923, military intelligence was little concerned with student dissent. Occasionally, corps area intelligence officers would forward a report on the National Student Forum (NSF). This group—which raised public issues, favored free speech, and generally became a voice for liberal viewpoints—had 25 college branches by October 1923. Although propacifist, it did not single out the military establishment for particular attack. Washington G-2 officers warned at least one ROTC officer early in 1923 not to let the military be drawn into local actions against the NSF. "You know how suspicious of MID activities many people are and that it is attacked on the slightest provocation for 'military interference' in civilian matters," the officer wrote. G-2 in Washington usually referred ROTC officers to the Justice Department's Bureau of Investigation if they wanted information on civilians. A G-2 memorandum of this time labeled National Student Forum activity as "not thought to be worthy of serious concern."[17]

Later, however, the Fellowship of Youth for Peace (FYP) began its drive to organize educational programs and to support student opposition to ROTC. Fellowship of Youth for Peace was, of course, only part of the pacifist upsurge following World War I. Determined to cut back military spending and to end the armaments race, chemical warfare, and compulsory military training of any type, pacifists organized on a scale larger than ever before to influence the military policy of the government. Pacifists became the first group of citizens to develop public concern over expansion of surveillance by the federal government. Unfavorable publicity about the activities of G-2 officers caused the War Department to curtail all regular investigation of civilians after 1922 and to restrict its surveillance activities to liaison with civilian agencies. Unfavorable publicity in 1924 also caused the Justice Department to withdraw the Bureau of Investigation from investigation of proponents of unpopular political doctrines who had violated no laws.[18]

The War Department did not retreat willingly before the pacifist uprising. Under the leadership of John D. Weeks, a former senator from Massachusetts, the War Department fought back between 1922 and 1924 with speeches, criticism of pacifists, and attacks on specific groups and individuals, particularly women's groups that were forming coalitions with church and civic groups to roll back defense spending. By 1925, however, the pacifists had seemingly triumphed. The War Department, concerned about still further cuts, retreated.[19]

Pacifists now focused on the ROTC. In 1923 progressive reformers swept the legislature of Wisconsin and passed a bill making ROTC voluntary at the University of Wisconsin. The War Department responded by seeking a ruling from the Secretary of the Interior regarding the intent of the Morrill Act. The secretary replied that nothing in the act indicated that land grant colleges must require military training of their students. The colleges merely had to offer such training. War Department officials decided that funds could not be withheld from the university, and the University of Wisconsin became the first major land grant college in the country with a voluntary ROTC program. With this precedent, a coalition of pacifists, liberals, socialists, and educators united in 1925 to form the Committee on Militarism in Education (CME) with the goal of eliminating compulsory military courses in colleges and ending federal subsidies for military training. During the next few years this powerful group of well-known citizens (it included John Dewey, Jane Addams, and Reinhold Niebuhr), published pamphlets, organized state committees, lobbied for federal and state legislation to make ROTC voluntary, and sent speakers to campuses. The Committee on Militarism in Education gave support to campus Christian pacifist groups such as the Fellowship of Youth for Peace.[20]

Agitation over ROTC increased. Colonel Reeves, the officer in charge of G-2 in Washington, pressed for a policy ruling on opposition to the pacifists. The FYP appeared to him to be the core of the student movement to abolish compulsory ROTC. He urged that intelligence be collected to give the War Department reasons for ROTC training and reasons for public opposition that might be used in case it was "necessary in combating radical and pacifist propaganda." Reeves proposed that the War Department adopt a policy of using civilian contacts and publicity agencies to counter the activities without publicly aligning itself against pacifist and radical organizations. Dwight F. Davis, the new Secretary of War, approved his suggestions in November 1925.[21]

The Secretary of War's approval of the Reeves policy brought war plan WHITE to the campus. The War Department did not officially notify all agents of its policy that "anti-military propaganda should be combatted through publicity agents," but whenever agents reported growing anti-ROTC activity, Reeves told them to recruit reserve officers and civilians to make addresses or write articles. If these tactics were not successful, corps area G-2s could call on G-2 in Washington. "We have certain contacts with patriotic organizations which can be used when the local agencies are unable to handle the problem," Reeves advised. The policy was thus systematically to use politically conservative patriotic groups to counter pacifist groups that criticized military training programs for students.[22]

War Department tactics successfully confused student pacifists, as shown by an exchange between O. A. Dickinson, G-2 of the II Corps Area, and Abraham Wirin, Secretary of the Fellowship of Youth for Peace. Dickinson, following policy, either encouraged or allowed an officer on duty at II Corps Area headquarters to speak out against FYP. Wirin wrote to Dickinson in protest. Dickinson replied that the officer spoke entirely as an individual member of the American Legion and that the attack had nothing to do with the military, which had no concern about various "isms." This use of patriotic front groups left the FYP unable to face the War Department as its real opponent. Meanwhile, though feigning disinterest, Dickinson kept close watch on the FYP, and subsequent correspondence indicates that Dickinson subscribed to FYP literature through an "outsider," attempted to track down the FYP as a distributor of anti-ROTC postcards, and forwarded at least one detailed report of an April 1926 FYP meeting. This report included the names of speakers and indicated what was said, how many attended, and the names of signers of a petition for abolition of conscription, also describing plans for a regional anti-ROTC conference for students. Dickinson also gave advice unofficially, as a member of the veterans' organization to which he belonged, to members of patriotic groups organizing to challenge pacifist leadership in Armistice Day celebrations. He furnished to these patriotic groups copies of FYP literature so that they could be informed of radical activities. All these actions could be taken within the guidelines laid down by the War Department policy.[23]

While work with patriotic groups off campus was undoubtedly the most effective action, it was not the only one that intelligence officers could take. As criticism spread, the War Department allowed these officers to take the initiative in forming "student defense leagues." One of the predominant features of campus life in the 1920s was the tendency of students to organize. An expanding student population fragmented the older loyalty to the college, leaving students with a greater need to bond together in small social groups. Pacifist groups spread in response to this social need as much as to idealistic concern with war. While administrators found themselves battling students who used these organizations to challenge campus authority, administrators themselves had originally encouraged organizations as a way of ordering and disciplining their growing family of students. The student defense leagues were an obvious way to counter organized pacifist activity.

These defense leagues were composed of students pledged to support compulsory military training in schools. Usually drawn from first- and second-year ROTC students, the leagues gave ROTC officers an additional vehicle to use in disseminating War Department views and countering pacifist arguments against compulsory military training. Groups soon had their own magazines, which supplemented literature distributed by ROTC officers. How many such groups formed and how many members they attracted is not clear form G-2 documents. Henry Rexach, G-2 at V Corps Area headquarters, covering Ohio, Indiana, Kentucky, and West Virginia, reported in March 1926 that he had 2,000 students already organized at the University of Indiana at Bloomington. Rexach provided ROTC professors in his corps area with copies of pro-ROTC literature published by the Reserve Officers Association and the National Security League, a G-2 compendium of opinions of leading citizens on military training in colleges, and copies of editorials and speeches favoring ROTC.[24]

Not all ROTC officers had to organize students. Some could depend upon administrators to take the initiative in countering pacifists, as at the University of Illinois. In 1914, the University of Illinois at Champaign-Urbana had the largest military department of any land grant college. By 1917, the department had enrolled 1,800 students. During 1919, Brig. Gen. Marlborough Churchill, the director of the military intelligence, asked ROTC officers at Illinois to use student informants to find out whether professors were teaching pro-Bolshevik ideas in the class-rooms. By the time of the 1926 anti-ROTC campaign, however, the president of the college seems to have had the situation firmly in hand.

President David Kinley took the lead in countering the 1926 move-ment. He sent letters to members of Congress and to influential clubs and citizens, asking for support in defeating a bill of the Committee on Militarism in Education, which was being proposed in Congress, to make ROTC voluntary. When ROTC officer Col. W. T. Merry warned Kinley that the YMCA had scheduled Sherwood Eddy, an anti-ROTC pacifist, to speak, Kinley replied that he had already "attended to the matter." Eddy did not speak. No sooner had Eddy been scotched than pacifists formed an Illinois CME unit to investigate military training in the state. In May, they asked the board of trustees to make ROTC option-al. Finley used G-2 tactics. He marshaled the American Legion, the Daughters of the American Revolution, and delegates from other patriot-ic groups to speak before the board. The board voted to continue compulsory ROTC. Kinley announced that ROTC was university policy, "not to be criticized or even discussed by any loyal member of the facul-ty," and the policy remained firmly entrenched despite some scattered opposition in the 1930s.[25]

During the 1920s, the MID's use of patriotic groups, help from ad-ministrators, and public speeches thus generally turned the tide against anti-ROTC drives. Occasionally, ROTC officers employed direct action against their opponents. One reported that he had been tearing down posters put up by students. "We go on the theory that we have as much right to take them down as he has to put them up," he said.[26] In addition, Mershon, a wealthy Ohio engineer who had helped create the ROTC, established the Civilian Military Education Fund (CMEF) and in 1928 set up the Mershon Fund to channel large sums of money to the board of that group. The CMEF's purpose was to encourage civilian military training for young men and to help counteract efforts to undermine ROTC in land grant colleges. Col. Ralph C. Bishop, who headed the CMEF, arranged to print copies of a tract stating incorrectly that under the Morrill Act land grant colleges were legally required to make ROTC compulsory. He dis-tributed these pamphlets in states with anti-ROTC movements.[27]

The depression brought a shift in student anti-ROTC tactics. De-spite the fears of G-2 about student radicalism, religious students led the movement during the 1920s. While religious groups continued their activities, the anti-ROTC movement received increasing support from secular liberal-radical students during the 1930s. These liberal-radicals brought to the movement mass action tactics borrowed from the labor movement. They influenced more moderate students at the University of Minnesota, City College of New York, Oregon, Oklahoma, and even Ohio State through organizing optional drill leagues. These leagues planned demonstrations on annual ROTC drill review days, calling them "Jingo Days," urged students to boycott the reviews, and circulated anti-ROTC petitions. At the University of Minnesota 1,500 students held a protest meeting, and 2 weeks later the board of regents declared drill optional. Mass action seemed to work.[28]

Mass action provoked drastic responses on some campuses, however. At the University of California, Berkeley, the American Legion organized student vigilantes to spy on and rough up student activists, and ROTC remained. At Ohio State, behind-the-scenes pressure by ROTC officers and administrators quelled the revolt. At City College of New York (CCNY), after a long conflict, ROTC became optional. These controversies at Berkeley, at Ohio State, and at CCNY exemplify types of responses the War Department could use in opposing mass anti-ROTC action.

The University of California at Berkeley made military instruction a requirement for all undergraduate males shortly after its establishment in 1866 as a land grant college. By 1917, when 1,160 students drilled, it ranked fourth, after Illinois, Ohio, and Cornell, in numbers. In 1919, David Barrows, who had been a colonial administrator in the Philippines and was a colonel in the California National Guard, became president. He dismissed two professors who engaged in amnesty activities for young men who had refused military duty in World War I. The IX Corps Area G-2 officer reported the dismissals and the fact that the conservative Better America Federation, one of the patriotic groups used by G-2 to counter pacifists, had several members among the faculty, but he concluded that pacifist attempts to influence the student body were having little effect. The student newspaper, the *Daily Californian* believed that some government agency had undergraduates conducting secret investigations of "Bolsheviks" in 1924 and coined the name "Billy Stiffs" for these informants. No documents exist that directly link this early surveillance to the military. It is possible that this network was a part of army surveillance, but in any event there was little student dissent on which to report during the 1920s and virtually no opposition to ROTC.[29]

The 1930s were different at Berkeley. During 1933, students petitioned the regents to end compulsory ROTC. By early 1934, the *San Francisco Examiner* was running a series of articles about campus "reds." That year, a long and bloody maritime strike, eventually broken by the National Guard under Barrows, polarized the Bay area. The role of the military in breaking the strike deeply affected students at Berkeley, and radical students mobilized considerable support for the abolition of ROTC. The National Student League had taken a strong stand against ROTC at the end of 1933, and in 1934 the Berkeley chapter began to sponsor anti-ROTC activities. A Social Problems Club poll in 1934 showed students opposed to compulsory ROTC two to one, and the student body asked that it become optional. The administration rejected the request. According to C. Michael Otten, who has studied the administration of the University of California at Berkeley in detail, the dean of students then encouraged fraternity men to form a vigilante group to oppose radical activity. When radicals gathered to protest the formation of similar vigilante groups at other California campuses, the Berkeley vigilantes heckled speakers, threw eggs and tomatoes, and disrupted the protests.[30]

In November 1934 the *Daily Californian* announced that Americanism groups had appointed 22 students as agents to procure information on campus radicals, both students and faculty. According to the newspaper account, these informants were working with the state and federal government through a committee set up by the American Legion. The next day the American Legion confirmed that it was conducting investigations.[31]

Again, there are no documents explicitly linking these student informants to G-2, but in view of the policy of the 1920s—a policy reconfirmed in 1934 by the Chief of Staff, General Douglas MacArthur, that G-2 officers combat anti-ROTC movements through patriotic groups such as the American Legion—it seems likely that the reports did go to the G-2 at VIII Corps Area headquarters. Since these reports were filed at the local level, there would be no mention of them in regular reports to Washington. The intelligence officer in San Francisco did report the formation of the Berkeley Nationals and other vigilante groups in the area who would operate in an emergency under the control of the civil authorities. This officer reported that one effect of his policy of using publicity to increase intolerance of both communists and fascists had been to make it difficult to control the antiradical policies of the Californians. The officer himself saw fascists as far more of a threat than communists.[32]

The vigilante and surveillance controversies of 1934 triggered wider support among Berkeley students. In a 1935 strike against war and fascism, 3,500 students, more than 25 percent of the student body, attended a rally at Sather Gate. Radicals of the 1930s believed that ROTC officers in California had aided and inspired the formation of the vigilantes, but they could never prove it. Instead of challenging the War Department, anti-ROTC groups rallied to the support of a student conscientious objector who brought suit against the university after being suspended for refusing to drill. In *Hamilton et al. v. Regents of the University of California*, the Supreme Court held that the fourteenth amendment rights of students had not been violated by mandatory drill. The court decision put an end to anti-ROTC activity at Berkeley.[33]

At Ohio State, students appealed to the faculty rather than to the courts to support their freedom from compulsory ROTC. Ohio State had experienced little anti-ROTC agitation in the 1920s. During the 1930s, however, the revolt on campus reached not only students but also faculty. Seven undergraduates, expelled for defying the drill rule, left quietly without appeal to the courts, but the rest of the students lobbied the faculty to support their overwhelming opposition to drill. The faculty voted 83 to 79 to recommend that the board of trustees make ROTC voluntary. Following the faculty decision, the administration called a special meeting at which ROTC officers warned faculty members that opponents of military training had communist sympathies. Administration officials let their promilitary training views be known and then lectured the faculty about supporting university rules. The faculty reversed its vote 144 to 9. That same day, an Ohio State representative introduced a bill to investigate any faculty opposing military training at Ohio State University. The next day, the board of trustees decreed that students and faculty must espouse the fundamental purpose of the university if they wished to remain. The president subsequently reminded the faculty that they had a duty to encourage sound thinking and respect for university policies. He then dismissed a sociology professor who persisted in his opposition to ROTC. Students continued opposition into 1934, as a report monitoring a meeting of the National Student League that was forwarded by the V Corps Area G-2 officer indicates, but drill remained mandatory. Only North Dakota joined Minnesota in making drill optional at land grant colleges in the 1930s.[34]

Among the non–land grant colleges that dropped compulsory ROTC in the 1930s, the biggest controversy developed at City College of New York. CCNY students finally won their battle against compulsory ROTC with the assistance of the community rather than the courts or faculty. Opposition to ROTC developed at CCNY almost as soon as the unit had been established in 1919, and the board of trustees made 2 years of training compulsory for every male student. In the early 1920s, a majority of students at CCNY were Jewish, many from communities with a strong tradition of working-class socialism. G-2 watched the anti-ROTC movement at CCNY carefully in 1925 when the student curriculum committee asked the faculty to eliminate compulsory military training and to replace it with athletics. Both faculty and the board of trustees voted to retain compulsory drill. Students then attacked the ROTC manual for condemning internationalism as an "impractical and destructive idealism" having as its goal the "destruction of nationalism." Complaints were to come from many pacifists about this definition of internationalism, and intelligence officers admitted to each other that the statements of this sort were unfortunate, since there were two types of internationalism in the United States, one the then popular idea of international cooperation and the other a movement toward international cooperation of the working classes. The War Department had actually been referring to the latter definition but feared that such a correction would only increase criticism; it decided to withdraw the offending manual and to allow local ROTC instructors to create their own definitions of citizenship.[35]

Although the CCNY Board of Trustees voted to retain ROTC in 1925 as inculcating principles of self-discipline and physical and mental training, members were not so sure by 1927. In that year, they established civilian drill as an alternative option. When students complained about the expense of buying uniforms for this civilian drill, the board abolished it and made military drill optional with the proviso that students who did not enroll in the 2-year military training course had to take 3 years of athletics instead. Students considered this an artificial prop to maintain ROTC enrollment and continued demands to make ROTC completely optional.[36]

ROTC officers at CCNY, like officers at other colleges, organized ROTC students into campus groups as a result of the criticism of the 1920s. By 1931, 90 advanced students belonged to an Officer's Club, and basic students were being organized by officers into a Cadet Club, which soon began publishing a magazine called the *Lavender Cadet* to promote ROTC. That year some students circulated a pro-ROTC petition that 1,500 students signed. Whether the ROTC instructor instigated the petition or not, he received a copy of it and reported to G-2 that fraternities and scientific students supported compulsory ROTC.[37]

At CCNY, administrators seem to have generally welcomed student groups of the 1920s as a way of organizing and controlling student activities in a burgeoning student body and a decreasing faculty-student ratio. Frederick Bertrand Robinson, the president of the university, formed a Liberal Club for the evening students and approved a Social Problems Club for students enrolled in the day session. Both clubs focused on contemporary issues. By 1931, radical students had assumed leadership of both groups. Although Robinson refused to allow affiliation with national groups, many members of these two clubs joined the NSL and advocated increased anti-ROTC activities.[38]

Open conflict over ROTC began in the fall of 1931 when the Social Problems Club supported a student supposedly expelled for refusing to take ROTC. During the subsequent flap, ROTC students rallied to support the military science department, while the New York–based

THE LAVENDER CADET

COLLEGE OF THE CITY OF NEW YORK

WELCOME FRESHMEN!

*I*N 1847, led by Townsend Harris, the people of the City of New York set up the Free Academy. That institution has grown into The College of the City of New York. Believing that a democracy needs to educate all of its citizens, the people of the City offer to e a c h p r o p e r l y qualified High School graduate the privileges of the College. Our curriculum is planned to affer the best possible preparation, both for the individual student and for the community. It perpetuates the best of the earlier traditions of education. It examines our present surroundings in the light of the earlier tradition and in the face of the existing situation. It looks to the future with faith and confidence.

You come to us with an enviable record of work in the High School. The capacity you have shown there,

FREDERICK B. ROBINSON
President

if properly applied to the work in the College, will enable you to perform well the tasks which will fall upon you. You are mature enough not to be swayed by passion. You have intelligence to weigh all factors in college life. You should plan a program well balanced in work, in recreation, and in relaxation. No longer will you be required to sit in a particular place, except in recitations, or to report each hour in an assigned room. Your time must be planned by yourself. .You may even waste it,—but not for long. Every requirement of the College encourages the development of self-control and self-discipline. Every officer of the College will assist in the accomplishment of these aims, and all hope you will succeed.

DANIEL W. REDMOND.
Dean of the College of Liberal Arts and Science.

Vol. I, No. 2   10c   September, 1931

September 1931 *Lavender Cadet* of the City College of New York
(Source: Military Intelligence Division, Records of the War Department General and Special Staffs, National Archives)

Committee on Militarism in Education used copies of the Social Club's newspaper *Frontiers* to oppose ROTC on other campuses. Robinson expelled the president of the club and 10 members for their part in the controversy. Dismissals further polarized the students and popularized the anti-ROTC movement. At fall registration, an ROTC officer counted 24 radical and pacifist anti-ROTC circulars and pamphlets that were being distributed. ROTC enrollment fell, and that September 3,000 copies of the *Lavender Cadet* mysteriously disappeared.

During spring registration, ROTC Capt. Leon L. Kotzebue reported to campus officials unauthorized persons distributing anti-ROTC circulars on campus. Campus security guards expelled the young people. Police later arrested one student, and student newspapers reported that Kotzebue had asked the policeman to arrest the young student for distributing literature without a license. The *New York Times* picked up the story, as did New York Congressman Ross Collins. The War Department asked for an explanation. The military science department replied with what today would be called a "plausible denial." Without disclaiming any involvement, the head officer replied that "no member of the military personnel was present at the time of arrest, nor spoke to the arresting officer, nor appeared either as a witness nor complainant in court in this case." This "plausible denial" together with approval by President Robinson of Kotzebue's conduct as in accordance with faculty obligations, and personal assurance by Robinson to the corps area commander of his support, ended the incident.[39]

The department cleared itself, but campus unrest intensified. At Easter in 1932, students and faculty visited embattled miners in Harlan County, KY. A few weeks later, the Liberal Club began to organize student protests against tuition increases. Robinson did not rehire the faculty sponsor of the club in the fall. Students held a protest rally at which police arrested several students, whereupon students rallied to protest the arrests. The anti-ROTC movement now became part of an expanding spiral of student protest. In May 1933, 500 students demonstrated at "Jingo Day" to oppose the annual ROTC review. Robinson became enraged and with an umbrella attacked—some accounts say defended himself against—several students. Protestors began to stage "umbrella parades." A student referendum that year showed 2,093 opposed and 345 for compulsory ROTC.[40]

At this point, according to James Wechsler, a participant and later a chronicler of the student movement of the 1930s, Maj. Herbert Holton of the military science department organized vigilantes to combat radical students with "controlled force." Again, there is no evidence that Holton did, in fact, organize vigilantes. If he did, they only intensified the conflict and united the student body against the military. Confrontations escalated during 1934, culminating in a student demonstration against visiting Italian Fascist students. When Robinson expelled students for this protest, the Officer's Club was the only student organization to endorse the expulsions. Masses of students demonstrated for reinstatement. In 1935 almost the entire student body boycotted the annual ROTC day, and in June students hooted an ROTC colonel off the commencement stage when he attempted to make ROTC awards. In 10 years, Wechsler wryly observed, Robinson had not succeeded in stamping out "subversive activities." In September 1935, the general faculty finally voted to make ROTC purely elective. Student discontent at Robinson's policies also gained enough support from alumni and the community to end Robinson's tenure in 1938. He fled to Arizona on a sabbatical leave, pleading poor health, and resigned soon after.[41]

G-2 should have learned something from these three battles. Like guerrilla warfare, student protest was difficult to contain once it had begun. Clumsy attempts to escalate control of student protest drove students to the left. While administrators who could maintain their authority, such as the presidents of Ohio State and the University of California at Berkeley, might buttress the military, an authoritarian, such as Robinson, who lost the respect of students could further discredit the military on campus. The policy of using patriotic societies, organizing ROTC students, even using vigilantes, if that was done, proved useful mainly where the students were relatively isolated and had little political support from the community. The G-2 maintained a low profile on campus for most of the 1920s and 1930s because it was on the defensive against pacifism. There is no evidence that it considered interference in civilian politics wrong, only that publicity might bring further cutbacks if it was exposed by critics. The War Department approved countering political movements that criticized military policy, but it believed that, since popular ideology limited military activities during peacetime, patriotic societies had to be used as a front.

Defenders of compulsory ROTC have pointed to the fact that 90,000 officers who had been trained in colleges served in World War II. Defenders of voluntary ROTC, with equal justice, have maintained that, during a period of great economic upheaval, the United States did not employ military force to solve its political problems. The same groups that opposed ROTC also exerted pressure to keep the Civilian Conservation Corps, although trained by officers, without military drill. While neither side would recognize the legitimacy of the claims of the other, and both sides resorted at times to unfair tactics, the two traditions survived side by side.[42]

The conflict between proponents of these two traditions undoubtedly influenced Gen. George C. Marshall's April 1940 announcement that in any future war the War Department did not intend to revive the SATC of World War I. The attempt to combine an intensive military training program with an academic program would disrupt the academic program, he said. If the government, in extreme emergency, had to take over the universities, then the regular academic program would be discontinued. The army established separate officer candidate schools, and ROTC languished on campus during the war. Marshall's decision kept military-civilian disputes at a minimum but left unsettled the question of just how far the military could go in its surveillance of students. This issue became a postwar problem.[43]

Compulsory ROTC died on major land grant colleges following World War II. It died before the wave of student protest hit major college campuses and with relatively little student struggle. Pacifist and radical groups like the Student Federalists, the National Council of Methodist Youth, the student Peace Union, and the Young Socialist League continued to oppose ROTC, but these minuscule groups had little impact on most students in the 1950s. The end of compulsory ROTC came rather because of the changing needs of college administrators and the newly formed Department of Defense. Perhaps the most important factor was the increase in student population to 3 million in the late 1950s and a projected student population of 5 million to 6 million by 1970.[44]

After World War II, administrators at land grant colleges experienced a growing disenchantment with federal military training policies. Land grant colleges lost their special relationship to ROTC when private colleges, seeking a way to weather a drop in enrollment caused by the Korean war, applied for ROTC units. With the loss of this primary responsibility to train officers, military training began to appear to be a financial burden. While most of the old administrators and many boards of trustees still favored compulsory training, younger administrators trained in management saw the program as obsolete. These administrators considered a shift to research and development a surer route to federal money. The responsibility, if any, of land grant colleges was no longer to inculcate obedience to authority but to produce young people capable of maintaining the technological superiority of the United States. Administrative managers also wanted greater flexibility in controlling the program of undergraduates.[45]

Administrators now felt less dependent upon military training as a mechanism for instilling student loyalty and obedience. As students began pouring onto the campus in the late 1950s, administrators shifted emphasis to academic requirements as a way to control and organize them. Since high schools had not properly prepared students for college courses anyway, academic requirements provided an easy way of organizing students. At the same time, heavy academic pressure reduced student time for activities, which might have been difficult for administrations to control. As academic pressure increased, students began to complain about the military training requirements, which seemed to take time from academic work and often gave no course credit in return.[46]

While student numbers grew and administrators lost interest in ROTC programs, changes in military policy during the late 1950s also affected the interest in ROTC that was taken by the Department of Defense (DOD). The Eisenhower administration shifted emphasis away from mass armies to dependence on more sophisticated weaponry. In 1960, the DOD estimated that, in 1970, it would need only 122,000 ROTC students, while ROTC programs would be enrolling 300,000. Because of new weaponry, the army needed 14,000 career officers a year. The ROTC supplied these needed officers but it also provided, at great expense, an excess of reserve officers. The DOD wanted a preprofessional program that would supply career officers and only a few reserves.[47]

Although the army continued to announce its commitment to ROTC as necessary in order to have a large enough pool from which to draw advanced cadets, the high command admitted that the old system was no longer adequate for postwar needs. Students needed broader training by more carefully selected instructors. The navy, air force, and DOD all signaled their lack of interest in continuing compulsory ROTC. Therefore, when students and faculties began to request voluntary ROTC and boards of trustees began to approve the requests, the military did not support ROTC as it had before the war. In schools where major controversies had occurred in the 1920s and 1930s, where officers had rallied around the program and had marshaled students and group support, the programs quietly became voluntary. In June 1961, Ohio State's board of trustees dropped compulsory training. The University of California soon followed. By the fall of 1963 the University of Illinois had joined the lengthening list of land grant colleges that no longer considered ROTC a necessary requirement for undergraduate male students.[48] As compulsory ROTC withered away, enrollments declined. By the time the DOD had made all ROTC programs voluntary in 1970, enrollment in the major northern universities had fallen off so much that the DOD transferred many northern ROTC programs to smaller southern schools where criticism of military policies was relatively minor.[49] When expansion of military surveillance on campus began in the mid-1960s, ROTC programs were only a small part of the general student criticism of military policy.

Expansion of campus surveillance began in 1965 with the merging of two domestic intelligence missions within the army. A legitimate type of surveillance—the investigation of people being considered for security clearances in the military—was handled through an intelligence command at Fort Holabird, MD. A second mission, never clearly defined, was the collection of information for civil disturbance situation reports. This mission was also legitimate if it was limited strictly to the collection of tactical information. Under the crisis of urban riots and growing antiwar dissent, however, the vague limits placed on this second type of intelligence gathering gradually eroded. By 1967, a thousand plainclothes military agents operated from 300 posts spread across the United States, gathering personal and political information on citizens. Agents soon turned their attention to student dissent.[50]

Most historians mark the 1964 free speech movement at Berkeley as the opening battle of the student movement of the 1960s. Student protest spread eastward from Berkeley and California state colleges to eastern campuses in a wave that by April 1969 had engulfed even Harvard University. During 1968–69, state officials called police and guardsmen to 127 campuses to quell student dissent. By spring 1969, thousands of students had been arrested, hundreds had been injured, and five southern students had been killed. Despite student turmoil, only a remote possibility existed that federal troops might be called onto campus. Police had, by this time, developed sophisticated riot control equipment and tactics. National Guardsmen stood ready as backup forces. Why, then, did military intelligence agents become concerned about the campus revolt? They were apparently worried because students challenged the legitimacy of the war in Vietnam, the army's conduct of the war, the draft, war-related research on campus, and ROTC programs, where such programs still existed.[51]

The FBI had clear jurisdiction over any student surveillance considered necessary by the federal government. The only reason for army agents to be on campus was to conduct investigations for security clearances. Army agents visited large campuses almost daily to check with clerks and registrars on educational records. College staff and officials cooperated, usually giving little thought to the privacy of students. Clerks were soon handing over to agents entire student dossiers. Army agents later said that the University of Dayton had furnished the results of psychological tests and the University of Notre Dame had given them free access to student disciplinary files. At the University of Michigan, agents obtained letters of recommendation, personal essays, names and addresses of character references, and financial aid records. As army agents became known to clerks and officials, they seldom questioned the legitimacy of these inquiries. Agents did not have to prove they were conducting specific security clearances. They began to check files of students who had not requested clearance but who were active in political protests.[52]

Without the knowledge or approval of civilian officials of the Department of the Army, intelligence agents expanded their campus activities. Agents tore down posters and peeled photographs off applications for admission. They posed as reporters and television newsmen to cover protests and as students to infiltrate campus groups. In Colorado, a military intelligence captain infiltrated chapters of Students for a Democratic Society (SDS) at the University of Denver and at the University of Colorado. A sergeant who replaced the captain attended the SDS National Council meeting at Boulder in October 1968 with at least four other army agents. In March 1969, this same sergeant threw a chair at S. I. Hayakawa during a speech at the University of Colorado. Police arrested the agent and five other students, but the agent was never prosecuted. The army simply reassigned him elsewhere. Some ROTC students found it difficult to remain aloof from the growing controversies. At the national headquarters of the Pershing Rifles, an elite ROTC honor unit, the G-2 ordered all regimental intelligence officers to forward information on the New Left movement, including membership, expansion, and attitudes, because of the threat that the group felt the New Left posed. Two weeks later the commander of the Pershing Rifles ordered this request to be "disregarded and destroyed if possible," but other surveillance continued.[53]

The worst fears of army intelligence officers were realized when, in June 1969, the SDS splintered, and one faction, the Weathermen, began to encourage the systematic use of violence, targeting ROTC units. Bombing and arson soon rocked campuses. Surveillance extended far beyond self-defense, however. Predicting disturbances in the fall of 1969, military intelligence agents gathered reports on SDS activities in colleges and on members of underground newspaper staffs and compiled lists of persons alleged to be active in the Progressive Labor Party. At Fort Holabird, officers kept track of college disorders with red pins stuck into a large wall map.[54]

Army agents covered the fall 1969 moratorium in which more than 1 million Americans in more than 500 cities and towns and on most college campuses protested. At Rock Island, IL, where two church-related colleges planned candlelight vigils, four agents carried candles in the procession. Two agents stood ready in cars to monitor reports of violence. Special agents in Minneapolis were ordered by a captain to monitor a parade from the College of St. Thomas to Macalaster College, including speeches by Minnesota Senator Walter F. Mondale. That November, when town and gown came together to stage the largest antiwar demonstration in the nation's history and 250,000 people marched on Washington in a peaceful demonstration, army agents were out in force.[55]

Civilian officials of the Department of the Army apparently never knew the extent of military surveillance. The reason for the action taken, they believed, was that civilian agencies had not provided the material the intelligence officers wanted. Nevertheless, civilian surveillance activities seemed to be weakening the intelligence command by diffusing manpower, and eventually high army officials moved to curtail surveillance of civilians. The structure for surveillance remained in place, however, and computers kept the records of civilian protestors intact. The army now had 350 record centers on civilian political activity and an elaborate network to give and to receive information from other agencies, including FBI, police, and campus security officers.[56]

One of the main reasons why the army expanded its surveillance during the 1960s was that so little public criticism existed. During the 1920s, pacifists had consistently kept the public aware of any attempt to expand the role of the army into surveillance. During the 1970s, antiwar protestors seldom attacked military surveillance. In part this silence occurred because protestors did not know which bureaucracy the agents represented. Most protestors knew little about either the civilian or the military bureaucracy that they battled in opposing war policies. Sometimes they lumped all agents together as government agents. At other times, dissident and antiwar newspapers and magazines reported without criticism incidents in which army agents were clearly involved in civilian politics. Like top DOD officials, top college administrators apparently did not know the extent of investigations of student politics, but administrators, staff, and faculty cooperated to some extent on all college campuses.

Public controversy began to surface only when former army intelligence officers began blowing the whistle in early 1970. Both House and Senate committees then began hearings on bills designed to curtail surveillance by legislation. The Nixon administration promised closer supervision. Attorney General William Rehnquist defended "self-discipline on the part of the executive branch" as the solution to any excesses. In 1972, the Supreme Court in *Laird* v. *Tatum* added that it did not consider army surveillance harmful to first amendment rights.[57]

After the *Laird* v. *Tatum* decision the American Civil Liberties Union tried unsuccessfully to have the military prohibited from playing any role in the surveillance of civilians and from collecting information on either civilian or military personnel who were exercising their constitutional rights. The new House Select Committee on Intelligence recommended that the Defense Intelligence Agency, which now oversaw all military surveillance, be prohibited from any military intelligence operations in the United States. In May 1977 Secretary of Defense Harold Brown did order military intelligence agencies to keep their operations within the law and asked that any violations be reported at once, but 10 months after the Senate Intelligence Committee had introduced a draft charter for reform of intelligence agencies, the Carter administration had failed to approve any proposals, and congressional support for a comprehensive law to reform the intelligence agencies was faltering.[58]

The executive branch has successfully maintained control of surveillance. Thus, it has become necessary for universities to take an increasing role in defining the intelligence activities that they would allow on campuses, as they have begun to do in the case of Central Intelligence Agency activities. In the future universities will have to closely scrutinize the history of military surveillance on campus and define civilian-military relations more carefully. Much research is needed on the role of military surveillance on campus, but this research is likely to show far more involvement than citizens have suspected and far more than most high military officials would readily condone. Until the relations between army intelligence, the ROTC, and students are clearly defined by policy, any future crisis is likely to bring increased public criticism of the military if it becomes involved in civilian politics on campus.

Notes

1. Joan M. Jensen, *Military Surveillance of Civilians in America* (Morristown, NJ: General Learning Press, 1975), pp. 1–8.

2. Col. J. H. Reeves, "Problems of the Military Intelligence Division," lecture delivered at the Army War College, January 4, 1927, MID 10560-757/16, Military Intelligence Division Correspondence, 1917–1941. Records of the War Department General and Special Staffs, Record Group 165, National Archives. Hereafter records in the National Archives are indicated by the symbol NA preceded by the record group (RG) number.

3. Joan M. Jensen, *The Price of Vigilance* (Chicago: Rand McNally, 1968) and *Military Surveillance*, pp. 8–16.

4. Reeves, "Problems of the Military Intelligence Division," and speech by Reeves on the MID, September 4, 1924, MID 10560-737, RG 165, NA. The number of officers had decreased from 282 to 25.

5. Lt. Col. John R. Kelly, memorandum undated but stamped June 16, 1924, and various memoranda concerning definition of duties are in MID 10560-736 and MID 10560-731, RG 165, NA.

6. Col. Stanley H. Ford, Assistant Chief of Staff (hereafter ACS), G-2, memorandum for Chief of Staff, July 13, 1927, MID 10110-2512/3, MID 10560-731, RG 165, NA; Jensen, *Price of Vigilance*, pp. 270–292; and *Military Surveillance*, pp. 16–21.

7. Joan M. Jensen, "The 'Hindu Conspiracy': A Reassessment," *Pacific Historical Review* 48 (Feb. 1979):65–84.

8. Capt. Ira L. Reeves, *Military Education in the United States* (Burlington, VT: Free Press, 1914), pp. 113–150, gives a variety of programs and instructors. On at least two campuses women also drilled in the late 19th century. See Phillip Reed Rulon, "Plowboys and Blacksmiths," *Phi Kappa Phi Journal* 53 (Fall 1973): 36, for Oklahoma State and Mary Gray Peck, "Mrs. Catt at College, 1880–1930," *Woman's Journal* 16 (September 1930): 40–41, for Iowa State.

9. Correspondence relating to Lt. Richard Rowan is in file 367 ACP 85, Letters Received by the Appointment, Commission, and Personal Branch, Records of the Adjutant General's Office, 1790s–1917, RG 94, NA.

10. James E. Pollard, *Military Training in the Land-Grant Colleges and Universities* (Washington, DC: Association of State Universities and Land Grant Colleges, n.d.), p. 5.

11. For World War I, see Pollard, *Military Training*, pp. 9–10; Gene M. Lyons and John W. Masland, *Education and Military Leadership: A Study of the ROTC* (Princeton: Princeton University Press, 1959), pp. 40–43; and Calvin B. T. Lee, *The Campus Scene, 1900-1970* (New York: McKay, 1970), p. 21.

12. C. Michael Otten, *University Authority and the Student: The Berkeley Experience* (Berkeley: University of California Press, 1970), pp. 38–76, and Joseph R. DeMartini, "Student Culture as a Change Agent in American Higher Education: An Illustration from the Nineteenth Century," *Journal of Social History* 9 (Summer 1976):526–541.

13. Reeves, *Military Education*, p. 91.

14. Pollard, *Military Training*, pp. 4–9.

15. Reeves, *Military Education*, pp. 115–116, 147–148; Pollard, *Military Training*, pp. 25–26; Joseph Raphael DeMartini, "Student Protest During Two Periods in the History of the University of Illinois: 1867–1894 and 1929–1942" (Ph.D. diss., University of Illinois, 1974), p. 78; and Philip G. Altbach, *Student Politics in America: A Historical Analysis* (New York: McGraw-Hill, 1974), p. 26.

16. On the 1920s, see Mollie Camp Davis, "Quest for a New America: Ferment in Collegiate Culture, 1921–1929" (Ph.D. diss., University of Georgia, 1972).

17. S. Heintzelman, ACS, G-2, memorandum to ACS, G-3, May 23, 1922. See also Amos A. Fries, Chief, Chemical Warfare Service, to Major W. H. Cowles, January 2, 1923, for the comment that the NSF was "doing the work of the Bolsheviks" and P. H. Bagby, MID Washington, to Capt. W. J. Niederpruem, Coe College, Cedar Rapids, IA, February 17, 1923, in MID 10110-2473/4 and 10110-2473, RG 165, NA.

18. Jensen, *Military Surveillance*, pp. 21–23.

19. Joan M. Jensen, "All Pink Sisters: The War Department and the Women's Movement in the 1920s" in Lois Scharf and Joan Jensen (eds.), *Decades of Discontent: The Women's Movement, 1920–1940* (Westport, CT: Greenwood Press, 1983), pp. 199–222, and Robert D. Ward, "Against the Tide: The Preparedness Movement of 1923–1924," *Military Affairs* 38 (April 1974):59–61.

20. James H. Hawkes, "Antimilitarism at State Universities: The Campaign Against Compulsory ROTC, 1920–1940," *Wisconsin Magazine of History* 49 (Autumn 1965):41–54.

21. Col. James H. Reeves, memoranda for ACS, G-3, October 25, 1925, and November 10 and 11, 1925. The Chief of Staff did not approve a request by Reeves to have ROTC officers regularly forward reports to Washington, March 18, 1926, memorandum from Reeves to Chief of Staff, MID 10314-556, RG 165, NA.

22. James H. Reeves, ACS, G-2, to Col. Tenney Ross, G-2, VII Corps Area, December 1925, MID 10314-556, RG 165, NA.

23. O. A. Dickinson to Abraham Wirin, July 7, 1925; O. A. Dickinson to Washington, G-2, September 22, 1925; Dickinson to Lt. Col. Mark Brooke, Acting Executive Officer, G-2, October 1 and 13, 1925; and Dickinson to Lt. Col Walter O. Boswell, Executive Officer, G-2, January 1926, with enclosed report, MID 10314-574, RG 165, NA.

24. Henry C. Rexach, ACS, G-2, V Corps Area, to Chief of Staff, March 29, 1926, MID 10314-556/144, RG 165, NA.

25. Hawkes, "Antimililtarism at State Universities," pp. 43–46.

26. Capt. W. J. Niederpruem, ROTC officer, Coe College, to P. H. Bagby, MID, Washington, February 10, 1923, MID 10110-2473, RG 165, NA.

27. Pollard, *Military Training*, p. 9.

28. Altbach, *Student Politics in America*, pp. 8, 46–47; James Wechsler, *Revolt on the Campus* (New York: Covici, Riede, 1935), pp. 147–148.

29. Situational Survey, IX Corps Area, April 27 to May 4, 1922, MID 10110-C-15. A number of reports from this corps area regarding professors and students are in MID 10314-556, MID 10110-2473/7, and MID 248-20/169, RG 165, NA. See also Otten, *University Authority*, pp. 77 and 83.

30. Otten, *University Authority*, pp. 109, n. 3, and 110.

31. Ibid., p. 11, n. 7.

32. William H. Wilson, Acting ACS, G-2, memorandum for Chief of Staff, March 23, 1932, MID 10314-556/298, and G-2 IX Corps Area, to Major General Malin Craig, Army War College, June 20, 1935, MID 10110-2452, RG 165, NA.

33. Max Heirich and Sam Kaplan, "Yesterday's Discords," in *The Berkeley Student Revolt: Facts and Interpretations*, eds. Seymour Lipset and Sheldon S. Wolin (New York: Doubleday, 1965), pp. 11-16; Hawkes, "Antimililtarism at State Universities," p. 52; and Wechsler, *Revolt on the Campus*, pp. 268-286.

34. Doris Galant Rodin, "The Opposition to the Establishment of Military Training in Civil Schools and Colleges in the United States, 1914-1940" (M.A. thesis, American University, 1949), pp. 118-119. H. M. Pool, ACS, G-2, V Corps Area, to ACS, G-2, Washington, October 20, 1934, and report of meeting on October 12, 1934, MID 10314-556, RG 165, NA.

35. S. Willis Rudy, *The College of the City of New York: A History, 1847-1947* (1949; reprint ed., New York: Arno, 1977), pp. 404-405; Wechsler, *Revolt on the Campus*, pp. 379-395. MID 10314-556 contains a May 16, 1925, clipping on the anti-ROTC movement from the *New York Tribune;* James Asa White to Secretary of War, April 3, 1930; and W. H. Wilson, memorandum for Acting ACS, G-2, September 15, 1930, MID 10314-611, RG 165, NA.

36. Rudy, *College of the City of New York*, p. 408.

37. CCNY Department of Military Science and Tactics to Commanding General, II Corps Area, February 18, 1932, MID 10314-556/296, RG 165, NA.

38. Oakley C. Johnson, "Campus Battles for Freedom in the Thirties," *Centennial Review* 14 (Winter 1970): 342.

39. CCNY Department of Military Science and Tactics to Commanding General, II Corps Area, February 18, 1932, MID 10314-556/296, RG 165, NA.

40. Rudy, *College of the City of New York*, pp. 413-420; Johnson, "Campus Battles," pp. 355-367.

41. Wechsler, *Revolt on the Campus*, pp. 387-395. For other campus activities in the 1930s, see Ralph S. Brax, "When Students First Organized Against War: Student Protest During the 1930s," *New York Historical Quarterly* 63 (July 1979):228-255.

42. Hawkes, "Antimilitarism at State Universities," p. 54, and Robert W. Coakley, Paul J. Scheips, and Emma J. Portuondo, *Antiwar and Antimilitary Activities in the United States, 1846-1954*, mimeographed (Washington, DC: Office of the Chief of Military History, 1970), p. 94.

43. Pollard, *Military Training*, pp. 100 and 103.

44. Hanson W. Baldwin, "The ROTC," *New York Times*, August 21, 1960, 29:3; August 23, 1960, 15:3; August 27, 1960, 8:3-3; and August 28, 1960, 31:2.

45. Otten, *Authority and the Student*, pp. 159-188.

46. Lyons and Masland, *Education and Military Leadership*, p 126.

47. Baldwin, "The ROTC," *New York Times*, August 23, 1960, 15:3; and Lyons and Masland, *Education and Military Leadership*, p. 123.

48. *New York Times*, June 9, 1961, 28; Pollard, *Mililtary Training*, p. 24.

49. Larry W. Reed and L. Anthony Loman, "The Future of ROTC on the Small College Campus," *Journal of Political and Military Sociology* 3 (1975):229-230.

50. Christopher Pyle, "Military Surveillance of Civilian Politics, 1967-1970" (Ph.D. diss., Columbia University, 1974), 5:21-28.

51. Robert Justin Goldstein, *Political Repression in Modern America: 1870 to the Present*

(Cambridge, Mass.: Schenkman, 1978), pp. 511–513, 520–521.

52. "Intelligence/Counterintelligence," *Daily Cardinal* (University of Wisconsin), May 14–16, 18, and 20, 1970; and Pyle, "Military Surveillance of Civilian Politics," 5:21–28.

53. Jensen, *Military Surveillance*, pp. 31–39.

54. Pyle, "Military Surveillance of Civilian Politics," 5:21–28.

55. Ibid.

56. Ibid.

57. Jensen, *Military Surveillance*, p. 39.

58. Christine M. Marwick, "Reforming the Intelligence Agencies: Proposals of the American Civil Liberties Union, the Ford Administration, the House Select Committee on Intelligence," *First Principles* 1 (March 1976): 3–13; *New York Times*, May 9, 1977, 1:3; and May 19, 1977, 1:1, 16:1.

The Army
and Civil Disturbances:
Oxford and Detroit

Paul J. Scheips

According to a student examination paper quoted by David Grimsted a few years ago, "Americans have always been a *beneviolent* people."[1] The student unwittingly called attention to the peculiar mixture of benevolence and violence that has marked both our national and our international life. Although most of our domestic violence has been dealt with by state and local forces, federal forces have been involved in many instances.[2] Here I shall discuss two recent instances that contrasted considerably with those of the army's earlier days and indeed differed one from the other, although together they demonstrated a certain constancy of federal policy. They are the troubles at Oxford, MS, in 1962 and at Detroit, MI, in 1967.

The troubles at Oxford in 1962 evolved from the efforts of James H. Meredith, a young black veteran of the air force, to enroll in the University of Mississippi. On September 13, 1962, after months of litigation, a sweeping federal injunction prohibited any interference with his admission to the university and his continued attendance.[3] Meanwhile the army had known for at least 5 days that it might have to support federal marshals in effecting Meredith's enrollment because of the intransigence of Governor Ross R. Barnett and other Mississippi officials who opposed it.[4]

The constitutional basis for forcible federal intervention in cases of this kind is to be found in the supremacy clause of the Constitution, the

179

President's duty to see that the federal laws are executed, and the responsibilities of Congress to provide the means for protecting the federal interests. The statutory authority, as found in the *United States Code*, provides for the use of federal troops to deal with violence that obstructs the enforcement of federal law or interferes with rights secured by the Constitution.[5]

To understand the Kennedy administration's approach to the Oxford intervention fully, we should recall that, when President Dwight D. Eisenhower used troops to enforce school integration in Little Rock, AR, in 1957, "a strong revulsion" swept over the country "against . . . use of military might against civilians." Even many persons who approved of integration "condemned the use of the military" and the absence of any attempt to use "alternative procedures."[6] On the eve of the Oxford riot, Eisenhower himself believed that the Kennedy administration should use what he called "reserve marshals," which he said were unavailable to him at Little Rock.[7] Eisenhower doubtless meant federal deputy marshals (hereafter generally called marshals), for federal marshals and, hence, deputy marshals, had early been given the same powers in executing federal law that sheriffs exercised in executing the laws of their states. Through subsequent years marshals retained these powers.[8]

The use of marshals brings to the control of a disturbance the civil rather than the military arm of the government, perhaps thereby making the use of troops unnecessary . It is an approach that much appealed to the administration of President John F. Kennedy, particularly to his brother, Attorney General Robert F. Kennedy, who was strongly opposed to the use of troops in civil disturbances.[9] Indeed, earlier administrations had also been reluctant to use troops, and there is a considerable history of the use of federal marshals in civil disturbances, including the Kennedys' own use of marshals during the freedom rides in Alabama in 1961. The Kennedys, at that time, prudently planned for the use of troops to support the marshals, but troops did not have to be used. Their handling of the crisis in Alabama encouraged the Kennedys to use much the same approach in handling the Oxford crisis the next year.[10]

The army's contingency planning in 1962 was in two parts. One part provided for a "tent city" near Oxford as a housing facility for the federal marshals, and the other provided for operational forces. Both the marshals and troops would be staged at the Memphis Naval Air Station at Millington, TN, about 90 miles from Oxford. Meanwhile, by early September, the Department of Justice had planned for a force of several hundred men to include highway patrolmen and men from the Bureau of Prisons who would be sworn in as special deputy marshals under Chief U.S. Marshal James J. P. McShane.[11]

Operational planning led to the preparation of five task forces of regular troops, formed around military policy battalions and infantry battle groups with support forces. These forces would be under Brig. Gen. Charles Billingslea. The Tactical Air Force would provide airlift to the staging area (although some troops would move by land), and the marine corps would provide helicopters to guarantee adequate airlift from the staging area to Oxford. Consideration was given to federalizing the Mississippi National Guard, which would then come under Billingslea.

The army's mission would be to remove obstructions to the arrest of the governor and other state officials, if necessary, and to Meredith's enrollment and attendance at the university: in short, to clear the way for and support the marshals, who would apprehend the troublemakers. In accomplishing its mission, the army would "use minimum strength and force." The same policy would control the use of weapons, which would normally follow a five-step priority from unarmed rifles without bayonets to loaded rifles. Heavy weapons would not accompany the troops.[12]

Overall policy direction was in the hands of Attorney General Robert F. Kennedy, and coordination between the Department of Justice and the army was to be effected through William A. Geoghegan, assistant deputy attorney general, and Maj. Gen. Creighton W. Abrams, who would become the personal representative of the army chief of staff for Oxford matters.

Despite the continued opposition to Meredith's enrollment, Washington authorities tried to bring the matter to a lawful conclusion peaceably. Three times they sought to register Meredith by using a small party of officials of the Department of Justice, and three times the way was barred, twice by Governor Barnett in person. On a fourth try, with an escort of 25 marshals, the party, with Meredith, turned back before reaching the campus. Nevertheless, the Kennedys kept trying. President Kennedy himself spoke with Barnett three times and agreed to a devious proposal by the governor under which Meredith would be registered in Jackson on Monday, October 1, while the governor and lieutenant governor would go to Oxford where, appearing tricked, they would yield and would then take steps to provide for Meredith's safety on the campus the next day.[13] In anticipation of Barnett's refusal to follow this plan, and then because of his refusal, which became known at about 10 p.m. Saturday, September 29, preparations went forward to force Meredith's registration on Monday if necessary. Orders therefore went out to hold one task force on alert at Fort Benning, GA, and to move the other four forces to the staging area, two of them to be there by noon on Sunday, September 30.

It now being all but certain that Barnett would not yield, President Kennedy, at 1 minute past midnight, Sunday morning, September 30, issued a proclamation commanding "all persons" obstructing justice in Mississippi to cease their obstruction and retire peacefully. He immediately followed the proclamation with an executive order, based, as he said, on the Constitution and laws, instructing Secretary of Defense Robert S. McNamara to take steps to enforce the court orders in the Meredith case, including the use of the active armed forces and federalization of the Mississippi National Guard.[14] Accordingly, a call soon went out to the guard and orders went to three of its units to prepare for movement to Oxford, to close there not later than 10 o'clock Monday morning, October 1. Oxford was the home station for Troop E of one of these units, the 108th Armored Cavalry Regiment.

On Sunday there were still further negotiations with Governor Barnett. From them came Barnett's proposal to place Meredith on the campus that afternoon before the President's scheduled address that evening. The Mississippi highway patrol would assist federal officials in keeping the peace, Barnett said. To this proposal Robert Kennedy agreed, but he apparently saw no need to alter the existing military plans, which still looked toward Monday.[15]

By Sunday afternoon, when the new plans respecting Meredith were made, the Department of Justice had assembled a force of about 500 federal marshals in the staging area. At the same time there were enroute, on alert, or already in the staging area and the tent city, 4,582 federal troops, counting those of a marine air unit with helicopters. In addition, more than 3,000 federalized Mississippi guardsmen were on alert for possible movement to Oxford on Monday, October 1.

As Sunday afternoon wore on, the marshals began moving by air from the staging area to the University-Oxford airport, from which army trucks from the tent city transported them to the university campus. At the campus they formed around the Lyceum, the revered old administration building, which was some distance from Baxter Hall, where Meredith arrived safely, under escort, late Sunday afternoon, and where he was to live. Deputy Atty. Gen. Nicholas Katzenbach also arrived to serve as the senior Department of Justice representative at the university.

The marshals had gas masks and tear gas. They carried billy clubs, and they had side arms in shoulder holsters under their jackets. As they arrived and deployed about the Lyceum, a crowd gathered. It grew to a mob of 1,000 persons by early evening and later, with more and more outsiders crowding in, to a maximum of perhaps 2,000. Persons shouted obscenities at the marshals, spat at them, and tossed lighted cigarette butts at them—but that was not all. Some hurled bottles containing acid and some bottles that had been made into Molotov cocktails. Lengths of pipe and pieces of brick and cinder blocks from a nearby construction site also flew through the air. The state highway patrol was at best of very limited help. At about 8 o'clock, as the President began his television address to the people of Mississippi, McShane finally ordered his hard-pressed marshals to use tear gas. For about 2 more hours they held off the mob unaided. Until early the following morning, violent rioting continued about the Lyceum. Most of the streetlights

Guard Post Number 2, West Entrance, First Floor, Baxter Hall, University of Mississippi, October 1962 *(Source: National Archives)*

about the campus were broken or shot out. From the darkness there was gunfire that took the lives of two men, a French newspaper reporter and a local jukebox repairman, and almost killed a marshal. Other marshals also suffered gunshot wounds, but at no time did they fire anything in return except tear gas.

Deputy Attorney General Katzenbach finally advised Washington sometime before 10 o'clock Sunday night that troops had better be called in. The first troops on the scene were the guardsmen in Capt. Murry C.

Falkner's Troop E, about 70 strong, who were at the Oxford armory. Later, at about 2 o'clock in the morning, Company A, 503d Military Police Battalion, commanded by Capt. Fred J. Villella, which flew from the staging area to the University-Oxford airport, was the first of the active army troop units to reach the scene of the riot. Subsequently, other troops arrived. As daybreak approached, a skirmish line of about 400 troops and 200 marshals, the latter of whom had volunteered, moved against the rioters and soon cleared the campus. Tear gas was used, but no soldier fired his weapon until Monday morning, when a small force of guardsmen fired about 15 rounds over the heads of a menacing remnant of the previous night's mob. According to official reports, Sunday night's rioting injured 166 marshals, 48 military personnel, and 31 other people, including 3 state highway patrolmen.[16]

With Meredith now on the campus and amid uncertainty about what might happen next, Washington authorities continued the troop buildup far beyond the level contemplated earlier. By October 6, the troops earmarked for the Oxford operation, including the federalized guard, totaled 30,656, of which about 20,600 had been deployed, partly to the staging area and partly to Oxford. Deployments to Oxford itself reached a peak of about 12,000 on October 2, of which 9,300 were troops of the active army and the rest guardsmen.

The marshals redeployed rapidly, leaving only a small number of men (12 by mid-October) to guard Meredith around the clock. In case of further trouble the army would take charge, and no large force of marshals would return. When it appeared that there was no immediate threat of large-scale violence, the army also redeployed rapidly, leaving only a relatively small force at Oxford. There were only 502 troops in Oxford in November 1962 and only 151 when the army withdrew the last of its troops in July 1963, a month before Meredith's graduation. The years from 1962 to 1967 saw the death of President John F. Kennedy and the succession to the Presidency of Lyndon B. Johnson in 1963. They also saw the rise of serious domestic disorders in the great urban centers of the West and North, including Los Angeles in 1965 and Newark and Detroit in the summer of 1967.[17]

A serious racial disturbance in Detroit in 1943 had led Michigan Governor Harry F. Kelly to request and receive the help of federal troops.[18] Although race relations were believed to have improved considerably by 1967, grievances and tensions nevertheless built up to such an extent that only a small incident was needed to cause trouble. In Detroit, the incident was an early morning raid on Sunday, July 23, on a so-called "blind pig," an after-hours drinking club in the black ghetto, which drew a crowd. The violence began when someone threw a bottle at a departing police cruiser and then spread as the crowd moved down the street breaking windows. By 6:30 the first of many fire reports had come in, and by 8 o'clock there was widespread looting. In the evening there was a new element in the form of gunfire, or sniping, as it was called.[19]

Meanwhile, city officials delayed asking for state assistance until shortly after 2 o'clock Sunday afternoon, when Mayor Jerome P. Cavanagh asked for and received the help of the state police. Then, shortly after 4 o'clock, he asked Governor George Romney for the National Guard. Romney quickly complied with the request. On Sunday evening and Monday the 46th Infantry Division, Michigan National Guard, moved to the support of the city police, of whom there were about 1,100 and of the several hundred state police on duty. By late Monday afternoon there were about 7,000 guardsmen in Detroit.[20]

The Guard patrolled on foot, accompanied policemen and firemen, and guarded fire stations. Their weapons included rifles and machine guns (some of .50 caliber), and they had a supply of chemical agents. Their equipment included armored personnel carriers and tanks.[21] Maj. Gen. Cecil L. Simmons, who commanded the 46th Infantry Division, declared, in accordance with instructions from Governor Romney, that "the laws of the State will be obeyed. We will use whatever force is necessary." Guardsmen were issued ammunition and were ordered to fire when fired upon. The guard's orders with respect to looters were that, if they could not be stopped in any other way, they were to be shot. As Simmons later put it, this was in accordance with custom "from time immemorial."[22]

By 2 o'clock Monday morning, July 24, Governor Romney, who was in Detroit, was worried. The problem was no longer limited to the western part of the city, for arson, looting, and sniping were moving into the eastern part, and "a 2½ by 3½ mile area" was in flames. Against a background of such violence, Romney reached the conclusion that federal assistance was required. Accordingly, he set out to obtain 5,000 federal troops but found himself in disagreement with Att. Gen. Ramsey Clark over how to go about it.[23]

Attorney General Clark wanted Governor Romney to put the matter precisely and in writing. The two men were particularly at odds over Romney's failure to "request" rather than to "recommend" federal troops and to declare that there was an "insurrection" that the state and local authorities could not control with their own resources. Clark's efforts to persuade Romney to use the terms "request" and "insurrection" were based upon the provisions of the controlling law that, in the case of an "insurrection," "the President may" render military aid to a state "upon the request of its legislature or of its governor if the legislature cannot be convened."[24] Curiously, though, the constitutional provision on which this law is based uses the term "domestic Violence" instead of "insurrection."[25] Finally, Governor Romney agreed to request federal troops and so phrased a telegram to President Johnson shortly before 11 o'clock Monday morning. In it he stated that Mayor Cavanagh joined him "in this request" and that "there is reasonable doubt that we can suppress the existing looting, arson and sniping without the assistance of federal troops."[26]

Already alert to the possible need for federal troops, Secretary of the Army Stanley R. Resor, with President Johnson's approval, had initiated a series of actions to prepare for the movement of troops. President Johnson, however, was not satisfied that Romney's request for troops fulfilled the legal requirements and that federal troops were necessary. He therefore ordered troops composing Task Force Detroit to Selfridge Air Force Base, MI, about 25 miles from Detroit, and sent Cyrus R. Vance, the former Secretary of the Army, to investigate the Detroit situation and report to him. Later, Vance would serve, although without the title, as the presidential representative "in charge of . . . Federal operations" in Detroit.[27]

In Detroit, Vance and Lt. Gen. John L. Throckmorton, the commander of Task Force Detroit, conferred with Romney and others and then toured the city. Vance also pressed Romney concerning his unwillingness to certify that there was an "insurrection" or "domestic violence," and Romney explained his fear that his use of the word "insurrection" would render many insurance policies valueless. As Monday evening progressed and reports of incidents began to rise, Throckmorton, with Vance's approval, moved three battalions of regular troops from Selfridge to the state fairgrounds, about a half hour's march from the riot area. There were now 15 deaths, and as the reports of incidents continued to rise, and all available police and guardsmen were on the street, Vance recommended to the President the commitment of federal troops.[28]

President Johnson responded affirmatively to Vance's recommendation by issuing late Monday evening, July 24, the required proclamation to cease and desist and, shortly before midnight, an Executive order authorizing the use of federal troops and federalization of the Michigan National Guard, most of which was quickly called into the federal service.[29] President Johnson then broadcast to the nation an explanation of his actions in which he declared "that Governor Romney of Michigan and the local officials in Detroit have been unable to bring the situation under control."[30]

Whatever the truth may be with respect to Romney's belief that President Johnson's remarks and his slowness in committing federal troops were politically motivated,[31] it must be said that the President's reluctance to use troops in Detroit accorded with the historic experience of the Presidency until that time. According to one survey of the subject, there had been a "full and immediate response" by Presidents "in only about half of the cases" in which such requests had been made, including the 1967 Detroit riot itself.[32]

The units comprising Task Force Detroit under General Throckmorton included a headquarters staff drawn from the XVIII Airborne Corps headquarters, two airborne brigades (one from the 82d and the other from the 101st Airborne Division), and most of the Michigan National Guard, army and air. Active army troops had begun moving to Selfridge Air Force Base around 2 o'clock Monday afternoon. None was on the streets of Detroit until sometime after 2 o'clock, Tuesday morning, July 25, and the last of them did not reach Selfridge until after 3 o'clock that morning. By 9 o'clock Tuesday morning, there were 7,725 troops on the streets, including those of both the active army and the Guard from a total available force of 15,031. On July 29, when the troops in the area were at their peak strength, there were 9,613 troops deployed and an available force of 15,339.

One of General Throckmorton's first actions after receiving orders to execute his instructions as commander of Task Force Detroit was to divide responsibility for the city between the active army forces, organized into subordinate Task Force 82, and the National Guard. At 4 o'clock Tuesday morning, July 25, the active army forces became responsible for the area to the east of Woodward Avenue and the guardsmen for the area west of the avenue. When Throckmorton placed the active army troops in the eastern sector, there was a rising incidence of trouble in that sector, but in subsequent days most of the difficulties were in the Guard's sector on the west.[33] Upon assuming command in Detroit, Throckmorton and Col. Alexander R. Bolling, another early arriving army officer, had found the city fear ridden. Now, with troops in place, their first duty "was to reduce the fear and restore an air of normalcy."[34]

The problem of bringing about a disciplined use of weapons by the federalized guardsmen, who had been making frequent use of them, was doubtless the most important single command and operational problem that General Throckmorton faced. As was customary, his letter of instruction stressed the use of the minimum force consistent with carrying out his mission and provided that the normal use of weapons would range through four steps, from "unloaded rifles with bayonets fixed and sheathed" to "loaded rifles with bare bayonets fixed."[35]

In accordance with his instructions and assessment of the situation, Throckmorton issued on July 25, as one of his first orders after federalization, a verbal order to General Simmons, the Guard commander, that all guardsmen should unload their weapons and put the ammunition in their pockets. Until that time they had been carrying loaded rifles with live rounds in the chambers. Thereafter they were not to fire except when authorized to do so by an officer, and they were to stop shooting looters. They were also to stop shooting out streetlights, which they had been doing from a fear of snipers.

Despite General Simmon's assertion that he enforced the order (even though he disapproved of it), it seems to have been widely ineffective, for both Throckmorton and his deputy, Maj. Gen. Charles P. Stone, subsequently found guardsmen who had never heard of it and who consequently were not obeying it. Indeed, Stone claimed that 90 percent of the approximately 500 guardsmen with whom he talked still had loaded rifles as late as Thursday and Friday, July 27 and 28. On one corner, he said, there was a machine gun loaded as late as Thursday. Simmons asserted, as did Stone, that the problem was one of dissemination of the order. Compliance vastly improved when, on Friday, July 28, Simmons finally put the order in writing, stipulating that rifles normally be unloaded and saying that if troops were fired upon they were to take cover and "await [the] arrival and instructions of an officer." By that time, the general situation in Detroit had eased considerably, and federal officials anticipated restoration of full responsibility to the state and local authorities.[36]

The so-called sniper fire, which was a source of much of the fear that Throckmorton and Bolling found in Detroit and was the cause of much of the firing by guardsmen, is believed to have been greatly exaggerated. General Stone testified that it was not real sniper fire. "What I believe we had," he said, "were individuals armed with rifles, sometimes under the influence of liquor firing often without purpose" and firing ineffectually.[37] According to what John Hersey has called a "brilliant piece of team journalism," three Detroit Free Press reporters concluded that "only one sniper is among the riot victims and only three of the victims may possibly have been killed by snipers, two of them doubtful."[38]

For whatever reasons, guardsmen of the 46th Infantry Division, according to official figures, had expended 156,387 rounds of ammunition by the early morning of July 29 and 156,391 rounds by late Sunday afternoon, July 30, that is, during the first 7 days of their commitment. In the Newark riot the New Jersey National Guard had fired an estimated 10,414 rounds in about 3 days. Active army troops of the 82d and 101st Airborne Divisions, admittedly in a relatively quiet sector, had fired 202 rounds by early July 29 and 206 rounds by late Sunday afternoon, July 30, which was their total expenditure for about 5½ days.[39]

Guard units began relieving troops of Task Force 82 in the area east of Woodward Avenue on July 28, as the federal troops began a phased withdrawal, which they completed on August 2, when Task Force Detroit was disestablished. At noon on August 2 the guardsmen returned to state control but maintained their street deployment until August 5, when Governor Romney revoked his declaration of a state of emergency.[40]

When the violence in Detroit was over, official figures put the dead at 43, of whom 33 were black and 10 were white. Police officers were responsible "for 20 and, very likely, 21 of the deaths," the National Guard for 7, or "very likely," 9, and the army for 1. Other deaths were caused variously. Some persons believed that many deaths were unreported. There were more than 600 injured, property damages of $40 million to $45 million, and "an untold and incalculable loss in wages and tax revenues to the city." Arrests from July 23 to July 31, 1967, totaled 6,528, of which 4,881 went to prosecution. Federal troops sustained 3 injuries, and the Michigan National Guard 15 injuries and 1 death, the latter from a gunshot wound in the back. Altogether the Detroit riot may have been "the worst civil disorder of any American city in the 20th century."[41]

The history of the U.S. Army's role in civil disturbances, as exemplified in the Oxford and Detroit riots, throws light not only on the history of certain complex social problems but also on certain relationships of our federal system of government to which I hope that this paper has brought some perspective. There were a number of differences in the two riots and in the ways in which the federal government and the army dealt with them. At the same time, two aspects of policy were common to both Oxford and Detroit and are especially worth noting. One is the reluctance to use troops that was exhibited by both President Kennedy at Oxford and President Johnson at Detroit despite the legal and other differences in the two cases. This reluctance accorded with traditional policy even if it was colored by politics in the Detroit case. At Oxford the reluctance to use troops took a notable turn in the use of marshals, which demonstrated in concrete terms the deep-rooted philosophical, if not legal, implication of constitutionalism—that troops should not be used against free men except in the most extreme circumstances. The second aspect of policy common to Oxford and Detroit was the restraint with which the active army conducted itself at both places, restraint that to this day has become its hallmark in civil disturbances, as befits the army of a democracy.

Notes

1. David Grimsted, "Rioting in Its Jacksonian Setting," *American Historical Review* 77 (April 1972):361 (emphasis added).

2. On violence in an early period of our history, including the little-known riots in Baltimore, MD, and Washington, DC, in 1835, which resulted in the use of federal troops, see ibid., pp. 361–397; and Leonard L. Richards, *"Gentlemen of Property and Standing": Anti-Abolition Mobs in Jacksonian America* (New York: Oxford University Press, 1970). For figures on the incidence of domestic violence in the late 1960s, see Urban America, Inc.,

and the Urban Coalition, *One Year Later: An Assessment of the Nation's Response to the Crisis Described by the National Advisory Commission on Civil Disorders* (New York: Frederick A. Praeger, 1969), p. 66. The uses of federal troops in civil disturbances down to World War II can be traced, with some omissions, in Frederick T. Wilson, *Federal Aid in Domestic Disturbances, 1787–1903,* S. Doc. 209, 57th Cong., 2d sess. (Washington, DC: U.S. GPO, 1903); Office of the Judge Advocate General, *Federal Aid in Domestic Disturbances, 1903–1922 (Supplemental to Senate Document 209, 57th Congress, 2d Session),* S. Doc. 263, 67th Cong., 2d sess. (Washington, DC: U.S. GPO, 1923); Marlin S.Reichley, "Federal Military Intervention in Civil Disturbances" (Ph.d. diss., Georgetown University, 1939); and Bennett Milton Rich, *The Presidents and Civil Disorder* (Washington, DC: Brookings Institution, 1941). The following three-part chronological survey is useful for the period from World War II through 1976: Robert W. Coakley, Paul J. Scheips, and Vincent H. Demma, *Use of Troops in Civil Disturbances Since World War II, 1945–1965,* Office, Chief of Military History (hereafter, OCMH) Study 75, rev. ed. (Washington, DC: OCMH, 1971); Scheips, Supplement I (1966), Center of Military History (hereafter, CMH) Study 75, rev. ed. (Washington, DC: CMH, 1973); and Scheips and M. Warner Stark, *Supplement II* (1967), CMH Study 75, (Washington, DC: CMH, 1969; reprinted 1974).

3. The Meredith case (*Meredith v. Fair*) and the related opinions, orders, and other documents can be found in 6-7 *Race Relations Law Reporter* 1028–1032 (1961), and 70–80, 423–440, 739–765 (1962). Accounts of this litigation are in James H. Meredith's autobiographical *Three Years in Mississippi* (Bloomington: Indiana University Press, 1966), pp. 104–173; and in *The University of Mississippi and the Meredith Case* (University, Mississippi, 1962), pp. 3–10.

4. Paul J. Scheips, *The Role of the Army in the Oxford, Mississippi, Incident, 1962–1963,* OCMH Monograph 73M (Washington, DC: OCMH, 1965), p. 11. The following account of the Oxford riot is drawn from this monograph (except where supplemented by other works, as cited), which is largely based upon the official records, particularly those of the army action officer, Office of the Deputy Chief of Staff for Operations (ODCSOPS), Department of the Army (hereafter DA). These records include the related field records and are remarkably complete. They are now filed as records of the Oxford, MS, Operation, 1962–1963, among the Domestic Disturbance Files, ODCSOPS, Records of the Army Staff, RG 319, National Archives, Washington, DC. Hereafter records in the National Archives are indicated by the symbol NA, preceded by the record group (RG) number.

5. "Statement of Martin F. Richman, First Assistant, Office of Legal Counsel, U.S. Department of Justice," U.S. Congress, House, Committee on Armed Forces, *Hearings Before Special Subcommittee to Inquire into the Capability of the National Guard to Cope with Civil Disturbances,* 90th Cong., 1st sess., August 10, 11, 15, 22, 23, 24, and 25 and October 3, 1967 (Washington, DC: U.S. GPO, 1967), pp. 5815–5816 (hereafter cited as *Capability Hearings*). The codification of the particular statutory authority to which I refer is found in 10 *United States Code* (hereafter *U.S.C.*), secs. 332–333 (1976).

6. Robert S. Rankin, *The Impact of Civil Rights Upon Twentieth-Century Federalism,* University of Illinois Bulletin, 60 (1963):13. Although little known, this lecture by a prominent political scientist and member of the U.S. Commission on Civil Rights is an important contribution to our understanding of alternative procedures in cases such as those of Little Rock and Oxford. Also see Frank E. G. Weil, "Use Federal Agencies Instead of the Army," *American Bar Association Journal,* 44 (November 1958):1024 and 1030. Details of the widespread revulsion that followed the use of troops are in the press reports of the day. An interesting and pertinent outcome of the Little Rock affair was the debate in legal journals on the legality of the military intervention, for citations to which see Paul J. Scheips, "Enforcement of the Federal Judicial Process by Federal Marshals: A Comparison of Little Rock and Oxford," in *Bayonets in the Streets: The Use of Troops in Civil Disturbances,* ed. Robin Higham (Lawrence: University Press of Kansas, 1969), pp. 52–53, nn. 8–9. On the lesser amount of legal comment inspired by Oxford, see *Bayonets,* pp. 53–54, n. 10.

7. *New York Times,* September 28, 1962.

8. Congress first provided for federal marshals in the Judiciary Act of 1789 (1 *Statutes at Large* 73). Their present status and that of deputy marshals who are now under civil service is described in 28 *U.S.C.,* secs. 561 and 569–570 (1976).

9. Victor S. Navasky, *Kennedy Justice* (New York: Atheneum, 1971), p. 196; and Walter Lord, *The Past That Would Not Die* (New York: Pocket Books, Pocket Cardinal, 1967), p. 126. Navasky thinks (pp. 24, 110–111, 198–199, and 227–231) that, in situations such as those at Montgomery and Oxford, agents of the Federal Bureau of Investigation should be used. He also notes (p. 228) that Jack Greenberg of the Legal Defense Fund of the National Association for the Advancement of Colored People believed that troops should have been used at Oxford at the outset.

10. Robert V. Bruce, *1877: Year of Violence* (Chicago: Quadrangle Books, 1970), pp. 258, 287–290; Gerald G. Eggert, *Railroad Labor Disputes: The Beginnings of Federal Strike Policy* (Ann Arbor: University of Michigan Press, 1967), pp. 37–38, 60ff., 139–146, 158–163, 213, 280 (n. 45); and Rich, *The Presidents and Civil Disorder,* pp. 87–91, 92–102. All three studies describe instances of civil disorder in our earlier history in which federal marshals were used, sometimes in substantial numbers. Brief accounts of the use of marshals in Montgomery appear in Edwin Guthman, *We Band of Brothers* (New York: Harper and Row, 1971), pp. 172–174; Lord, *The Past That Would Not Die,* p. 127 (where the text incorrectly states: "This was the first time they had been employed on a large scale"); Burke Marshall *Federalism and Civil Rights* (New York: Columbia University Press, 1964), pp. 65–69; and Navasky, *Kennedy Justice,* pp. 20–24. The military preparations can be followed in the (mistitled) file on "Alert of Troops, Birmingham, AL—Freedom Riders," which is among the records of the Oxford, MS, Operation, 1962–63, ODCSOPS, RG 319, NA. Rankin, *The Impact of Civil Rights Upon Twentieth-Century Federalism,* pp. 12–15, puts the use of marshals at Montgomery and Oxford in perspective.

11. Walter Lord, who had access to Department of Justice sources, describes the preparation of the force of marshals in *The Past That Would Not Die,* p. 127.

12. The instructions prepared for use in planning (DA message [by Abrams] to commanding general, 2d Infantry Division, Fort Benning, GA, September 28, 1962 [DA 919735]), soon became the operational instructions (DA message to Billingslea, September 30, 1962 [DA 919745]), records of the Oxford, MS, Operation, ODCSOPS, RG 319, NA.

13. On the early efforts thus far to enroll Meredith and to secure Barnett's cooperation, see Russell H. Barrett, *Integration at Ole Miss* (Chicago: Quadrangle Books, 1965), pp. 105–119, 123–124; Guthman, *We Band of Brothers,* pp. 185–198; Lord, *The Past That Would Not Die,* pp. 132–153, 164–167; Meredith, *Three Years in Mississippi,* pp. 184–206; Navasky, *Kennedy Justice,* pp. 165–225, including extended quotations from transcripts of Kennedy-Barnett telephone conversations; and Arthur M. Schlesinger, Jr., *A Thousand Days: John F. Kennedy in the White House* (Boston: Houghton Mifflin, 1965), pp. 941–946.

14. Proclamation No. 3497, "Obstruction of Justice in the State of Mississippi" (September 30, 1962), 27 *Federal Register* 9681 or 3 *Code of Federal Regulations* 225 (1959–1963 Compilation), citing particularly 10 *U.S.C.,* secs. 332–34, and Executive Order 11053, "Assistance for Removal of Unlawful Obstruction of Justice in the State of Mississippi" (September 30, 1962), 27 *Federal Register* 9691 or 3 *Code of Federal Regulations* 645 (1959–63 Compilation).

15. Barrett, *Integration at Ole Miss,* pp. 126–128; Guthman, *We Band of Brothers,* p. 200; Lord, *The Past That Would Not Die,* pp. 172–173; and Navasky, *Kennedy Justice,* pp. 231–234, using material taken from an affidavit prepared for a contempt case against Barnett but not filed.

16. The following accounts of the riot are especially useful: Barrett, *Integration at Ole Miss,* pp. 123–162, by a political science professor who had taken refuge in a campus building near the riot; Guthman, *We Band of Brothers,* pp. 200–205, by Robert Kennedy's special as-

sistant for public information, who was in the Lyceum with Katzenbach; Lord, *The Past That Would Not Die*, pp. 174–204, by an able writer who, although not at the riot, had early access to Department of Justice sources; Michael Dorman, *We Shall Overcome* (New York: Delacorte Press, 1964), pp. 51–109, by a veteran *Newsday* reporter who was on the scene; and James W. Silver, *Mississippi: The Closed Society* (New York: Harcourt Brace and World, 1966), by a professor of history who was an eyewitness to many of the events. For an official Mississippi view of the "occupation" of the university campus, see *A Report by the General Legislative Investigative Committee to the Mississippi State Legislature Concerning the Occupation of the Campus of the University of Mississippi, September 30, 1962, by the Department of Justice of the United States* (Jackson, MS: n.p., 1963).

17. See the various relevant works cited in n. 2, and the following: Robert Conot, *Rivers of Blood, Years of Darkness* (New York: Bantam Books, 1967), on the Los Angeles, or Watts, riot; and Governor's Select Commission on Civil Disorder, State of New Jersey, *Report for Action* (n.p., 1968), on the Newark riot.

18. On the 1943 Detroit riot, see Robert Shogan and Tom Craig, *The Detroit Race Riot: A Study in Violence* (Philadelphia: Chilton, 1964).

19. Hubert G. Locke, *The Detroit Riot of 1967* (Detroit: Wayne State University Press, 1969), pp. 23–34. At the time of the riot, Locke was an administrative assistant to Detroit Police Commissioner Ray Girardin. See also *Report of the National Advisory Commission on Civil Disorders* (Washington, DC: U.S. GPO, 1968), pp. 47, and 68–69 (hereafter cited as the *Kerner Report*, after the commission's chairman, Governor Otto Kerner of Illinois).

20. After Action Report, Task Force Detroit, July 24, 1967–August 2, 1967 (1967), Annex B, p. B2, and Annex D, TF Operational Report, 46th Infantry Division, August 7, 1967, pp. D2–D3; and Final Report of Cyrus R. Vance, Special Assistant to the Secretary of Defense, Concerning the Detroit Riots, July 23 through August 2, 1967 (released Sept. 12, 1967), pp. 13–14. All of these items are in the Civil Disturbance Files in the custody of CMH, DA, Washington, DC. Billy B. Dansby, "Operation Sundown: Devastation in Detroit," *National Guardsman* 21 (September 1967):6; and Locke, *The Detroit Riot of 1967*, pp. 34–36.

21. Dansby, "Operation Sundown," p. 6; David W. Jordan, "Civil Disturbance: A Case Study of Task Force Detroit, 1967," *Perspectives in Defense Management* 2 (Aug. 1968):23, a very useful work; *Kerner Report*, pp. 27 and 55, on the use of .50-caliber machine guns by guardsmen; and After Action Report, TF Detroit, Annex D, pp. D3, D4, D11, Civil Disturbance Files, CMH, DA, Washington, DC.

22. *Capability Hearings*, p. 5805. Simmons is quoted in Dansby, "Operation Sundown," pp. 6–7.

23. Transcript of press conference by Governor Romney, July 31, 1967, in *Capability Hearings*, pp. 6310 and 6311; and Final Report of Cyrus R. Vance, pp. 3–5, Civil Disturbance Files, CMH, DA, Washington, DC.

24. 10 *U.S.C.*, sec. 331 (1976).

25. U.S. Constitution, art. IV, sec. 4. On August 7, 1967, Attorney General Clark, at the President's request, sent a letter to each governor setting forth the "basic prerequisites to the use of federal troops in a state in the event of domestic violence." The first prerequisite, he said, using the constitutional rather than the statutory wording, is certification of the existence of "serious 'domestic Violence.'" This letter, with an enclosure, is reproduced in its entirety in various places, including the *Kerner Report*, pp. 292–293, and the *Capability Hearings*, pp. 5758–5761. The Kerner commission recommended (p. 288) in 1968 that the law should be amended by changing the word "insurrection" to "domestic violence" so as "to eliminate any possible difficulties." For discussion of these terms and the other statutory and constitutional language associated with them, see "Riot Control and the Use of Federal Troops," *Harvard Law Review* 81 (January 1968):639–647; and Final Report of Cyrus R. Vance, pp. 27–28, Civil Disturbance Files, CMH, DA, Washington, DC.

26. Romney's efforts to secure federal troops are described in the transcript of his press conference of July 31, 1967, *Capability Hearings,* pp. 6311–6313; and in Final Report of Cyrus R. Vance, pp. 1–6, Civil Disturbance Files, CMH, DA, Washington, DC. Also see n. 31, below.

27. Final Report of Cyrus R. Vance, pp. 5–6 (quotation), and 7–8 Civil Disturbance Files, CMH, DA, Washington, DC; Lyndon Baines Johnson, *The Vantage Point: Perspectives of the Presidency* (New York: Holt, Rinehart and Winston, 1971), pp. 167–169; and Johnson to Romney, July 24, 1967, Romney Name File, White House Central Files (hereafter WHCF), Lyndon Baines Johnson Library, Austin, TX (hereafter LBJL). The author acknowledges, with thanks, the prompt, helpful, and friendly assistance of Tina Lawson, supervisory archivist of the Johnson Library.

28. Final Report of Cyrus R. Vance, pp. 7–8, and After Action Report, TF Detroit, pp. 3–5, Civil Disturbance Files, CMH, DA, Washington, DC; *New York Times,* July 25, 1967; and *Washington Post,* July 29, 1967.

29. Proclamation No. 3795, "Law and Order in the State of Michigan" (July 24, 1967), 32 *Federal Register* 10905 or 3 *Code of Federal Regulations* 137 (1967 Compilation), citing 10 *U.S.C.,* sec. 331 and 334; and Executive Order No. 11364, "Providing for the Restoration of Law and Order in the State of Michigan" (July 24, 1967), 32 *Federal Register* 10907 or 3 *Code of Federal Regulations* 309 (1967 Compilation).

30. *Public Papers of the Presidents of the United States: Lyndon B. Johnson . . . 1967,* 2 vols. (Washington, DC: U.S. GPO, 1968), 2:716.

31. Governor Romney, a prospective candidate for the Presidency, and others believed that President Johnson allowed political considerations to influence him, specifically that Johnson offered help to Governor Richard J. Hughes of New Jersey, a Democrat, during the Newark riot but was reluctant to aid Romney. From the record it appears that Johnson wanted Hughes "to know that the President, the Attorney General and everyone here wants to support you and give you any aid." Hughes recalled in an oral history interview in 1969 that Attorney General Ramsey Clark had been "helpful" and that during an earlier riot in Jersey City Johnson had called to ask: "Do you need the army, or can we help?" Also, it may be noted, Governor Edmund G. Brown of California, also a Democrat, recalled in an oral history interview in 1970 that the White House offered help during the Watts riot of 1965. Like Hughes, Brown did not request federal troops, but the administration alerted troops and gave logistical support to the California National Guard. See transcript of the Romney press conference of July 31, 1967, *Capability Hearings,* pp. 6316–6318; Harry McPherson, *A Political Education* (Boston: Little, Brown, and Co., 1972), pp. 359–360; Romney, Hughes, Clark, and Brown materials, including oral history interviews with Hughes and Brown by Joe B. Frantz and with Clark by Harri Baker, together with Name and Diary Backup Files, WHCF, LBJL; and Coakley, Scheips, and Demma, *OCMH Study 75,* pp. 114–115. Johnson is quoted from the record of a telephone conversation between Hughes and Johnson on July 14, 1967, with memorandum, Jones to Watson, July 14, 1967, Diary Backup File, WHCF, LBJL.

32. "Statement of Martin F. Richman," *Capability Hearings,* p. 5817, referring to a list of formal state requests enclosed with Attorney General Clark's letter to the various governors, August 7, 1967, as cited in n. 25. Also see "The Law and Tradition Governing the Use of Federal Troops in Cases of Domestic Violence," Final Report of Cyrus R. Vance, pp. 31–33, Civil Disturbance Files, CMH, DA, Washington, DC.

33. Final Report of Cyrus R. Vance, pp. 18a–20; and After Action Report, TF Detroit, Civil Disturbance Files, CMH, DA, Washington, DC, as follows: pp. 2 and 7; Annex A, p. A3, maps and strength figures in Annex B, particularly pp. B5 and B9; Annex K, pp. K1–K5 (message, DA to Commander, Selfridge AFB, MI [for Throckmorton], July 24, 1967, subj.: Letter of Instruction GARDEN PLOT 1-67 [DA 824879]; and Annex L, p. L3 (message, DA to

Commander, Selfridge AFB, MI [for Throckmorton and Maj. Gen. Carl C. Turner, Chief of Staff of the Army Liaison Officer], July 25, 1967, subj.: LOI GARDEN PLOT 3-67, from Chief of Staff of the Army, signed Johnson [DA 824899]). Closing times at Selfridge AFB for the troop airlifts appear in [Brooks E. Kleber], "Chronology, Detroit Civil Disturbance, 23 July–2 August 1967" [HQ, U.S. Continental Army Command, 1967], pp. 11, 12 (hereafter cited as Kleber Chronology).

34. As quoted in *Kerner Report*, p. 56. Bolling, a retired major general, had some sharply etched recollections of that night, which he related to the author in a telephone interview, April 30, 1979.

35. DA message for Throckmorton, July 24, 1967 (DA 824879), After Action Report, TF Detroit, CMH, DA, Washington, DC.

36. Testimony by Schnipke, Simmons, Stone, and Throckmorton in *Capability Hearings*, pp. 5805, 5876, 5877, 5880, 5889, 5891, 5892, 6066, and 6068 (quotation); *Washington Post*, August 23, 1967; and Final Report of Cyrus R. Vance, pp. 23–24, Civil Disturbance File, CMH, DA, Washington, DC. On the National Guard's operations in general, see memo for Chief of Staff of the Army from Stone, August 4, 1967, sub.: Report of the Deputy Commander Task Force Detroit—Operations and Observations, in *Capability Hearings*, pp. 5966–5973 (hereafter cited as Stone Report). Compare the other versions of this report in the *Capability Hearings*, pp. 5683–5689; and in *Bayonets in the Streets*, pp. 189–203, with an editorial introduction, pp. 185–189.

37. Stone Report, *Capability Hearings*, pp. 5967–5968. Compare the somewhat different wording of Stone's statement on sniping, pp. 5684–5685; and in *Bayonets in the Streets*, p. 193. There are descriptions in the *Kerner Report* (pp. 54–60) of a number of incidents.

38. John Hersey, *The Algiers Motel Incident* (New York: Bantam Books, 1968), pp. 286–291, particularly pp. 287 (first quotation) and 290 (second quotation as rendered by Hersey). According to official Detroit figures, "2663 or 54.6% of Prosecution Arrests were for LOOTING," while only "26 . . . were for SNIPING," in Statistical Report on the Civil Disorder Occurring in the City of Detroit, July 1967, p. 3.

39. DA message to Joint Chiefs of Staff, White House, and others, 6 A.M., EDT, July 29, 1967 (DA/SITREP No. 9, DA 825736), p. 5; Kleber Chronology, p. 26; and *Report for Action*, p. 135. In the summer of 1979, following presentation of this paper, General Throckmorton, learning for the first time of the reported ammunition expenditure by the Michigan Guard, expressed doubt concerning the accuracy of the report, believing it to be overstated (author's telephone interview with Throckmorton, August 27, 1979). Even if the figures are inaccurate, however, other available evidence, including Throckmorton's own testimony, suggests an excessive use of weapons by the guardsmen.

40. After Action Report, TF Detroit, pp. 11–13, and Annex A, pp. A5–A8; Final Report of Cyrus R. Vance, pp. 23–27, 100–103 Civil Disturbance Files, CMH, DA, Washington, DC; and *Civil Rights, 1967–68* (New York: Facts on File, Inc., 1973), 2:34.

41. Kerner Report, pp. 60–61, 66, 197, 202. Compare Hersey, *The Algiers Motel Incident*, pp. 287–288, and Garry Wills, *The Second Civil War: Arming for Armageddon* (New York: New American Library, 1968), pp. 55–57. Also see: Dansby, "Operation Sundown," pp. 6 (death of guardsman from gunshot wound) and 40; Locke, *The Detroit Riot of 1967*, pp. 23 and 51; and Statistical Report on the Civil Disorder Occurring in the City of Detroit, July 1967, pp. 1, 5. Civil Disturbance Files, CMH, DA, Washington, DC. For other arrest and damage reports, see *Civil Rights*, 2:32–33.

Biographical Sketches

Edward M. Coffman is a professor of history at the University of Wisconsin-Madison. He earned his B.A., M.A., and Ph.D. from the University of Kentucky. He was a visiting professor of history at the U.S. Military Academy, 1977-78, at the U.S. Air Force Academy, 1982-83, and at the U.S. Army War College, 1986-87. From 1983 to 1985 he was president at the American Military Institute. He has written two major works on American participation in the First World War—*Hilt of the Sword: The Career of Peyton C. March* (1966) and *The War to End All Wars: The American Military Experience in World War I* (1968), and recently completed *The Old Army: A Portrait of the American Army in Peacetime, 1784-1898* (1986).

Jerry M. Cooper has a B.A. from Western Michigan University and an M.A. and Ph.D. from the University of Wisconsin. He is an associate professor of history at the University of Missouri-St. Louis and during 1986-87 was a visiting professor at the University of East Anglia, Norwich, England. He is the author of *The Army and Civil Disorder: Federal Military Intervention in American Labor Disputes, 1877-1900* (1979) and is currently preparing *The Rise of the National Guard: The Evolution of the American Militia, 1815-1920*, for publication.

Elaine C. Everly graduated from California State College (Pennsylvania) and received an M.A. from the University of West Virginia, and a Ph.D. from George Washington University. She has worked with military records in the National Archives for over twenty years and is currently the chief of the Military Field Branch, Military Archives Division. Dr. Everly has long been interested in documentation relating to the impact of military installations on local communities,

195

an interest reflected in her active participation in the Council on America's Military Past.

Elizabeth M. Finlayson, retired in 1985 as Dean of Summer Session at James Madison University, where she had held a number of important administrative positions. She has a B.S. and M.S. from the University of Wisconsin and an Ed.D. from George Washington University. Dr. Finlayson has published a number of articles on the role and current status of the army wife.

Ernest F. Fisher, Jr., graduated from Boston University before serving as an airborne infantry officer in Europe during World War II. Following wartime service he received an M.A. from Boston University and a Ph.D. from the University of Wisconsin. In 1986 he retired as a historian from the Center of Military History, Department of the Army, where he most recently prepared a study on the non-commissioned officer in the U.S. Army. He has written several articles on military operations and doctrine for *Military Review* and is the author of *Cassino to the Alps* (1977), a volume in the *United States Army in World War II* series.

Andrew J. Goodpaster was recalled from retirement in 1977 after thirty-five years of military service to become the 51st Superintendent of the U.S. Military Academy, a position he held until 1981. General Goodpaster is a graduate of the Military Academy and holds M.A. and Ph.D. degrees from Princeton University. Following combat duty in Italy during World War II he served in the Office of the Joint Chiefs of Staff, on the staff of Supreme Headquarters Allied Powers Europe, and on the White House staff during the Eisenhower administration. In 1961 and 1962 he commanded the U.S. 8th Division in Germany after which he again served with the Joint Chiefs. He has served as the senior member of the Military Staff Committee with the United Nations, as Commandant of the National War College, and as Deputy Commander of the U.S. Military Assistance Command-Vietnam. At the time of his "first" retirement in 1974 he was Supreme Allied Commander in Europe. In 1985 he became the chairman of the American Battle Monuments Commission.

Joan M. Jensen is a professor of history at New Mexico State University. She received her B.A., M.A., and Ph.D. degrees from the University of California-Los Angeles. In addition to New Mexico State, she has taught history at the University of California-Los Angeles, Arizona State University, and United States International University. Her major publications are *The Price of Vigilance* (1965), *Military Surveillance of Civilians in America* (1975), *With These Hands: Working Women on the Land* (1981), and *Decades of Discontent: The Women's Movement, 1920-1940* (1982).

Richard H. Kohn graduated from Harvard University and received his M.S. and Ph.D. from the University of Wisconsin. He taught American history at the City College of New York and Rutgers University. He has written many articles and essays in the fields of American military history and the history of the American Revolution. During the 1980-81 academic year he was the Harold K. Johnson Visiting Professor of Military History at the Army War College. He is the author of

Eagle and Sword: The Federalists and the Creation of the Military Establishment in America, 1783-1802 (1975). Since 1981 he has headed the Office of Air Force History.

Jack C. Lane, a B.A. graduate of Oglethorpe University, earned an M.A. from Emory University and a Ph.D. from the University of Georgia. He has taught American history at Georgia State College and Rollins College, where he currently holds the rank of professor. In addition to numerous articles and reviews, he is the author of a biography of Leonard Wood, *Armed Progressive: General Leonard Wood* (1973), the editor of Wood's journal of the Geronimo campaign of 1886, *Chasing Geronimo: The Journal of Leonard Wood, May-September 1886* (1970), and the compiler of *America's Military Past: A Guide to Information Sources* (1980).

Gerald F. Linderman graduated from Yale University and served for ten years as a foreign service officer in Nigeria, India, and the Congo. He received his M.A. and Ph.D. from Northwestern University and now is an associate professor of history at the University of Michigan. He has published *Mirror of War: American Society and the Spanish-American War* (1974).

Anton Myrer attended Harvard University for one year before serving in the Pacific from 1942 to 1945 with the Marine Corps. After the war he returned to Harvard and graduated magna cum laude. He is the author of eight novels, including *The Big War* (1957), *The Last Convertible* (1978), *Green Desire* (1982), and *Once An Eagle* (1968). The latter, a selection of Book-of-the-Month Club and Reader's Digest Condensed Books, portrays the life of a professional soldier— from private in the First World War to lieutenant general in the Second.

Armstead L. Robinson graduated with honors from Yale University and received his Ph.D. from the University of Rochester. He has taught Civil War and Afro-American history at the State University of New York-Stony Brook, the State University of New York-Brockport, and the University of Virginia, where he is now the director of the Carter B. Woodson Institute for Afro-American and Afro Studies. He has written and lectured extensively on the demise of slavery in the Mississippi Valley during the Civil War.

Paul J. Scheips has a B.A. from Evansville College, an M.A. from the University of Chicago, and a Ph.D. from The American University. He was a historian with the U.S. Army Signal Corps Historical Division from 1952 to 1962 and was with the Center of Military History, Department of the Army, from that year until his retirement in 1986. His publications include numerous articles and essays on American military and social history in a variety of journals and books of readings. He is currently completing (on contract) a history of the use of troops in civil disturbances since the Whiskey Rebellion for the Center of Military History.

Frank N. Schubert obtained his B.A. from Howard University and his M.A. from the University of Wyoming and Ph.D. from the University of Toledo. He is a historian with the Office of the Chief of Engineers, U.S. Army. In addition to a dissertation and several articles on the frontier army, he has edited the journal of Lt. William B. Franklin, Corps of Topographical Engineers, *March to South Pass: Lieutenant William B. Franklin's Journal of the Kearny Expedition of 1845* (1978) and is the author of *Vanguard of Expansion: Army Engineers in the Trans-Mississippi West, 1819-1879* (1980).

William B. Skelton is a professor of history at the University of Wisconsin-Stevens Point. His B.A. is from Bowdoin College, his M.A. and Ph.D. from Northwestern University. He has written extensively on the institutional and social history of the ante bellum army and is preparing a book on the army officer corps, 1784-1861.

Merritt Roe Smith is a professor of the history of technology at Massachusetts Institute of Technology. He has taught at Ohio State University and the University of Pennsylvania. A graduate of Georgetown University, he received his M.A. and Ph.D. from Pennsylvania State University. He has written many articles and reviews on the history of early American technology. His book, *Harpers Ferry Armory and the New Technology: The Challenge of Change* (1977), won the Frederick Jackson Turner Award from the Organization of American Historians and was a Pulitzer Prize nomination.

Russell F. Weigley received his B.A. from Albright College and his M.A. and Ph.D. from the University of Pennsylvania. He is a professor of history at Temple University where he has taught since 1962. He is a past president of the American Military Institute and was a visiting professor of military history at the Army War College, 1973-74. His major works are *Towards an American Army: Military Thought from Washington to Marshall* (1962), *History of the United States Army* (1967), *The American Way of War: A History of United States Military Strategy and Policy* (1973), and *Eisenhower's Lieutenants: The Campaign of France and Germany, 1944-1945* (1981).

Index

(Army wives *cont'd.*)
  effect on, 50–51
  See also Women
ARU, *See* American Railway
  Union

B

Barbour, Alfred, 89
Barbour, James, 8
Barnett, Ross R., 179, 181–182
Barrows, David, 163
Batchelor, Joseph B., 139
Beatty, John, 123–124
Bell, John H., 86
Bennett, William, 50
Benning, Henry L., 110
Berry, Mary, 119
Better America Federation, 163
Bigelow, John, 31
Billingslea, Charles, 181
Bishop, Ralph C., 162
Black Americans
  in Columbus, GA after Civil
    War, 109
  at Fort Benning, GA, 112
  at Fort Robinson, NE, 98
  integration of University of
    Mississippi, 179–184
  at West Point, 10
  See also Emancipation; Civil
    rights movement; Race
    relations
Blake, Jacob E., 65
Bolling, Alexander R., 187
Bomford, George, 84, 85, 86
Bradford, William, officer's com-
  mission, 63 (illus.)
Bradley, Omar, 72
Brady, Elias, 126
Bragg, Braxton, 68
Brown, Harold, 174
Brown, John, 126–127
Bruer, John, 98, 100

Bunker Hill and Sullivan Mining
  Co., 138, 139
Bunker Hill Strike, 138–139
  army intervention, 139–142
  congressional investigation,
    146, 147
  newspaper coverage of, 140
    (photo)
  political oversight, 143–146
Burke, Kenneth, 17
Butler, Benjamin, 122

C

Cabanillas, Claude E., 48, 50
Calhoun, John C., 8, 22
Calmer, Ned, 71
Camus, Albert, 71
Cavanagh, Jerome P., 185
CCNY, *See* City College of New
  York
Chadron, NE, 100
Chaffee, Adna R., Jr., 36
Chase, William H., 67
Christie, Walter, 35
Church, James, 99
Churchill, Marlborough, 162
Cincinnati, Society of, 4
City College of New York
  (CCNY), 163, 165–166, 167,
  168–169
Civil rights movement
  and army wives, 50–51
  integration of University of
    Mississippi, 179–184
  See also Black Americans;
    Race relations
Civil War
  emancipation policy during,
    118–121
  "jayhawking" by soldiers,
    126–127
Civilian Conservation Corps,
  169